HABITUAL ETHICS?

What if data-intensive technologies' ability to mould habits with unprecedented precision is also capable of triggering some mass disability of profound consequences? What if we become incapable of modifying the deeply-rooted habits that stem from our increased technological dependence?

On an impoverished understanding of habit, the above questions are easily shrugged off. Habits are deemed rigid by definition: 'as long as our deliberative selves remain capable of steering the design of data-intensive technologies, we'll be fine'. To question this assumption, this book first articulates the way in which the habitual stretches all the way from unconscious tics to purposive, intentionally acquired habits. It also highlights the extent to which our habit-reliant, pre-reflective intelligence normally supports our deliberative selves. It is when habit rigidification sets in that this complementarity breaks down.

The book moves from a philosophical inquiry into the 'double edge' of habit – its empowering and compromising sides – to consideration of individual and collective strategies to keep habits at the service of our ethical life. Allowing the norms that structure our forms of life to be cotton-wooled in abstract reasoning is but one of the factors that can compromise ongoing social and moral transformations. Systems designed to simplify our practical reasoning can also make us 'sheep-like'.

Drawing a parallel between the moral risk inherent in both legal and algorithmic systems, the book concludes with concrete interventions designed to revive the scope for normative experimentation. It will appeal to any reader concerned with our retaining an ability to trigger change within the practices that shape our ethical sensibility.

Habitual Ethics?

Sylvie Delacroix

·HART·
OXFORD · LONDON · NEW YORK · NEW DELHI · SYDNEY

HART PUBLISHING

Bloomsbury Publishing Plc

Kemp House, Chawley Park, Cumnor Hill, Oxford, OX2 9PH, UK

1385 Broadway, New York, NY 10018, USA

29 Earlsfort Terrace, Dublin 2, Ireland

First published in Great Britain 2022

Open Access was funded by Mozilla Foundation.

A catalogue record for this book is available from the British Library.

A catalogue record for this book is available from the Library of Congress.

Library of Congress Control Number: 2022935434

ISBN: HB: 978-1-50992-041-9
ePDF: 978-1-50992-043-3
ePub: 978-1-50992-042-6

Typeset by Compuscript Ltd, Shannon

Foreword

FOR A LONG time habits have had a bad reputation. In the Christian tradition our habits are those of fallen creatures, only to be redeemed, if at all, by strenuous exercises of faith and piety. Greek thought had a more optimistic view of our habits, particularly in its utopian tendency to suppose that virtuous habits always served one's own interest best. But it has in turn been accused of a rather suffocating complacency, particularly given some of the unpleasant habits prevalent in Athens. With the Enlightenment came more optimistic views of human nature, but only as it could perhaps become, not so much as it was in its unrefined, natural state. And even before the Enlightenment had run its course habits were made subservient to their proper master, reason, either in its Kantian role of rightly dominating everything else, or at any rate in its capacity to give us the calculations of Benthamite utilitarianism. These two philosophies have thankfully had to abdicate, but habits cannot be said to have occupied the thrones they vacated. Reason thought of as a transcendent faculty, a captain we must obey above and beyond the rest of our natures has largely kept its Kantian place, and too few philosophers have understood that in our practical reasonings it is the mutinous crew of sentiments and habits that dictate what we take to be the pronouncements of reason. What we regard as reasonable is itself a function of our habits and dispositions. This is not widely understood, so Professor Delacroix's title can be expected to have a shock effect.

Yet as she well shows, an awareness of the immense role that habit plays in our lives is surely a gateway to any self-awareness of ourselves as practical agents. Most of our lives are spent doing what we do out of habit. The ordinary mores of everyday life which make social existence possible are as habitual as the words in which we describe what we are doing. The everyday decencies with which we avoid generating friction and insult, and the everyday considerations and kindnesses with which we lubricate social spaces are second nature to us. Any moral philosophy which is preoccupied with heroic deeds or intractable dilemmas is in danger of overlooking the ordinary routines when we know what needs doing and without thinking do it: the landscape of little decencies which form life's background. Fortunately enough perhaps human beings have been able to construct worlds with few trolley problems and tragic dilemmas for most of us, most of the time. Except in moments of stress the habitual ways we feel about things quietly see us through. It suits the dramatist and the film maker to highlight the chaos when values clash and violent decisions must be made, but it suits the rest of us to avoid it as much as we can.

Nevertheless life has risks, and the traditions that worried about habits were not wholly misguided. As Professor Delacroix rightly goes on to emphasize, we can be lured into bad habits, not so much in the way that the Christian story supposes, through personal defects such as vanity, pride, greed, envy, or willful attraction to what we know is the wrong thing to do, but by cultural norms and reinforcements. Really bad people are relatively rare, but misguided, misled, careless and docile people are common. An atmosphere can then engender bad habits. One highlighted here is the deformation when the prevailing ethos of a profession, such as secrecy or loyalty to misguided ideas about leadership or hierarchy, spread bad habits through its practitioners. Even institutions that depend on our trust, such as parliament or the medical services, are badly, or in some cases hopelessly infected by habits of entitlement or by the expectation of deference and the inability to brook criticism, and it takes courage to hold a mirror up to give Caliban a good look at himself. It is always easier to go along with the flow.

Secondly there is the way in which our natural tendencies to chime in with others are recruited by the commercial algorithms governing social media, that direct us to whatever misinformation or propaganda seems to attract us.

Of course, something has gone wrong if only entitled twerps are elected to parliament, or the social media are cesspits of refuse and litter, and although it may often be difficult to pinpoint malevolence as the origin of these misfortunes, it is obviously bad habits that bring them about, and the bad habits they engender that sustain them.

Being aware of the possible deformations of our habits is, of course only the beginning. We need to be self-critical, self-cultivating, and receptive to the voices of others. What we do not need is an 'Archimedean point' from beyond, on which we can stand and view and winnow out all our sentiments and habits in one fell swoop. As Delacroix says in Chapter 5, 'When it comes to explaining our capacity to step back from the habitual, all the naturalist has at its disposal are socially conditioned emotions, practices and habits of evaluation'. This is no counsel of scepticism, for in exactly the same holistic way, we cannot evaluate all our empirical beliefs in one fell swoop, but we can stand on relatively firm ground in order to test others of them. And this is enough. So even when our habits are unthinking, they are not insulated from thought. Delacroix follows a great tradition of philosophers from Shaftesbury through Hume to Adam Smith who have highlighted the ways in which critical appreciation and encounters with others enable us, if we are careful, diligent, and perhaps a little lucky, to learn to face the gaze of the impartial spectator, and thereby learn to be better able to face others and to bear our own survey. And it is salutary to be shown that it is not only our own habits, but those prevalent in our own milieus, that we must interrogate as we do so.

Simon Blackburn
Trinity College, Cambridge.

Acknowledgements

THE QUESTIONS AT the root of this book were born while I was on a Leverhulme funded research leave in UCL in 2011. When they were formulated in terms of moral change, these questions induced recurrent cases of 'thinking in circles'. Many friends transformed what could have remained some lost at sea, circular experience into a colourful journey: written thanks cannot do justice to the significance of their role. Through generous conversations, a long list of colleagues helped turn inchoate concerns into the arguments at the heart of this book. Crucial among these colleagues was John Gardner, who is sorely missed. In alphabetical order, I would like to thank: Rudolf Bernet, Simon Blackburn, Jude Brown, Gavin Byrne, Clare Carlisle, Sean Coyle, Maks Del Mar, Mette Eilstrup, Sarah Fine, Jakob Holtermann, Kristjan Kristjansson, Maria Lee, Margaret Martin, Manolis Melissaris, Jonathan Montgomery, Bence Nanay, Georgios Pavlakos, Carolyn Pedwell, Dan Priel, Lubomira Radoilska, Andrea Sangiovanni, Philip Schofield, Bosko Tripkovic, Jana Van Grunsven, Michael Wilkinson and Lorenzo Zucca.

Given the importance attributed to our ability to learn from human encounters throughout this manuscript, a few are worth relating outside the confines of an alphabetical list. They were unlikely yet had significant impact. Some involved years-long detours that did shape the more concrete aspects of this book. Meeting Xueni Pan and Mel Slater, the potential of immersive virtual reality as a way of throwing light on the non-cognitive underpinnings of morally-loaded, professional judgment proved hard to resist. Born from the challenges inherent in sharing 'smart', personalisable objects, my conversation with Mireille Hildebrandt has triggered enduring concern for the effect of optimisation tools on our non-reflective agency. My collaboration with Neil Lawrence took shape through a string of chance coffees, which led us from Laplace's demon to flying teapots via bottom-up data trusts. I am forever grateful for the research time that enabled the ebullience of such transformative encounters. This gift of time stemmed from a Leverhulme Trust Prize, followed by a professorial research fellowship at the University of Birmingham and a Mozilla Foundation fellowship.

Valuable feedback was provided during the talks and workshops that punctuated the book writing process. I am especially indebted to Rae Langton for making an in person, early manuscript workshop in Newnham College, Cambridge possible. Participants to this workshop (and the virtual version that followed) included: Anna Boncompagni, Clare Carlisle, Mario De Caro, Christos Douskos, Cecilie Erikssen, Sarah Fine, Hans Fink, Richard Holton,

Rae Langton, David MacArthur, Georgios Pavlakos, Carolyn Pedwell, Gerald Postema, Komarine Romdenh-Romluc, Andrea Sangiovanni and Lorenzo Zucca. Each of their interventions helped me rethink key arguments, sometimes buoying up under-developed ideas, at other times shining light on gaping holes. I am deeply in their debt. I am also grateful for the support of a wide range of colleagues in both UCL and Birmingham, as well as the precious research assistance of Jessica Sutherland, Meagan Parent and Kelsey Ridge.

My biggest thanks go to my beloved 'optimistic pessimist', Chris Pickard. Aside from his eye-opening research assistance as a ridiculously well-read physicist, this book would not have been completed without his rock-solid support and the many early-morning weekend writing sessions he made possible. Finally, I will never forget the solemn emotion with which Luke sent off a manuscript that so often diverted my attention throughout his (thankfully not over yet) childhood: even when it stood in the way of far more entertaining options, Luke poignantly cheered me on. This book is dedicated to him.

The open access publication of this manuscript was made possible by a community-development grant from the Mozilla Foundation.

Contents

Introduction

FEW THINGS MOVE us as surely – or as universally – as habits do. Habits pervade every aspect of our existence: without carefully cultivated habits you would not be able to read this book or have a conversation about it. Yet we know remarkably little about the habits that structure our life, whether at an individual or collective level. In that sense habits may be deemed the 'black holes of social sciences': just like black holes, what we know about them is mostly inferred from the observed behaviour of those it impacts – us. Because habits are not easily disentangled from the deliberative determinants of our behaviour, that inference process is both complex and haphazard. Fancy tech may not help with the visual portrayal of habit (unlike black holes), but it has already had a dramatic impact on our ability to capture habits we were previously unaware of. How?

The multitude of tracking schemes and devices we rely on has turned even the most innocuous aspects of our existence into data points. Where the human mind might only see noise, algorithms trained to detect patterns within vast amounts of data can yield insights. Initially leveraged to anticipate things like consumer behaviour, those insights are now the building blocks of sophisticated behavioural interventions. The latter are designed to exploit the fact that we are creatures whose habits can be moulded by the shape of our environment. The manifold legal, political and ethical issues that stem from these increasingly fine-tuned behavioural interventions are only starting to be grappled with. What if data-intensive technologies' ability to mould habits with unprecedented precision is also capable of triggering some mass disability with profound consequences? What if we become incapable of shifting or modifying the deeply rooted habits that stem from our increased technological dependence?

On a narrow, impoverished understanding of habit, the above question is easily shrugged off. Habits are rigid by definition: as long as our deliberative selves remain capable of steering the choice or design of data-intensive technologies, we'll be fine. To question this assumption, one needs to articulate the various ways of having a habit, and the extent to which the habitual stretches all the way from unconscious tics to purposive, intentionally acquired habits. One also needs to highlight the extent to which our habit-reliant, pre-reflective intelligence normally supports our deliberative selves. It is when the nature of the automaticity underlying these habits degenerates – thereby allowing rigidification to set in – that this complementarity breaks down. Given the extent to which our ability to find our way around the world often presupposes some informal, experienced-based 'know-how', habit rigidification is bad news – never more so than when it comes to the ethically loaded aspects of our lives.

I. WHAT IS A HABIT?

Habit requires repetition – whether it be repeated movement, or posture, or frame of thought. In the pattern shaped by this repetition,[1] at some point a habit is formed. To try to identify a precise moment in time when a habit is born is notoriously difficult, since diminished awareness of the pattern underlying it is key to its emergence. You do not have a habit unless it has at least momentarily escaped your conscious awareness. This emergence condition need not confine habits to mere conditioned reflexes or Pavlovian automatisms.

Habits can be acquired in many ways: intentionally (for instance to foster the realisation of a particular goal) or unintentionally (through learned responses to particular environmental features or contexts). The intentional acquisition of a habit can be difficult: one may repeat a particular pattern of behaviour – for example, I go jogging every day at 7am, rain or shine – and fail to develop the desired habit. Even though I have been careful to never stray from that jogging pattern for weeks, I know I still haven't developed the desired habit because today nothing prompts me to put my trainers on: I have to will myself out, remind myself of my fitness goals etc. But if, upon stepping onto the pavement the next day, I realise with a sudden pang that here I am, all clad in running gear when I am meant to take a long-scheduled video call in 5 minutes, I might celebrate despite the inconvenience. I have finally developed the desired habit! That I am on the pavement all geared up when I had been preparing for that video call only the night before testifies to the birth of a running habit.

My going running this morning (unlike yesterday) was not 'goal-mediated',[2] to use psychologists' jargon. I am in a celebratory mood because I know that my fitness goals are now much more likely to be achieved. My being in the habit of jogging means I can now free myself from the need to consider my fitness goals to shape the requisite behaviour. I can focus instead on the news of the day or my scheduled video call. Of course, habits cut both ways: I will feel a lot less celebratory later when I realise I have travelled halfway to my son's school even though I am meant to pick up my son from the other side of town that day. In this case, the habitual pattern of behaviour has led me to loose sight of the goal that prompted my hopping on my bike.

The bulk of experimental research in neuroscience has been dominated by this negative, 'goal-blind(ing)' side of habit. In contrast to teleologically driven actions, habits are often defined by their insensitivity to the outcome they lead to.[3] If an animal's pattern of behaviour persists despite the fact that the goal that initially prompted that behaviour is absent (or of diminished value), it is deemed

[1] See notably Nathan Brett, 'Human habits' (1981) 11 *Canadian Journal of Philosophy* 357.

[2] Wendy Wood and David T Neal, 'A new look at habits and the habit-goal interface' (2007) 114 *Psychological Review* 843.

[3] Christopher D Adams and Anthony Dickinson, 'Instrumental responding following reinforcer devaluation' (1981) 33 *The Quarterly Journal of Experimental Psychology* Section B 109.

a habit.[4] The appeal of this purported opposition between goal-directed actions and habits is not difficult to understand. For experiments that often have to make do with a study of animal – rather than human – habits, this distinction has the merit of providing a neat, observable condition. Yet when one switches from animal to human habits, this 'diminished goal-sensitivity' condition proves neither necessary nor sufficient to the existence of a habit.[5]

Similar difficulties are encountered with any singular condition purporting to neatly distinguish habits from non-habits. Availability to conscious awareness or to cognitive control are sometimes put forward as purported demarcation criteria, yet while drafting this book I am acutely aware of – and seek to correct – all sorts of writing habits. The only 'safe', necessary conditions when trying to define habit have to do with its emergence conditions. The repetition that gives rise to a habit is as important as the fact that a habit is only born if it momentarily escapes our awareness. After that, habits come in all shapes and colours. Most are essential to our physical and mental well-being. Many make us capable of wondrous things, including the art of living together. Some hold us back, sometimes painfully so.

Careful readers will rightly point out that these emergence conditions are not specific enough. These conditions fail to highlight one important by-product of having a habit: once something has become a habit, that 'something' requires less effort. The nature of that effort will vary. In the above jogging example, I am saved the effort of not only reminding myself to go running, but also overcoming the many conflicting desires or propensities that would otherwise keep me in bed a while longer. Once one pays attention to the degree of cognitive effort that is bypassed by the birth of a habit, one is soon led to the distinction between skill and habits. There is only partial overlap between the two: just as some habits have nothing skilful about them, only some skills have habitual components.

Some skills are innate. Some people are lucky enough to be born with natural social skills, or an ability to put skis on and immediately go down a slope. In such cases, those skills can be said to have less habitual components. Others need to laboriously train themselves to look people in the eye, shake hands, ask for a name and so on, until one day they do so without realising. Suddenly they don't have to go through their mental 'to do' list. In such cases, the skills are acquired through a process of habituation. That process is gradual. The 'to do' list will progressively shrink as different components are chunked together: I might

[4] Henry H Yin and Barbara J Knowlton, 'The role of the basal ganglia in habit formation' (2006) 7 *Nature Reviews Neuroscience* 464.

[5] To show that such a condition is not necessary, Bernacer and Murillo refer to shoelaces tying as an 'outcome-oriented' habit: Javier Bernacer and Jose Ignacio Murillo, 'The Aristotelian conception of habit and its contribution to human neuroscience' (2014) *Frontiers in Human Neurosciences*. To show that diminished goal-sensitivity is not sufficient, one need only contemplate those occasions when one sets out to do something (for instance getting a book downstairs) only to find oneself wondering, once downstairs, what prompted that trip down the stairs.

start automatically asking for a name as soon as I shake hands, for instance. Or I might start moving my ski poles as soon as I shift my weight from one ski to the other.

Considered from this perspective, automaticity may be said to be the 'glue' that allows habit to come into existence. Left unattended this 'glue' can also be the cause of habit degenerating into rigid addiction or other pathologies. Yet automaticity was not included in the emergence conditions mentioned earlier. This is to avoid a frequent misunderstanding: automaticity is too often presented as a necessary condition[6] for the existence of habits. That is misleading.[7] Being an emergence condition does not entail being an existence condition. Having developed the habit of greeting people by looking them in the eye, shaking their hands and asking for a name, I may find myself deliberating about the appropriateness of doing so in particular circumstances without necessarily having lost that habit. The existence of a habit is compatible with ongoing deliberative control and intervention: in the middle of a pandemic, I might train myself to greet people with a loud 'I am sorry we can't shake hands' to remind all concerned (including myself) of the need to avert shaking hands. If this lasts long enough, the habit of shaking hands may be transformed beyond recognition.

Now to go back to the emergence conditions mentioned so far: a habit emerges once a repeated pattern of behaviour (or thought) at least momentarily escapes the subject's awareness. This is made possible by the fact that that behaviour (or train of thought) is not dependent anymore upon the conscious activation of its constituent parts or steps (such as 'make eye contact / shake hands / ask for name'). Many skills, dispositions, addictions – and even some social practices – satisfy those emergence conditions too. Rather than hankering for some elusive demarcation criterion, this book pays attention to the habitual elements in each.

Many – but not all[8] – skills, dispositions and social practices develop on the back of habits: whether they do so depends in large part on the quality of the automaticity inherent in the underlying habit. When it degenerates – leading to a rigidification of the underlying patterns of behaviour – a habit may for instance

[6] Within the psychology literature, 'automaticity' tends to be deemed such a central feature as to allow habit and automaticity to be used interchangeably (this is highlighted in Wendy Wood and Dennis Rünger, 'Psychology of habit' (2016) 67 *Annual Review of Psychology*), even if the concept of 'automaticity' itself admits of several definitions. See for instance: '[habit is a] form of automaticity in responding that develops as people repeat actions in stable circumstances': Bas Verplanken and Wendy Wood, 'Interventions to break and create consumer habits' (2006) 25 *Journal of Public Policy & Marketing* 90. Things are more nuanced in the philosophical literature, which will be discussed in chapters one, two and five.

[7] For a critique of such automaticity-centred definitions of habit, see notably Christos Douskos, 'Deliberation and automaticity in habitual acts' (2018) 9 *Ethics in Progress*.

[8] Some skills, dispositions and even addictions are 'innate', in that they are not acquired through behaviour repetition. Some social practices are born out of purely deliberative interventions: this will be unpacked in chapter six.

give rise to some form of addiction. If, by contrast, these patterns remain plastic enough to successfully adapt to changing environments or aspirations, they are more likely to be conducive to the development of dispositions or skills.

The birth of a disposition (or skill) does not entail the disappearance of the underlying habit. In many cases, the same behaviour might be characterised as a habit, disposition or skill depending on one's vantage point. My messy eating habit might be apprehended as a disposition acquired under the influence of some implicit norm, while in other contexts it might be deemed a valuable skill. Those who insist on strictly demarcating 'mere habits' from dispositions often do so on the basis of an impoverished account of habit: the latter might for instance be presented as inflexible behaviours that are the result of direct conditioning.[9] These reductive accounts of habit not only struggle to accommodate our quotidian reliance on intelligent, highly adaptable habits, they also mask the contribution of the habitual to the 'small piecemeal business' constitutive of our ongoing 'moral life'.[10]

II. THE HABITUAL AND THE ETHICAL: UNHAPPY MARRIAGE?

Within the wide spectrum that leads from unconscious tics and compulsive behaviour all the way to collective, goal-driven endeavours developed on the basis of habits, one cannot identify a point where the habitual suddenly starts – or ceases. One can look for its absence. That we are creatures that are capable of stepping back from the habitual is significant. When we deliberate about the merits of doing X or Y, our deliberations will be affected by our habits of thought, yet with the requisite level of awareness and distanciation, we may claim to have reached a 'free', deliberate decision.[11] The conditions under which we may rightfully claim such autonomy have received huge amounts of philosophical attention. One need only consider how infrequent such instances of pure deliberative agency are – compared to the bulk of our non-deliberative, yet intelligent existence – to guess at the emotional stakes underlying this assertion of freedom.

Hence, for many, the provocativeness of this book's title: to argue that there can be such a thing as habitual ethics would be to admit defeat from the start.

[9] Gilbert Ryle, *The Concept of Mind: 60th Anniversary Edition* (Taylor & Francis 1949/2009).

[10] Iris Murdoch, *The Sovereignty of Good* (Routledge 2013) 36.

[11] The frequent reduction of the ethical to such deliberative instances will be criticised in chapter five along lines that echo Murdoch's own critique: 'If we ignore the prior work of attention and notice only the emptiness of the moment of choice we are likely to identify freedom with the outward movement since there is nothing else to identify it with. But if we consider what the work of attention is like, how continuously it goes on, and how imperceptibly it builds up structures of value round about us, we shall not be surprised that at crucial moments of choice most of the business of choosing is already over. This does not imply that we are not free, certainly not': ibid.

On this view, ethics – and our capacity for deliberative agency – is our 'way out' from routine selfishness and short-sightedness. On such accounts, the idea that there could be such a thing as habitual ethics makes little sense, since it is precisely because we are capable of distancing ourselves from the habitual way of doing things that we are in a position to address the ethical question: 'how should I/we live?'.

This book not only argues that there can be such a thing as habitual ethics; it also argues it is high time we paid attention to the conditions under which the possibility of habitual ethics becomes compromised. We will get a rather poor and incomplete grasp of these conditions if we only consider those compromising factors from an individual perspective, as in the first part of this book. The second part ventures into 'macro', collective factors to tease out the impact of 'system design' interventions on our capacity to sustain habits that are flexible enough to remain at the service of our ethical life. Two types of systems are considered. The algorithmic systems we have become so reliant on, and legal systems. Analysis of the former's ability to generate and mould habits is far more studied than the latter.

Legal theory scarcely mentions habits. When legal theory does refer to habits, it is mostly to contrast them to the kind of practices that are capable of giving rise to social (and legal) norms. This stark contrast is unhelpful in several respects. Not only does it encourage implausible accounts of the processes that lead to legal norms (they are implausible because deliberative all the way through). It also conceals the moral risks inherent in certain institutional designs, which will become apparent in chapter six. Borrowed from that chapter, the figure below provides an artificially linear, 'macro' perspective on the relationship between collective patterns of behaviour, habits, social practices, social norms and legal norms. While legal theorists will be familiar with the last three elements (on the right hand-side), the left-hand side is often 'left' to the province of sociology. By the time you've read this book, the amplitude of that mistake should become apparent.

Figure The two way movement from patterns of behaviour to legal norms, and back

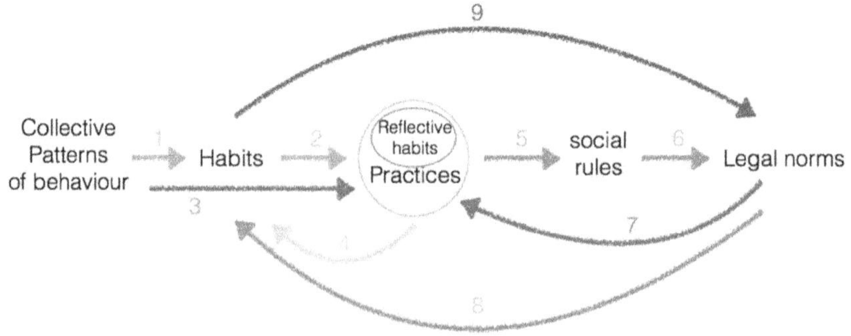

Note: Vectors 1 to 9 are defined in chapter six.

III. WHY DOES 'HABITUAL ETHICS' MATTER TODAY?

The adaptability of both our individual and collective habits is one of the central threads running through this book and its title: can there ever be such a thing as habitual ethics? Most would agree to say that a world in which 'the good' was done habitually (and hence effortlessly) would be an attractive one, yet most would also hesitate to say that acting ethically can ever be a matter of 'mere' habit. Why? While habits can enable wonders (I wouldn't be able to type this without a variety of carefully cultivated habits), they can also be what makes us oblivious to important features of the world we inhabit. Among the factors that may call into question the possibility of habitual ethics, the Christian distrust of the visceral features prominently, as does the intuitive – and warranted – association of ethics with the idea that living a good life demands that we be able to step up and question the usual.

For the ethical question to remain such – an open 'how should I / we live' question, rather than a source of rigid, ready-made responses – it needs to be able to yield malleable answers, shaped by our changing environment, needs and aspirations. The possibility of such continued flexibility – and hence of ethics, rather than ideology – can be compromised. A 'lack of aspiration'[12] or 'thoughtlessness'[13] can come in the way, as can situational factors. Featuring prominently among those factors is our increasing reliance on the tracking schemes and devices mentioned earlier. The very tech that promises to give us unprecedented insight into our habits may also be what spells the end of our ability to constructively adapt our habits in the light of changing needs or aspirations. This prospect brings urgency to a question that has divided philosophers since Antiquity.[14]

Among those who see habit as a source of moral and intellectual impoverishment, Parmenides' warning probably came the earliest (fifth century BC): 'let not habit do violence to you in the empirical way of exercising an unseeing eye and a noisy ear and tongue, but decide by reason'.[15] On this view, habit makes us blind, and it is the job of the philosopher (or artist) to lift this 'heavy curtain', which 'conceals from us almost the whole universe, and prevents us from knowing ourselves'.[16]

In contrast to this defiant take on habit, the Aristotelian tradition emphasises habit's positive and vitally important role: without carefully cultivated habits we would be incapable of living anything resembling a 'good' life. Along this line, Aristotle emphasises the complementarity of the 'virtues of character' – which are acquired through a process of habituation – and intellectual virtues,

[12] Julia Annas, *Intelligent Virtue* (Kindle Edition edn, OUP 2011).

[13] Hannah Arendt, *Eichmann in Jerusalem: A Report on the Banality of Evil* (Penguin 1994).

[14] Carlisle brilliantly outlines the contrast between two contrasting 'branches' of habit's intellectual history in C Carlisle, *On Habit* (Routledge 2014).

[15] AH Coxon (ed), *The Fragments of Parmenides* (Van Gorcum 1986) 58.

[16] Marcel Proust, *In Search of Lost Time*, vol 5 (Vintage 1996) 621. Cited by Carlisle, *On Habit* 2.

including *phronêsis*. Conceived as the art of figuring out some 'golden mean' in each particular case according to one's aims and who one is / who one wants to be, Aristotle highlights the extent to which *phronêsis* is not only made possible by the habit-dependent education of one's senses; it also reinforces virtues of character once established. As for what happens when the nature of habitually acquired traits or 'virtues' needs to adapt, Aristotle has less to say.[17] He is not alone in this respect.

To this day, relatively few philosophers have paid particular attention to the factors that condition the continued adaptability of both individual and collective habits. At the defiant end of the philosophical tradition, habits are seen as threats because of their assumed rigidity. At the other end, those who emphasise the empowering aspect of habit often underestimate the extent to which habits do need to change,[18] whether it is because they were bad habits in the first place or have become so through lack of adaptability. This book can be read as an endeavour to delineate the conditions under which habits remain plastic enough to be at the service of (rather than hampering) our ethical life.

In a world in which habits are exploited with more precision than ever before by technological and regulatory interventions, the delineation of these conditions cannot afford to focus only on individual ethical agency, or to rely solely on philosophical insights. While the second part of this book considers what underlies the possibility of moral change – and hence plastic habits – at a collective scale, the first part ties together psychological studies of expertise and skill acquisition with an account of ethical agency and its preconditions. This move from individual skill acquisition all the way to collective moral change does entail an unapologetically wide understanding of the habitual. From unconscious tics to social practices that are not only conscious of their habitual roots, but continually transform themselves in the light of some goal, the habitual vastly outstrips the behaviourist confines vainly imposed by some philosophical traditions.

These traditions tend to lay great store by what is sometimes referred to as 'Hume's challenge', which supposedly forbids 'any derivation of an ought from an is'.[19] Making room for a wide spectrum of habits – many of which gradually

[17] Save a reference to the importance of *sophia* as excellence in the art of contemplation (another 'Intellectual' virtue). This will be unpacked in chapter three.

[18] 'Nietzsche compares long-lasting habit to a "tyrant" – but, fearing that life without habit would be "intolerable", he recommends cultivating a succession of "brief habits"': quote from Carlisle, *On Habit* 3.

[19] It is unclear whether Hume is rightly understood to forbid such a 'derivation'. Putnam convincingly argues otherwise: 'The logical positivist fact/value dichotomy was defended on the basis of a narrowly scientistic picture of what a "fact" might be, just as the Humean ancestor of that distinction was defended upon the basis of a narrow empiricist psychology of "ideas" and "impressions". The realization that so much of our descriptive language is a living counterexample to *both* (classical empiricist and logical positivist) pictures of the realm of "fact" ought to shake the confidence of anyone who supposes that there is a notion of *fact* that contrasts neatly and absolutely with the

acquire normative significance – does not sit well with any such interdict. Since many habits irreverently bridge whatever gap was meant to exist between facts and values, they inherently call for the endorsement of some sort of naturalist premises.

These naturalist premises are outlined in chapter one. This meta-ethical opening is necessary in order to appreciate the nature of the problems lurking behind a non-reductive understanding of ethics that acknowledges the constructive role played by habit. For 'habitual ethics' to make sense, the habitual at stake needs to be malleable enough to allow the ethical question to remain such: as a question, it needs to admit changing answers. All sorts of factors can compromise this malleability. These factors do not typically receive much attention from philosophers interested in our capacity for ethical agency for a simple reason: this capacity is often taken as a given.

On such accounts, it is because we are creatures capable of confronting the 'how should I live?' question that we are capable of freedom; that we are not doomed to conform to the patterns of behaviour and thought that we find ourselves immersed into. If we do not take this capacity for ethical agency as a given, to ask instead what makes it possible in the first place, we are left with precisely the patterns of behaviour and thought which ethical agency was supposed to allow us to transcend. Chapter two unpacks the extent to which we acquire the know-how that makes us capable of ethical judgement through immersion in socio-cultural practices. Given that it is first and foremost through this immersion process that we come to internalise a complex web of expectations, the difficult question is: how do we account for our supposed ability to step back and critically consider those expectations?

That question is far from new. Any critical reflection on the way we learn to live together, and the way we often get it wrong, is likely to lead to the following: how do we live up to our ethical responsibility to see the need for – and enact – change when needed? Many philosophers have muddled through with relatively easy (even if complex-looking) answers, whereby we somehow reach for objectively delineated reasons and see the need for – or enact – change (whether it be via some fancy transcendental reflection structured around the categorical imperative or whether it be via some less fancy, voluntarist 'self-catapulting'[20]). We have gotten away with these fancy or less fancy meta-ethical ways of avoiding this quandary for a rather long time. Now that data-intensive technologies are helping us track and exploit our habits like never before, the worry is that the concrete cost of these theoretical avoidance strategies will become apparent. The non-naturalism that informs these avoidance strategies licenses a pervasive

notion of "value" supposedly invoked in talk of the nature of all "value judgments": Hilary Putnam, *The Collapse of the Fact/Value Dichotomy and Other Essays* (Harvard UP 2002) 26). In contrast, see for instance Scott J Shapiro, *Legality* (Harvard UP 2011) 2615 (loc).

[20] I borrow this image from Simon Blackburn, 'Normativity à la mode' (2001) 5 *Journal of Ethics: An International Philosophical Review* 139.

disregard for the need to account for what enables us to step back from the habitual. This makes non-naturalist accounts of ethical agency at least as perilous as the reductivist understandings of ethics – 'it's all a matter of attitudes' – that are too often associated with naturalism.

IV. CHAPTERS OVERVIEW

Chapter one outlines three of the philosophical battlegrounds that need to be visited if a viable, non-reductivist naturalism is to be put forward. In each case, a focus on 'what we do' as a starting point is key to the most promising solutions. It is also key to this book's endeavour to delineate the conditions under which there can be such a thing as 'habitual ethics'. To grasp these conditions, chapter two starts by delineating the way in which much of 'what we do' entails forming empowering habits. Such habits enable us to accomplish all sorts of things, from piano playing to developing an ethically responsive way of delivering care and services. Because studies of expertise pay particular attention to the factors that can contribute to a degradation in the nature of the automaticity underlying acquired skills (or habit), they help articulate the juncture between the empowering and compromising roles that habit can play when it comes to ethical agency. While chapter two focuses on the empowering aspect through the prism of skill acquisition, chapter three delves into habit rigidification in morally loaded contexts through the prism of professional responsibility. Because living up to this responsibility requires a combination of both skill and ethical judgement, professional practice is a helpful context in which to study what happens when the nature of the automaticity underlying morally significant habits degenerates.

Chapters four and five differ from chapters two and three in that they leave insights from psychology and expertise studies behind. Chapter four is rooted in the following question: what if habit plasticity is not enough, when ethical agency is concerned? What if the problem with the many who find themselves endorsing ideologies that back the 'legitimate' extermination – or mutilation – of fellow human beings is aptly phrased in terms of excessively plastic habits of thought? If ethical agency is to mean anything, it must have at its core an account of exactly what it is about us, human beings, that endows us with the capacity to stand back from and challenge accepted norms, rather than blindly adapt to them. How would a habit-centred account of ethical agency provide such an account? Chapter four throws light on the continued dominance of negative answers to the above question: for a wide strand of philosophy, ethical agency is all about the mechanisms that allow us to grow *out* of the habitual.

This emphasis on the necessity to grow *out* of the habitual through critical reasoning reflects an assumption that structures all non-naturalist accounts of ethical agency: there is a fundamental discontinuity between the natural and the ethical. To mark a departure from such accounts, chapter five critically considers the role played by 'responsiveness to the Other' as a pre-reflective form of situational discernment that is central to ethical agency. The significance of this capability has often been obscured by the dominance of overly abstract (and individualist) 'responsiveness to reasons' accounts.

Considered from a collective perspective, the normative challenges concomitant with an account of ethical agency that places habit at its core are the focus of this book's second part. This part delves into the structural, environmental factors that underpin the continued possibility of social and moral transformations. The latter's often being taken for granted stems from a tendency to treat our capacity for ethical agency as a given. That capacity can be lost. Just like a muscle that has gone limp through lack of exercise, ethical agency can be compromised to the point of dying out.

Chapter six takes its roots in what is often called the 'moral risk' inherent in law's institutional structure. Because of the sharp distinction drawn by one of the most influential figures of contemporary jurisprudence – HLA Hart – between habits on one hand and social practices on the other, neither Hart nor present-day jurisprudes have been able to substantiate the claim that law's institutional structure may be inherently conducive to 'sheeplike' patterns of behaviour. Chapter six starts where Hart left off and argues that what is distinctively alienating about a legal regime is the way in which it can be conducive to the development of rigid, unreflective habits. Unlike the goal-oriented habits that nurture legal practice, the rigid habits (potentially) cultivated by a legal system's institutionalised adaptation to change can be incapable of generating the type of practices that give rise to novel legal structures. Such unreflective habits are also all too easily exploited by unscrupulous shepherds bent on a 'slaughterhouse' ending, to use Hart's metaphor. This raises challenges both in terms of professional practice (as seen in chapter three) and in terms of institutional design.

Just like law, automated systems designed to simplify our practical reasoning can also undermine our ability to keep calling for better ways of living together and challenge 'the usual'. Chapter seven considers the impact of the design choices underlying the development of such systems on our ability to adapt deeply rooted habits. What if the personalised optimisation of our online environments ends up compromising what Jaeggi refers to as our 'inner mobility'?[21] Are we confronted with a form of alienation that is both less visible and more potent than that facilitated by the legal structures considered in chapter six? Chapter seven concludes by considering the potential inherent in two different types of design interventions. They both seek to reverse the passivity habits that are encouraged by current infrastructure. While 'bottom-up data trusts' empower groups to regain agency over their data (which may thereby become

[21] Rahel Jaeggi, *Alienation* (Columbia UP 2014).

a political and economic lever for change), 'ensemble contestability' features are designed to facilitate a continuous, critical feedback loop from end users to personalised optimisation tools.

The resolutely practical stance underlying this final chapter is important. Today the long-standing debate between those who deem habit an enabling force in our developing a capacity for normative agency versus those who don't is not merely theoretical. Because of the precise and powerful habit-shaping technologies that structure our quotidian lives, the implications of this debate are both forward-looking and momentous. As a wake-up call, this book would fail if it only spurred some philosophers on to further thinking about agency. If 'habitual ethics' is to remain a genuine, live possibility, rather than some dangerous form of ideology, we each have a role to play, whether through pro-active citizenry, institutional modifications or system design intervention. At stake in each of those interventions is the continued plasticity of the habits that shape our ethical life.

Part I

Habit and Individual Agency

1

From Facts to Norms (and Back)

Nature is never mere nature. That which is more than mere is nature, too.

Hans Fink, 'Three sorts of naturalism'[1]

WHATEVER ELSE IT is, naturalism involves at least one 'lowest common denominator' commitment. This commitment is often defined negatively: you are not a naturalist if you do not rule out any appeal to the supernatural or non-natural in your endeavour to account for X or Y. For many 'X and Y' nowadays, that commitment is not too burdensome. Yet when it comes to explaining things like ethics or morality, adhering to a naturalist stance does raise a set of challenges. Prime among these challenges is the need to determine what counts as 'natural'. Do we let our natural sciences – or social sciences – as they exist today dictate what can be safely included in our concept of 'Nature'? If ethics and morality are deemed part of 'what we do' – hence 'natural' through and through – does that condemn us to seeing ethics and morality as just a set of attitudes devoid of any objectivity?

Of those who would lean towards a positive answer to that question, many lay great store by the supposed need to demarcate 'facts' from 'values'.[2] On this view, it is because we are capable of rising above all sorts of causal constraints on our behaviour – like the way we have been brought up, and the habits we pick up along the way – that we are capable of freedom, and hence of moral responsibility. When we ask 'why is such and such morally wrong?' the answer needs to be formulated in terms of reasons. To answer in terms of natural facts – whether these facts pertain to our usual ways of doing things, or to facts about us, human beings – is to become subservient to such facts; hence, to lose our freedom as ethical agents.

In contrast, there cannot be any discontinuity between the ethical and the natural in an account of ethical agency that gives a central place to habit. And that is not because the ethical is 'merely' natural but rather because, as Hans Fink nicely puts it: 'Nature is never *mere* nature. That which is *more* than *mere* is nature, too'.[3] Since they stretch all the way from unconscious tics to the shared

[1] Hans Fink, 'Three sorts of naturalism' (2006) 14 *European Journal of Philosophy* 202, 217.
[2] See n 19.
[3] Fink, 'Three sorts of naturalism' 217.

practices they can give rise to, habits are among those things that are both nature and 'more than mere' nature. As such, a book exploring the possibility of 'habitual ethics' would either be very odd or very short if it didn't endorse some kind of naturalist premises. The short, non-naturalist version would just conclude that 'habitual ethics' is a contradiction in terms. The odd version would yawn at the idea of 'habitual ethics' since it would reduce ethics to a set evaluative attitudes that we develop as we try to find our way around the world. The latter endeavour would be exhausting if these attitudes didn't become habitual at least in part. Hence, on such a view, there would be nothing particularly intriguing about the possibility of 'habitual ethics'.

This book is not overly long, but it still counts as a 'long version' answer to the possibility of habitual ethics. The length of that answer is not only due to its endorsing some naturalist premises. It also stems from its rejecting the reductionist, 'it's all a matter of attitudes' understanding of ethics that is often associated with naturalism. As there are quite a few sophisticated, non-reductivist naturalist understandings of ethics out there, one could leave it at that. One could select some 'off-the-shelves' account with minor alterations, declare the meta-ethics 'done' and turn to the less dusty, more applied ethics that pervade the rest of this book. Going for that option was tempting. This book could have had McDowell's account with less insistence on 'reasons responsiveness' when characterising unreflective action. Or maybe Julia Annas' but with more attention paid to our non-reflective, non 'rational' intelligence. The alterations may have turned out to be bigger than planned. There would have been raised philosophical eyebrows, as well as irritation creasing less philosophically inclined foreheads.

Since such irritation would be warranted, this book does not take any 'off-the-shelves' shortcut. Nor does it foolishly claim to put forward some brand new non-reductive naturalist meta-ethics that is presupposed by the possibility of habitual ethics. The point of this chapter is more pragmatic. To delineate a plausible, 'liberal'[4] naturalism in ethics, one tends to need to visit some common philosophical battlegrounds and plant a flag or two. This chapter zooms in on three of those. Section I looks at the stakes underlying one's definition of Nature (and Science). Section II visits the so-called 'motivation problem'. Section III looks at what it takes to 'follow a rule'. These three battlegrounds are chosen because the complex debates they have given rise to are crucially impacted by one's understanding of habit. To understand the nature of this impact helps appreciate the nature of the difficulties addressed in the rest of the book in at least two respects. First, negatively, a naturalist commitment rules out many well-trodden solutions to the problems inherent in delineating the possibility of habitual ethics. Second, positively, the preferred stances in all three of the above

[4] The 'liberal' adjective is coined in Mario De Caro and David Macarthur (eds), *Naturalism and Normativity* (Columbia UP 2010).

'battlegrounds' have in common a methodological focus on 'what we do' as a starting point. This methodological focus runs throughout the book.

I. DEFINING 'THE NATURAL' (AND THE ROLE OF SCIENCE)

Much of the debate concerning science's purported role as an arbiter of what exists can be brought back to Sellars' provocative 'science is the measure of all things'.[5] Just how provocative Sellars' position ends up being depends in part on the way one defines 'science'.

A. When 'the Natural' is Restricted to that which is the Result of Elementary Forces

Sellars' position is often associated with a 'bald'[6] understanding of both science and nature, according to which 'reality is exhausted by the natural world, in the sense of the world as the natural sciences are capable of revealing it to us'.[7]

Unlike the first part of the above quote, its second part may strike many as unreasonably restrictive: why should social sciences' efforts to 'reveal the world to us' be dismissed as not worthy of the same attention as those of the natural sciences? The explanation lies in the enduring appeal of what many (too) respectfully refer to as a 'Naturalistic Conception of objectivity'.[8] This conception of objectivity is often deemed to be a desirable by-product of the 'natural scientific method'. This method, unlike its 'social sciences' counterpart, would be seeking to unveil a concept of nature maximally independent of human intervention. This drive to confine the natural to that which is the result of elementary, material forces – as opposed to human forces – is far from new.[9]

Such a restrictive understanding of nature has contributed to enduring anxiety about both the reality and objectivity of all sorts of things, especially ethics: how does one ascertain the objective truth of ethical judgements, in the absence of 'objects' which those judgements would be said to accurately track?[10] The sceptical conclusions encouraged by this line of thought were most famously instantiated in Mackie's 'argument from queerness'. Mackie rejects the

[5] 'In the dimension of describing and explaining the world, science is the measure of all things, of what is that it is, and of what is not that it is not': Wilfrid Sellars, 'Empiricism and the philosophy of mind' (1956) 1 *Minnesota Studies in the Philosophy of Science* 253, 303.

[6] John McDowell, 'Précis of "Mind and World"' (1996) 7 *Philosophical Issues* 231.

[7] John McDowell, 'Projection and truth in ethics', *Mind, Value and Reality* (Harvard UP 1998).

[8] Brian Leiter, *Naturalizing Jurisprudence: Essays on American Legal Realism and Naturalism in Legal Philosophy* (OUP 2007) 243.

[9] It plays a central role in Plato's endeavour to capture the tension inherent in *physis* in *Laws*' Book X: Plato, *Laws* (CUP 2016).

[10] Putnam forcefully criticises this understanding of objectivity in Hilary Putnam, *Ethics Without Ontology* (Harvard UP 2004).

possibility of ethical objectivity on the basis that 'if there were objective values, then they would be entities or qualities or relations of a very strange sort, utterly different from anything else in the universe'.[11] Mackie concludes that our ethical discourse is fundamentally flawed since it seems to presuppose precisely such strange, independent entities. These entities are 'queer', according to Mackie, because they are not susceptible to empirically grounded investigation.[12]

The key element in this 'argument from queerness' is the taken-for-granted divorce between the sphere of reasons – including ethics – and the sphere of our experiences. From that perspective, to argue that our ethical norms may be the gradual product of our own experiences while nevertheless being able to claim some objective status is not only presumptuous, it also completely misses the point. The point, for 'empiricist naturalists', as McDowell calls them, is to insist on a univocal, 'natural-scientific' concept of objectivity as 'non-subjective'.[13] Any claim to objectivity must be backed up by objects as they are found in a nature stripped bare of the human touch – in 'a world purged of meaning'.[14]

Yet for those embracing such a naturalism, it is not 'meaning' so much as 'non-material causes, and teleologies, and gods and ghosts'[15] which the world is (rightly) purged of. From such a 'purged' perspective, the reality of moral values may seem as questionable as other 'entities [that] have no causal explanatory power'.[16] Armed with the conviction that we 'know and understand more, as a result of this epistemically motivated cleansing',[17] a 'scientistic' naturalist *à la* Leiter will have no time for those arguing that what depends on human beings' responsive capacities is no-less real than the straightforwardly causal,[18] albeit in

[11] JL Mackie, *Ethics: Inventing Right and Wrong* (Penguin Books 1990) 38.

[12] I adopt this interpretation of 'queerness' on the basis of a passage where Mackie states that the only satisfactory reply to a counter-argument underlining that our knowledge of many things turns out to be queer and hence that queerness is not really objectionable (see Hilary Putnam, *Reason, Truth, and History* (CUP 1981)) is to 'show how, on empiricist foundations, we can construct an account of the ideas and beliefs and knowledge that we have of all these matters. I cannot even begin to do that here … I can only state my belief that satisfactory accounts of most of these can be given in empirical terms. If some supposed metaphysical necessities or essences resist such treatment, then they too should be included, along with objective values, among the targets of the argument from queerness': Mackie, *Ethics: Inventing Right and Wrong* 39.

[13] '[I]t is one thing to recognize that the impersonal stance of scientific investigation is a methodological necessity for the achievement of a valuable mode of understanding reality; it is quite another thing to take the dawning grasp of this, in the modern era, for a metaphysical insight into the notion of objectivity as such, so that objective correctness in any mode of thought must be anchored in this kind of access to the real': McDowell, 'Two sorts of naturalism' 182.

[14] 'It is a commonplace that modern science has given us a disenchanted conception of the natural world. … The tendency of the scientific outlook is to purge the world of meaning': ibid 174.

[15] Brian Leiter, *Moral Psychology with Nietzsche* (OUP, USA 2019) 106.

[16] Ibid.

[17] Ibid.

[18] '[N]ot everything that we take to be nonsupernatural, such as numbers or propositions, can be understood in unproblematically causal terms. One way of thinking about the difference between Scientific and Liberal Naturalism is as a dispute about how the complementary categories of the "natural" and the "supernatural" should best be understood. Scientific Naturalism interprets

a different way. Insofar as it presupposes ontological pluralism[19] (the development of different existence criteria for different kinds of things[20]), the latter line of argument is both unnecessary and problematic.

There is another way of addressing our 'Modern' anxiety about the reality and objectivity of ethics, and more generally those features of our world whose reality seems to be shaped by our responses to them. It consists in pointing out that the supposed precariousness of the 'response-dependent' only springs up in contrast to a peculiarly – and suspiciously – bare Nature. Since the real we have access to is necessarily infused with (our) meaning, we had better stop hankering after some ultimate grounding of our ethical convictions in a sphere 'constitutively independent of the structure of subjectivity'.[21] Not only is it far from clear whether such a Nature stripped bare of human responses is in fact available to us. Quite why we would want a concept of both nature and science that reduces so drastically the explanatory resources at our disposal to explain things that matter to us (like morality) warrants an explanation.

B. Inhabited Nature

Among the explanatory resources that become available within an 'inhabited' concept of nature are the multitude of habits, dispositions and practices woven in our natural world. To understand the way in which these practices yield the social and moral norms that inform our ethical judgements, we will need to develop a narrative that takes us from human beings with needs and desires to internalised standards of right and wrong. There are many different ways of developing such a narrative. In the *Ethical Project*, Kitcher develops an 'evolutionary' narrative that traces the emergence of distinctive, ethical standards to

the natural strictly in terms of the scientific image of the world, narrowly or broadly conceived, whereas Liberal Naturalism, or some versions of it, offers a broader, more expansive conception of nature that makes room for a class of non-scientific, but nonetheless nonsupernatural, entities': Mario De Caro and David Macarthur, 'Science, naturalism, and the problem of normativity' in Mario De Caro and David Macarthur (eds), *Naturalism and Normativity* (Columbia UP 2010) 3.

[19] Price defines ontological pluralism (in his attempt at rescuing some of Carnap's insights) as the view according to which: 'to the extent that different frameworks [at play in language] are independent, and doing different jobs, their existential quantifiers also seem to be doing different jobs – each framework seems to bring with it its own notion of reality': Huw Price, 'Carnap, Quine, and the fate of metaphysics' (1997) 5 *Electronic Journal of Analytic Philosophy* 6.

[20] Leiter for instance criticises Scanlon's attempted vindication of domain-specific epistemological and ontological criteria in Thomas M Scanlon, *Being Realistic About Reasons* (OUP 2014), to defend instead 'causal explanatory power as a marker of the real and the knowable even in the moral domain': Leiter, *Moral Psychology with Nietzsche*.

[21] Interestingly, McDowell suggests that our obstinate wish 'to acknowledge a role for the "in itself"' may have something to do with 'an intelligible wish to avoid responsibility. If something utterly outside the space of logos forces itself on us, we cannot be blamed for believing what we do': McDowell, 'Two sorts of naturalism' 181.

the need to remedy 'altruism failures'.[22] In a less evolutionary, Wittgensteinian vein, Blackburn suggests we turn our attention to ways in which we train ourselves to meet a variety of needs against a background of prior practices:

> Consider, for instance, someone taught to use a carpenter's plane to shave a piece of wood flat. The process is one of sticks and carrots until the skill develops. To the metaphysician's eye this is all just is's, so if, for instance, after the process the apprentice shaves a plank leaving it wavy or jagged, that is just the way the causal process developed. There are dispositions and events all the way down, but nothing that counts as or constitutes, or, in one ugly terminology, acts as a truth maker for correctness or incorrectness (as Kripke's skeptic famously laments). But against the background of the activities of which the technique is a part there is more than that. The jagged or wavy result is unskilled, unintended, and it gives rise to disappointment and rejection.[23]

Whether it be the process whereby we train ourselves to develop better, less wavy tables, or the process whereby we learn to be better friends, better parents or better citizens, there is nothing mysterious about the way in which these processes yield standards and expectations. Far from being 'queer' entities, the moral norms that structure friendship (or parenting) become salient as we hold each other to the expectations we have come to develop on the basis of ongoing practices. '[B]y the time we have these "is's" up and running we have all that our normative nature require.'[24] So there is 'no unmoved mover: no intervention of the divine spark, or gifts from unexplained quarters'.[25]

Does such a narrative leave us with a watered-down understanding of ethics, one that could be said to lack 'oomph' in any way? The following two sections consider the two main ways in which such 'lack of oomph' arguments are typically put forward: some worry that ethics thus naturalised can't explain the way it motivates us to act (or criticise others). Others worry that such narratives can only ever yield dispositions to act or behave in certain ways: these dispositions would not be enough to account for our rule-following practices (section III). In both cases, the answer to such worries hinges upon one's understanding of the internaliation process necessary to the birth of both habits and acquired dispositions.[26]

[22] Philip Kitcher, *The Ethical Project* (Harvard UP 2011).

[23] Simon Blackburn, 'Normativity à la mode' (2001) 5 *Journal of Ethics: An International Philosophical Review* 139.

[24] ibid 148.

[25] ibid 150.

[26] For our purposes, dispositions differ from habits only to the extent that some dispositions are innate, whereas all habits are acquired. In what follows, 'habits' and 'acquired dispositions' are therefore used interchangeably. On this interchangeability, see: 'The word habit may seem twisted somewhat from its customary use when employed as we have been using it. But we need a word to express that kind of human activity which is influenced by prior activity and is in that sense acquired; which contains within itself a certain ordering or systematization of minor elements of action; which is projective, dynamic in quality, ready for overt manifestation; and which is operative in some subdued subordinate form even when not obviously dominating activity. Habit even it its

II. THE 'MOTIVATION PROBLEM'

The following question instigated the present work: what enables us to periodically stand against commonly accepted norms to initiate change in the way we develop the standards governing our way of living together? Given the inertia inherent in even the most flexible habits, gaining a better understanding of the many ways of having a habit (and the mechanisms underlying both habit acquisition and habit metamorphosis) is crucial to the above. Both empirical investigations and philosophical analyses can contribute to it. The next three chapters relay some of those analyses. Chapter two highlights the extent to which deliberate, intentional action commands a degree of philosophical attention that is far from commensurate with its relative prevalence, even in domains traditionally associated with 'higher' forms of cognition.

It should be no surprise, therefore, if exclusively reflective answers to the above question are deemed unsatisfactory. To explain our capacity to step back from and question accepted normative frameworks, greater attention needs to be devoted to the intuitions that underpin occasional tensions between internalised socio-cultural expectations and what we instinctively feel ought to be done. This will occupy us in chapter five. The rest of the present section considers those scenarios where reflective deliberation does play a central role in the process of initiating normative change.

An example will help illustrate a possible transition from the unreflective to the reflective: when I had to witness my grandmother being fitted with a feeding tube months before she died (after years of valiantly enduring various cancer therapies), my instinctive reaction was a mix of alarm and concern. Her inability to have a say over such an invasive and uncomfortable procedure upset me. Surrounded as I was by eminent, unquestionably well-intentioned doctors, I only managed a meek 'Why? Are you sure?', which got me equally meek 'Don't worry' answers. A lugubrious, downbeat episode were it not for the fact that it has at least led me to join the growing numbers of those who call for (or actively seek to implement[27]) open, earlier and, ideally, collective discussions of end-of-life care aspirations. These calls go hand in hand with extensive debates about the values that should preside over end-of-life care, as medical interventions continue to shift the boundaries between life and death.

Are these debates merely pitching changing attitudes against others? Or are they trying to get at something important about us, as human beings; something that is true independently of human choices, however fallible we may be at grasping it? The former, 'attitudes pitching' view gained currency in part

ordinary usage comes nearer to denoting these facts than any other word. If the facts are recognized we may also use the words attitude and disposition': John Dewey, *Human Nature and Conduct: An Introduction to Social Psychology* (G Allen & Unwin 1922) 31.

[27] Zoë Fritz, Anne-Marie Slowther and Gavin D Perkins, 'Resuscitation policy should focus on the patient, not the decision' (2017) 356 *BMJ* j813.

because it seemed to offer a solution to what is sometimes called 'the motivation problem'.[28] Attitudes do reliably motivate us. Can the same be said about facts, or the beliefs they give rise to? Not necessarily.

Those who worry about the motivation problem worry that naturalists are trying to have their cake and eat it too. On this line of argument, our moral practices – such as the end-of-life care debates mentioned above – cannot be rooted in natural facts, since facts (or the beliefs they give rise to) on their own do not motivate us, and morality does have a motivational pull over us. To be plausible, any account of morality that does not deny that motivational pull – any account that endorses what is called 'internalism about reasons'[29] – must give an important role to desires and attitudes. The 'expressivist'[30] view of moral judgement takes that Humean insight to its extreme: moral judgements are but the expression of our attitudes, and one must denounce as disingenuous any attempt to back up such attitudes by reference to factual truths. On this view, naturalists can explain morality's motivational pull, but only if they endorse an expressivist understanding of moral judgements (so they cannot 'have' the possibility of objectively true ethical judgements too).

The attentive reader will – hopefully – have guessed the weak link in the above line of argument: the idea that facts on their own do not motivate us goes hand in hand with what section I referred to as a 'bare' conception of nature. Because such an understanding of nature is at the heart of all too many 'scientistic' kinds of naturalism, it is often thought that naturalism is incompatible with so-called 'internalism about reasons'.[31] This line of thought (mistakenly) assumes that the ontological cleansing demanded by naturalism leaves those attempting to explain how moral judgements *reliably* motivate us with only brute 'inert' facts[32] as explanatory resources.

Far from having only inert facts at its disposal, the naturalism defended here not only relies on habit to explain the reliable connection between the

[28] Alfred R Mele, 'Motivation: essentially motivation-constituting attitudes' (1995) 104 *The Philosophical Review* 387; Stephen L Darwall, 'Internalism and agency' (1992) 6 *Philosophical Perspectives* 155; Richard Joyce, 'Expressivism and motivation internalism' (2002) 62 *Analysis* 336.

[29] Williams' account of the 'internalism versus externalism about reasons' debate has been particularly influential: Bernard Williams, 'Internal and external reasons' in Bernard Williams (ed), *Moral Luck: Philosophical Papers 1973–1980* (CUP 1981).

[30] AJ Ayer, *Language, Truth and Logic* (London: Penguin 2001); AJ Ayer, 'On the analysis of moral judgements', *Philosophical Essays* (Springer 1972).

[31] Leiter's particular naturalism backs up this assumption: 'Of course, the NeoHumean naturalist has not explained real normativity, as Scanlon complains, because real normativity does not exist: that is the entire upshot of the naturalist view. There are no reasons whose existence and character is independent of human attitudes; there are only human attitudes which lead us to "talk the talk" of reasons. And if real normativity does not exist, if only feelings of inclination and aversion, compulsion and avoidance, actually exist, then that means that all purportedly normative disputes bottom out not in reasons but in the clash of will or affect.' Brian Leiter, 'Normativity for naturalists' (2015) 25 *Philosophical Issues* 64, 74.

[32] This assumed 'normative inertness' of facts is nicely captured in Dancy asserting that 'Facts, moral or otherwise, cannot have any sort of force': Jonathan Dancy, 'Nonnaturalism' in David Copp (ed), *The Oxford Handbook of Ethical Theory* (OUP 2006).

facts that inform moral judgement and motivation. It must also include an account of the kind of creatures we are, and how certain facts about us guide our fallible and habit-dependent attempts at constructing better ways of living together. Prominent among those facts is not only our sociable nature, but also our tendency to look beyond our immediate circumstances to make projects and seek meaning, in full cognisance of our finite lifespans. The experience of vulnerability that comes with our awareness of being 'wholly situated, forever, between birth and death'[33] may express itself differently in different cultures. That experience may give rise to myriad different ways of acknowledging, mitigating or celebrating it. Yet it is a fact that shapes our perception and assessment of other facts.[34]

Does that fact also motivate us to act? Formulated in this way, it is difficult to see how that fact could fail to motivate us. But what about other facts? Can a habit-centred naturalism explain the 'reliable' connection between the various facts deemed to inform our moral practices and our being motivated to act? The term 'reliable' indicates a 'relaxed'[35] approach to drawing a connection between moral judgement and motivation. This approach relies on the fact that 'most of us are creatures of the right sort'. The latter expression is Railton's. What follows leans on his account with one modification: internalism about reasons is not deemed to be invalidated by pathological cases – quite the opposite. That the connection between moral judgement and motivation is compromised in cases such as the chronically depressive tells us something important about the nature of the internalisation process that sits at the heart of both Railton's argument and this book's 'habitual ethics'.

In a nutshell, Railton's argument works like this: in order to 'permit plausible connections to be drawn between, on the one hand, what is good or right and, on the other, what characteristically would motivate individuals who are prepared to submit themselves to relevant sorts of scrutiny',[36] the naturalist may usefully compare two types of practices: the practice of belief-based, everyday conversation and moral practice. In both cases, it is the internalisation of shared norms that makes it possible for us not only to 'convey spoken and unspoken information',[37] but also to develop the sort of habits[38] and dispositions that

[33] Michel de Montaigne, *The Complete Essays* (Penguin Classics 1991) 680.

[34] It probably played a role in my alarmed reaction to my grandmother's feeding tube ordeal, even if this becomes apparent only upon careful, post-hoc reflection.

[35] James Lenman, 'Moral naturalism' (*plato.stanford.edu*, 2006) accessed 10 February 2022.

[36] Peter Railton, *Facts, Values, and Norms: Essays Toward a Morality of Consequence* (CUP 2003) 33.

[37] Railton draws upon Grice's 'complex theory of how the norms that govern conversational exchanges – internalized by speakers as mutually understood intentions to be cooperative in communicating – make it possible for what we literally say to one another to convey spoken and unspoken information': Peter Railton, 'Moral factualism' (2006) *Contemporary Debates in Moral Theory* 201, 209, referring to P Grice, *Studies in the Ways of Words* (Harvard UP 1989).

[38] While Railton does not delve much into habit, he comes close to it in his description of 'our capacity for such nonpropositional, bodily centered, grounded mental maps and expectations',

make us take an interest in the relevant facts. This internalisation process does not happen overnight. The process of growing up[39] involves developing a sensibility 'that includes not only ordinary cognitive and sensory capacities but also a motivating attitude – a capacity to find certain things simply "to be done"'.[40]

This sensibility can be compromised by all sorts of things. Railton refers to the examples of Brad, who suffers from depression, and Theresa, whose 'capacities for empathy and engagement on a universal scale are quite limited'.[41] Far from invalidating the purported link between moral judgement and motivation, these pathological examples point at the often forgotten, yet crucial role played by emotional responsiveness within ethical agency. Crucially for our purposes, this responsiveness can also be compromised by the not necessarily pathological rigidification of the habits underlying our ethical sensitivity. This is explored in more detail in chapter five.

For now, it is worth emphasising the following: the only sort of naturalism that does have a 'motivation problem' is the scientistic, reductive kind highlighted in section I.A. As soon as we make room for habits, dispositions, and practices within the 'natural' explanatory resources at our disposal, the problem we face is less one of accounting for the 'motivational pull' of morality and more one of accounting for its normative status. Unpacking the type of internalisation necessary to the birth of normatively significant habits turns out to be crucial to that endeavour. This is explored in the next section.

III. 'FOLLOWING A RULE'

Section I highlighted the extent to which our own definition of 'nature' and 'science' dictates the shape and colour of our version of naturalism. Because of some versions' scientistic excesses,[42] 'the tide of naturalism [which] has been rising since the seventeenth century' can be perceived as a threat: 'the regions under threat are some of the most central in human life'.[43] To protect these

thanks to which 'we are able to connect human propositional thought to the world via de re and de se beliefs and intentions': Peter Railton, 'The affective dog and its rational tale: intuition and attunement' (2014) 124 *Ethics* 813, 838.

[39] A book-length account of naturalism as a method would delve into the wide variety of evolutionary accounts, see for instance: David O Brink, *Moral Realism and the Foundations of Ethics* (CUP 1989); Jack Ritchie, *Understanding Naturalism* (Routledge 2014); Lynne Rudder Baker, *Naturalism and the First-Person Perspective* (OUP 2013).

[40] Railton, 'Moral factualism' 212. Note that, in this quote, Railton is referring to McDowell's 'internalist' naturalism, which Railton is distancing himself from (unnecessarily, in my opinion) because of the possibility of the pathological cases mentioned above.

[41] Ibid 215.

[42] 'Naturalism is easily confused with a stronger, scientistic position, in which one, or a few, areas of natural science are given priority and taken to constrain philosophizing: in the extreme version, philosophical problems are held to be reducible to some field of scientific inquiry, neuroscience, or psychology – or evolutionary biology – say': Philip Kitcher, *Preludes to Pragmatism: Toward a Reconstruction of Philosophy* (OUP 2012) xvi.

[43] Huw Price, 'Naturalism and the fate of the M-Worlds' (1997) 7 *Proceedings of the Aristotelian Society* 247.

regions – morality is one of them – an increasing number of contemporary philosophers[44] find themselves 'on the same [broad or liberal] side of the barricades'.[45] At stake is the ability to account for the difference between what we do and what we should do. When the explanatory resources at our disposal must fit within a 'scientistic' understanding of nature (as outlined in section I.A), it is difficult to explain that difference: 'what we should do' collapses into subjective preferences and attitudes.

Once room is made for the myriad ways in which we come to inhabit our natural world, we find that these habitation endeavours typically entail a variety of dispositions: not only dispositions to do things in a certain way, but also dispositions to deem certain ways of doing things appropriate. Here it helps to call back on Blackburn's apprentice carpenter example:

> Consider, for instance, someone taught to use a carpenter's plane to shave a piece of wood flat. The process is one of sticks and carrots until the skill develops. To the metaphysician's eye this is all just is's, so if, for instance, after the process the apprentice shaves a plank leaving it wavy or jagged, that is just the way the causal process developed. There are dispositions and events all the way down, but nothing that counts as or constitutes, or, in one ugly terminology, acts as a truth maker for correctness or incorrectness (as Kripke's skeptic famously laments). But against the background of the activities of which the technique is a part there is more than that. The jagged or wavy result is unskilled, unintended, and it gives rise to disappointment and rejection.[46]

This apprentice carpenter example is informed by Wittgenstein's remarks on the so-called 'rule-following paradox': 'This was our paradox: no course of action could be determined by a rule, because every course of action can be made out to accord with the rule'.[47] On Kripke's interpretation, Wittgenstein would have meant to point at the sceptical challenge that stems from the absence of facts capable of determining what counts as the 'correct' following of a rule. This sceptical challenge has three branches. Our disposition to be disappointed by (or criticise) the wavy plank or, say, a less than loyal friend, would only point at what we will do, not what we should do.[48] A 'dispositionalist' understanding of rule-following would not be able to justify our abiding by such rules.[49] Nor could it account for the possibility of mistakes.[50] Section III.A highlights how Ginsborg's reference to an 'attitude of primitive appropriateness'[51]

[44] From Price (ibid) to Putnam, *Reason, Truth, and History*, via McDowell, 'Projection and truth in ethics' and Blackburn, 'Normativity à la mode'.

[45] Paul Redding, 'Two directions for analytic Kantianism' in Mario De Caro and David Macarthur (eds), *Naturalism and Normativity* (Columbia UP 2010) 271.

[46] Blackburn, 'Normativity à la mode'.

[47] Ludwig Wittgenstein, *Philosophical Investigations* (Blackwell 1958) 201.

[48] Saul A Kripke, *Wittgenstein on Rules and Private Language: An Elementary Exposition* (Blackwell 1982) 29, 37.

[49] Ibid 37.

[50] Ibid 30–35.

[51] Hannah Ginsborg, 'Primitive normativity and skepticism about rules' (2011) 108 *The Journal of Philosophy* 227.

can go some way towards answering all three branches of Kripke's challenge. Section III.B unpacks the extent to which that attitude needs to be able to switch to one of 'primitive *in*appropriateness' as and when needed: grasping the normative dimension of a rule is also about grasping the circumstances when that rule needs to be broken – a key challenge for the delineation of some plausible 'habitual ethics'.

A. 'Primitive Appropriateness'

Our disposition to not only develop ways of doing things but also to deem those ways of doing things *appropriate* is central to answering all three branches of Kripke's sceptical challenge. This evaluative disposition emerges as a result of being 'inculcated' into ways of doing things, or what Wittgenstein refers to as 'custom' in a passage worth quoting in full:

> "But how can a rule show me what I have to do at this point? Whatever I do is, on some interpretation, in accord with the rule." – That is not what we ought to say, but rather: any interpretation still hangs in the air along with what it interprets, and cannot give it any support. Interpretations by themselves do not determine meaning.
>
> "Then can whatever I do be brought into accord with the rule?" – Let me ask this: what has the expression of a rule – say a sign-post – got to do with my actions?
>
> What sort of connection is there here? – Well, perhaps this one: I have been trained to react to this sign in a particular way, and now I do so react to it.
>
> "But that is only to give a causal connection; to tell how it has come about that we now go by the sign-post; not what this going-by-the-sign really consists in." On the contrary; I have further indicated that a person goes by a sign-post only in so far as there exists a regular use of sign-posts, a custom.[52]

In this passage, Wittgenstein lets the reader tease out the assumption that underpins his interlocutor's disappointment at being offered a merely 'causal' account of rule following. In a nutshell, this assumption comes down to 'the idea that rule following must involve a special mental process, one whose presence removes rule-following behaviour from the realm of natural reactions'.[53] On this view, there cannot be any overlap between 'doing what comes naturally' and following a rule.[54] Despite an abundance of counterexamples taken from our experience of everyday life, this idea is pervasive. Debunking it is not only central to the possibility of a non-reductive naturalism in ethics, it is also crucial to the delineation of the conditions under which there can be such a thing as 'habitual ethics'.

[52] Wittgenstein, *Philosophical Investigations*.

[53] Jason Bridges, 'Rule-following skepticism, properly so called' in James Conant and Andrea Kern (eds), *Varieties of Skepticism: Essays after Kant, Wittgenstein, and Cavell* (De Gruyter 2014) 46.

[54] For a further critique see Gertrude Elizabeth Margaret Anscombe, 'Rules, rights, and promises' (1978) 3 *Midwest Studies in Philosophy* 318.

For those in thrall to the idea that rule following presupposes some special mental process directing us from outside habits or impulsive reactions, Wittgenstein's suggested therapy is to focus on the 'concrete cases'.[55] Whether it be the disposition to go by a sign, perform a mathematical calculation or shave a plank in a certain way, in each case that disposition is accompanied by a conviction that this is the appropriate way of doing things. Ginsborg refers to that conviction as an attitude of 'primitive appropriateness'. It is primitive in that taking something to be appropriate in this sense does not require any prior grasp of the rule:

> we can reverse the relation between the awareness of normativity and grasp of a rule, holding that grasp of a rule is to be explained in terms of the consciousness of one's activity as appropriate to one's circumstances and hence as normatively constrained.[56]

The 'consciousness of one's activity as appropriate' results from a process of internalisation: in the process of learning to go by a sign or shaving a plank, we internalise the set of expectations inherent in that practice. This internalisation process not only entails that the performance becomes effortless; it also means we become prone to criticising deviation from those expectations. But is it also compatible with a capacity to change or deviate from that practice ourselves? What happens if at some point we become conscious of the activity we are disposed towards as '*in*appropriate to the circumstances'?

B. Dispositions, the Possibility of Mistakes and 'Primitive *In*appropriateness'

Suppose I have been criticising a fellow carpenter for shaving her planks of wood the wrong way, or with the wrong tools, until one day it becomes apparent that her way of doing things yields a better result. My criticisms will give way to a new-found conviction that this way of shaving wood is the appropriate way. When we switch from the art of wood shaving to practices of ethical significance, how do shifts of this kind take place? Can we ever point at the equivalent of 'superior wood shaving results'? If an equivalent, objective standard cannot easily be mustered, are our 'ethically loaded' dispositions merely pitched against another's in a sort of 'weight contest'?

Consider the end-of-life care scenario mentioned earlier. In many ways, the strength of our drive to save or prolong lives is to be celebrated. The widespread disposition to keep intervening therapeutically until it is undeniably too late

[55] In his 'Blue Book', Wittgenstein can be seen as encouraging 'the philosopher' to stop dismissing 'as irrelevant the concrete cases, which alone could have helped him to understand the usage of the general term': Ludwig Wittgenstein, *The Blue Book* (Harper & Row 1960) 19–20.

[56] Hannah Ginsborg, 'Normativity and concepts' in Daniel Star (ed), *The Oxford Handbook of Reasons and Normativity* (OUP 2018) 18.

is associated with a conviction that this is the decent thing to do as a matter of course. The relatively recent introduction of end-of-life care conversations nevertheless makes space for the articulation of aspirations that may call into question the desirability of certain therapeutic interventions. These conversations have been introduced on the back of growing unease on the part of both doctors and the general public about the sometimes brutal implications of relentless – and increasingly powerful – medical interventions. The shift enabled by the introduction of these conversations proceeds at several levels. There may be a new, explicit rule about the need to consult with the patient to understand and take into account the patient's end-of-life care aspirations. This explicit rule goes hand in hand with a transformation of both patients' and doctors' own pre-reflective dispositions when it comes to end-of-life care.

Was the shift that led to those more frequent end-of-life care conversations triggered by the dawning realisation of a 'mistake' – or the discovery that 'better results' can be achieved through those conversations? Unlikely. To understand the way in which a shift in pre-reflective dispositions can be triggered by 'imperfectly rationalised' intuitions[57] about the 'primitive inappropriateness' of certain ethical stances, Williams' 'axiological habitat' metaphor helps:

> we shall see their judgments as part of their way of living, a cultural artifact they have come to inhabit (though they have not consciously built it). On this, nonobjectivist, model, we shall take a different view of the relations between that practice and critical reflection. We shall not be disposed to see the level of reflection as implicitly already there.[58]

Seeing values – and the ethical stances they give rise to – as a kind of habitation helps to capture the way in which a conviction of primitive *in*appropriateness need not presuppose 'the dissolving force of [deliberative] analysis',[59] to use Mill's words. This *in*appropriateness can be perceived pre-reflectively, just like the suitability of a habitat. The environment or a way of living might change in such a way as to make our present habitation feel ill-suited or cramped: as can the values presiding over our ethically-loaded practices. Born 'pre-reflectively', this feeling of ill-suitability will be informed by the set of practical claims which our dynamic, evolving 'life form'[60] makes upon us. This dynamic dimension is important, since:

> species themselves are subject to change. This is of course important, and it means that Aristotelian categoricals must take account of sub-species adapted to

[57] Bernard Williams, 'Conflicts of value', *Moral Luck: Philosophical Papers* (CUP 1981).

[58] Bernard Williams, *Ethics and the Limits of Philosophy* (Fontana Masterguides 1985) 147.

[59] '[M]oral associations which are wholly of artificial creation, when the intellectual culture goes on, yield by degrees to the dissolving force of analysis; and if the feeling of duty, when associated with utility, would appear equally arbitrary … it might happen that this association also, even after it had been implanted by education, might be analyzed away' John Stuart Mill, *Utilitarianism* (Cambridge Library Collection – Philosophy, CUP 2014 [1863]) 46.

[60] This is a nod to Thomson' naturalism, which won't be unpacked here despite its pertinence: Judith Jarvis Thomson, *Normativity* (Open Court 2008); Judith Jarvis Thomson, 'The right and the good' (1997) 94 *The Journal of Philosophy* 273.

> local conditions. The history of a species is not, however, the subject with which Aristotelian categoricals deal. Their truth is truth about a species at a given historical time ...[61]

Coming from an author as explicitly committed to an Aristotelian type of naturalism as Foot, the above rejoinder is significant. A teleological, Aristotelian understanding of human nature is not particularly concerned with the need for dynamic adaptation, as a species shapes and is shaped by its environment. This is an important lacuna: the facts that guide our attempts to find our way around the world are not only a matter of who we are. These facts are also a matter of who we are becoming. Bracket that out and it becomes much easier to understand why the Aristotelian tradition pays relatively little attention to the fact that carefully cultivated habits and dispositions can become patently inadequate: that is also a fact about human nature.

It is in large part because of the above dynamic that it is perilous to ever deem the process of habituation at the root of ethically significant dispositions as 'having come to a close'. To be receptive to the occasional need to break rules, to distance oneself from what may otherwise still be perceived as 'primitively appropriate', habituation needs to be continuously honed. While our capacity to 'recognize reasons for action and to act on them'[62] can be relied on as a critical distanciation tool, from a naturalist perspective that capacity may not only be decried as 'already pervasively and substantively moralized'.[63] It can also prove inferior compared to our pre-reflective 'ethical intelligence', which is explored in the next chapter.

[61] Philippa Foot, *Natural Goodness* (Clarendon Press 2003) 29.
[62] Ibid 24.
[63] Matthew Lutz and James Lenman, 'Moral naturalism' (*The Stanford Encyclopedia of Philosophy*, 2021), plato.stanford.edu/archives/spr2021/entries/naturalism-moral accessed 8 February 2021.

2

Habit and Skill Acquisition

> We may be said to know how by means of our habits [...] We walk and read aloud, we get off and on street cars, we dress and undress, and do a thousand useful acts without thinking of them. We know something, namely, how to do them.
>
> John Dewey, *Human Nature and Conduct*[1]

THE INTERNALISATION ELEMENT that is necessary to the emergence of a habit is what makes habit powerful. Our ability to attend to the vast flows of information that structure our environment is limited; the extent to which we can process this information to shape current and future choices even more so. We need shortcuts. Section I endeavours to explain why we still have such a poor understanding of the factors that condition the extent to which 'unthinking activity' can play a role that supports deliberate, intentional action.

Our capacity to navigate and continually learn from our environment largely depends on the quality of the habits of thought and judgement built through experience. The latter hinges on two broad sets of factors. Section II highlights the impact of the two-way relationship between an agent's emergent abilities and environmental affordances: this two-way relationship can be structured in such a way as to be more or less conducive to the development of reliable habits. Section III focuses on the extent to which a habit's availability to conscious awareness (section III.A) and adaptability (section III.B) can be impacted by the agent's attitude.

I. SKILFUL COPING AND SKILFUL ACTION

When attempting to write this book, some would say[2] that I am driven by a mental representation of the concepts and ideas I am trying to communicate.

[1] John Dewey, *Human Nature and Conduct: An Introduction to Social Psychology* (G Allen & Unwin 1922).

[2] This formulation reflects my (detached) attempt to accommodate the language that would be used by philosophers such as Davidson or Searle – see below.

Roughly the same could be said about my endeavours to bake cakes or book family holidays. The mental representation of my goal – and the steps needed to achieve it – may be deeply flawed. It may also come in and out of focus, as my browsing may distract me enough to forget I meant to book a family holiday. Yet some appreciation for the quality of the steps taken and/or the end result may nevertheless warrant a description of these deliberate actions as skilful.

The above emphasis on mental representations is illustrative of a large strand of cognitive scientists and philosophers – Davidson is most often quoted in this respect. Within this philosophical strand, an action only counts as such if it is 'intentional under some description',[3] and this intentionality translates into some mental intentional content.[4] Concretely, this means that while the above book writing, cake baking and holiday booking probably count as actions on those accounts, my getting dressed this morning, eating the snacks on my desk and cycling to school do not. They could have; had I not quickly pulled on whatever came to hand, but carefully planned my outfit as I dressed instead, it would probably count as an action.

What is problematic in the above is not so much the intentionality condition (which lends itself to multiple interpretations) as the 'mental intentional content' requirement. The dominance of this 'representational' account of action has led to philosophical contempt for the myriad kinds of 'doings' that do not involve one's forming a mental representation of the goal driving those doings. Emblematic of this trend is Ryle's '[w]hen we describe someone as doing something by pure or blind habit, we mean that he does it automatically and *without having to mind* what he is doing'.[5] This quote is illustrative of a behaviourist stance[6] that has led to habit being all but dismissed within mainstream analytic philosophy.

McDowell's account of habits as 'embodied coping skills' which would – in mature human beings – '[be] permeated with mindedness' is one of the most notable exceptions. Yet this emphasis on the 'mindedness' that is meant to characterise unreflective agency betrays McDowell's eagerness to depict habitual actions in such a way as to acknowledge their 'participating in the space

[3] Donald Davidson, *Essays on Actions and Events* (Clarendon Press 1980) essay 3.

[4] 'To this day philosophers such as John Searle and Donald Davidson, who do not agree on much else, agree that action must be explained in terms of mental states with intentional content': Hubert L Dreyfus, 'Heidegger's critique of the Husserl/Searle account of intentionality' (1993) *Social Research* 17, 18.

[5] Gilbert Ryle, *The Concept of Mind: 60th Anniversary Edition* (Taylor & Francis 1949/2009) (my emphasis). Note that Ryle does distinguish between 'habits' and 'intelligent capacities' – the skills that together form the basis of our 'knowing how'. The grounds of Ryle's stark distinction between habits and such skills however remain questionable.

[6] Accordingly, this conception emphasises the lack of 'awareness, conscious control, cognitive effort, or deliberation' in habit performance: Benjamin Gardner, 'A review and analysis of the use of "habit" in understanding, predicting and influencing health-related behaviour' (2014) 9 *Health Psychology Review* 277.

of reasons',[7] rather than being wholly determined by causal chains of events.[8] The price of the metaphysical assumptions underlying this 'metaphor of two spaces'[9] (reasons versus causes) is not just an awkward fit with the experiential specifics of unreflective action: this 'responding-to-reasons' account also compromises McDowell's alertness to the fallibility – and hence need for modifiability – of habit. This inattentiveness to the extent to which habits can be or become compromising affects many other contemporary accounts, as unpacked in chapter five.

In contrast to the above, 'intellectualist' stance on habit, phenomenological accounts emphasise the extent to which we are capable of unreflective action that is skilful even in a complete absence of mindedness. Much of my life is spent 'sensing'[10] – and coping with – things in a purposive way that does not involve either 'mindedness' or my forming a mental representation of the goal driving those doings. As Dreyfus puts it:

> Phenomenological examination shows that in a wide variety of situations human beings relate to the world in an organized purposive manner without the constant accompaniment of a representational state which specifies what the action is aimed at accomplishing.[11]

It may only characterise a tiny part of our daily lives; yet the deliberate, focused stance is what we notice. Philosophers' captivation for that deliberative stance would be pretty harmless were it not frequently accompanied by some haughty indifference for the many forms of non-deliberate 'obscure intelligence(s)'[12] that make up the bulk of our existence.

Heidegger's key contribution in this respect was to challenge this traditional oversight and highlight the extent to which our non-deliberate 'coping' with the

[7] Charles Taylor, 'Foundationalism and the inner-outer distinction' in Nicholas H Smith (ed), *Reading McDowell: On Mind and World* (Routledge 2002) 115.

[8] McDowell confirms his need for a way of interacting with the world that is between the purely causal on the one hand, and the reflective on the other, to understand animal behaviour and human unreflective action: 'I agree with Taylor that there is something between spontaneity in what he calls "the strong Kantian sense, turning crucially on conceptual, reflective thought," on the one hand, and conformity to Galilean law, on the other. We need this middle ground for thinking about non-human animals, and it is what is supposed to be occupied by pre-understanding even in our case': John McDowell, 'Responses' in Nicholas H Smith (ed), *Reading McDowell: On Mind and World* (Routledge 2002) 283.

[9] For a critique of McDowell's reference to the 'space of reasons' (introduced in John McDowell, *Mind and World: With a New Introduction by the Author* (Harvard UP 1996)) and the dangers underlying this 'metaphor of two spaces', see Simon Blackburn, 'Normativity à la mode' (2001) 5 *Journal of Ethics: An International Philosophical Review* 139.

[10] The perceived object and the perceiving subject owe their thickness to sensing: Maurice Merleau-Ponty, *Phenomenology of Perception* (Routledge 2012) 53.

[11] Dreyfus, 'Heidegger's critique' 7.

[12] 'Habit produces not only a tendency to act and the diminution of the tendency to feel; above all, it produces an "obscure intelligence" that operates below the level of will, consciousness, intentionality or reflection, an intelligence in which all forms of life participate': Elizabeth Grosz, 'Habit today: Ravaisson, Bergson, Deleuze and us' (2013) 19 *Body & Society* 217, 223.

world ('*Verhalten*', often translated as 'comportment'[13]) is a background condition that makes deliberate, focused action possible.

Heidegger's insights – which he put forward in lectures given in 1927 – were not lost on Dreyfus, whose critique of the overly cognitive assumptions underlying early AI endeavours (in the 1960s)[14] proved prescient. Attempts to teach machines formal models of the world (under the now defunct assumption that intelligent behaviour is impossible in the absence of such *a priori* representational models) have long been sidelined. Yet we still have a relatively poor understanding of the factors that condition the extent to which 'unthinking activity' plays a role that is not only compatible with, but actually supports, deliberate action.[15]

Among these factors, the nature of an individual's participation in the environment that structures intentional action is crucial. Some environments are artificially configured so as to maximise the extent to which an individual is in a position to let herself be guided by her environment.[16] In ideal cases, 'one's body is solicited by the situation to get into the right relation to it. When everyday coping is going well, we experience something like what athletes call flow, or playing out of their heads'.[17]

While the nature of the possibilities for action provided by our environment – often referred to as 'affordances'[18] – clearly matters, the agent's ability and propensity to act on such affordances matters too, yet it is less commonly emphasised.[19] When one considers the acquisition of skills like the ability to

[13] 'Comportments have the structure of directing-oneself-toward, of being-directed-toward. […] Phenomenology calls this structure intentionality': Martin Heidegger, *The Basic Problems of Phenomenology* (Indiana UP 1988) 59.

[14] Hubert L Dreyfus, *Alchemy and Artificial Intelligence* (Rand Corporation Santa Monica, California 1965).

[15] David Owens, 'Habitual agency' (2017) 20 *Philosophical Explorations* 93; Joseph Raz, 'Intention and value' (2017) 20 *Philosophical Explorations* 109. For an account of habit that brilliantly outlines the Aristotelian alternative to the all too common understanding of habit as necessarily at odds with, or compromising autonomous, intentional action, see Clare Carlisle, *On Habit* (Routledge 2014).

[16] '[W]e do more and greater justice to it the more we let ourselves be guided by it, i.e., the less reserved we are in immersing ourselves in it and subordinating ourselves to it. We find ourselves in a situation and are interwoven with it': Aron Gurwitsch, *Human Encounters in the Social World* (Duquesne UP 1979) 67.

[17] Dreyfus, 'Heidegger's critique' 6. Dreyfus continues with the example of an expert tennis swing: 'If one is a beginner or is off one's form one might find oneself making an effort to keep one's eye on the ball, keep the racket perpendicular to the court, hit the ball squarely, etc. But if one is expert at the game and things are going well, what is experienced is more like one's arm going up and its being drawn to the appropriate position, the racket forming the optimal angle with the court […] One feels that one's motion was caused by the perceived conditions in such a way as to reduce a sense of deviation from some satisfactory *gestalt*'.

[18] James Jerome Gibson, *The Ecological Approach to Visual Perception* (Houghton Mifflin 1979); Anthony Chemero, 'An outline of a theory of affordances' (2003) 15 *Ecological Psychology* 181; Anthony Chemero, *Radical Embodied Cognitive Science* (MIT Press 2009); Claire F Michaels, 'Affordances: Four points of debate' (2003) 15 *Ecological Psychology* 135; Edward Reed, *Encountering the World: Toward an Ecological Psychology* (OUP 1996); Alan Costall, 'Socializing affordances' (1995) 5 *Theory & Psychology* 467; Harry Heft, *Ecological Psychology in Context: James Gibson, Roger Barker, and the Legacy of William James's Radical Empiricism* (Lawrence Erlbaum 2001).

[19] Erik Rietveld, Damiaan Denys and Maarten Van Westen, 'Ecological-Enactive Cognition as engaging with a field of relevant affordances' in *The Oxford Handbook of 4E Cognition* (OUP 2018).

play tennis, the extent to which the learning agent retains the willingness to respond to relevant affordances is less critical than when turning to the skills that underpin expertise in morally loaded contexts. In such contexts, 'broadening the notion of affordances' 'to include affordances for activities that people would traditionally classify as forms of "higher" cognition'[20] is necessary. This leads Rietveld to talk of non-propositional 'responsiveness to significance (including normative significance)'[21] instead of 'affordances'.

This move is significant for our purposes. A large part of this book is devoted to problematising precisely such 'non-propositional responsiveness to normative significance'. Chapter three analyses its import through the lens of morally loaded professional practice, while chapters four and five highlight the need to construct an account of ethical agency that places the challenge inherent in retaining such responsiveness at its core. Finally, Part II of this book analyses the impact of 'macro' factors – such as legal institutional design and computer systems design – on our retaining such 'responsiveness to normative significance'.

For now, the following two sections in this chapter highlight the impact of the two-way relationship between an agent's emergent abilities (section III) and environmental affordances (section II).

II. THE STRUCTURE OF THE ENVIRONMENT AND ITS IMPACT ON SKILL ACQUISITION

There are two broadly contrasting ways of envisaging the role played by an agent's environment when it comes to the process underlying judgement formation and skill acquisition. In most recent endeavours to challenge the contemptuous stance towards the non-reflective roots of judgement formation, the role played by the environment features front and centre. As an example, the so-called 'Skilled Intentionality Framework'[22]

> highlights the relevance of investigating the region of the landscape of affordances in which the individual is involved (e.g. by analyzing involvement in the sociomaterial practice over longer periods of time, see Brouwers and Rietveld 2016) and the structure of the resulting field of solicitations (including relevant place affordances and the current abilities of the individual) to learn something about the activity of the brain and body, and vice versa (Bruineberg and Rietveld 2014).[23]

[20] Ibid 6.

[21] Erik Rietveld, 'McDowell and Dreyfus on Unreflective Action' (2010) 53 *Inquiry* 183, 202.

[22] Aside from the work of Rietveld and others (below), Clark's 'embodied approach to cognition' pays particular attention to the way 'evolutionarily developed, domain-adapted' cognitive systems cope with their environments: see ch 8 of Andy Clark, *Being There: Putting Brain, Body, and World Together Again* (MIT Press 1997).

[23] Rietveld, Denys and Van Westen, 'Ecological-Enactive Cognition'.

In contrast to the above, more traditional cognitive studies tend to come at this environmental factor indirectly. The rest of this section is devoted to analysing the way in which two divergent takes on the role played by intuitive processes within judgement formation are (subsequently) explained by referring to differences in the structure of the environments considered. This 'post-hoc' inference is problematic in that it necessarily underestimates the extent to which the learning agent and her surrounding environment should 'co-evolve'.

A. The 'Skilled Intuitions' Stance

Many of the decisions we make on a daily basis involve some sort of prediction: from my choice of clothes this morning to my deciding how many courgettes to buy for dinner tonight. These decisions may not be experienced as decisions. When I hastily discarded sheer tights and unearthed some thick opaque ones sitting underneath a jumbled pile, my focus was on the train I'd just missed rather than any grandiose 'outfit decision', let alone 'outfit need' prediction. Yet that evening I silently lauded the intuitive switch when I discovered I was to sit on one of those dreaded 'podium with chairs' panels. Far from being random, this morning's hurried selection reflected rich priors acquired through experience. As Christian and Griffiths put it:

> Our judgments betray our expectations, and our expectations betray our experience. What we project about the future reveals a lot – about the world we live in, and about our own past.[24]

Beyond the mundane domain of tights choice and courgette shopping, our informal, tacit grasp of likely patterns of events also informs judgements and decisions associated with higher cognition skills. These skills have been the focus of the so-called 'naturalistic decision making' tradition (NDM),[25] which developed from an attempt to analyse the way fireground commanders make decisions under conditions of uncertainty and time pressure. Works within NDM studies tend to show that reliance on intuition to detect patterns of similarity between past and present situations can enable experts to perform much better than had they systematically sought to analyse and evaluate all feasible options.[26]

Because it is regular and provides ample feedback opportunity, chess is a paradigmatic example of a field where skilled intuition is essential to high

[24] Brian Christian and Tom Griffiths, *Algorithms to Live by: The Computer Science of Human Decisions* (Macmillan 2016) 2649 (loc).

[25] Gary Klein, 'Naturalistic decision making' (2008) 50 *Human Factors: The Journal of the Human Factors and Ergonomics Society* 456; Caroline E Zsambok and Gary Klein, *Naturalistic Decision Making* (Psychology Press 2014).

[26] '[S]imple heuristics that ignore information can be better – faster, more frugal, and more accurate – than complex strategies that use all available information': Gerd Gigerenzer and Henry Brighton, 'Can hunches be rational' (2007) 4 *Journal of Law, Economics & Policy* 155.

performance. Unsurprisingly, it was the focus of early NDM studies. These studies showed that, thanks to their 'perceptual skill' enabling them to recognise complex patterns,[27] chess masters were able to rapidly identify the most promising moves or the strength of a particular chessboard formation[28] while bypassing slow, cognitive processes.

In professional contexts, NDM has since studied many examples of such skilled intuition.[29] Crandall and Getchell-Reiter[30] for instance studied the intuitions that allow nurses in a neonatal intensive care unit to detect life-threatening infections even before blood tests came back positive. These intuitions draw upon tacit[31] rather than explicit knowledge: the nurses' remarkable ability is acquired through a process of gradual habituation, rather than any formalised training based on a set of rules or principles.

B. The 'Heuristics and Bias' Stance

In contrast to the positive, empowering role attributed to intuitive processes by NDM and other studies, Kahneman – and more widely the 'heuristics and biases' approach ('HB') – sees the latter with suspicion. 'HB' draws a distinction between 'System 1' (S1), which encompasses all the effortless impulses, instincts and intuitions that drive our non-cognitive responses with a greater or lesser degree of automaticity, and the slow and deliberate choices of 'System 2' (S2). This distinction is largely drawn to better raise our awareness of the vulnerability to biases and mistakes that is concomitant with uncritical reliance on S1.[32] Among such biases, Kahneman emphasises, for instance, the extent to which our 'confirmation bias'[33] makes us more likely to seek evidence that confirms the beliefs we already hold (for example when we are asked if someone is friendly,

[27] William G Chase and Herbert A Simon, 'The mind's eye in chess' (1973) Proceedings of the Eighth Annual Carnegie Symposium on Cognition, Held at the Carnegie-Mellon University, Pittsburgh, Pennsylvania, 19 May 1972.

[28] Evan Selinger, Hubert Dreyfus and Harry Collins, 'Interactional expertise and embodiment' (2007) 38 *Studies in History and Philosophy of Science* Part A 722; Dreyfus, *Alchemy and Artificial Intelligence*.

[29] Raanan M Lipshitz and others, 'Naturalistic decision making and organizations: Reviewing pragmatic science' (2006) 27 *Organization Studies* 925.

[30] Beth Crandall and Karen Getchell-Reiter, 'Critical decision method: A technique for eliciting concrete assessment indicators from the intuition of NICU nurses' (1993) 16 *Advances in Nursing Science* 42.

[31] For a study delving into the characteristics of such tacit knowledge see Nicky Priaulx, Martin Weinel and Anthony Wrigley, 'Rethinking moral expertise' (2014) 24 *Health Care Analysis* 1.

[32] The impact of Kahneman's dual-processing account based on S1 and S2 is such that the latter two categories – S1 and S2 – have come to acquire a definition of their own (whereby S1 stands for those broadly unreflective, 'fast' processes that impact upon our behaviour while S2 stands for the opposite: unreflective, slow processes): Daniel Kahneman, *Thinking, Fast and Slow* (Macmillan 2011).

[33] Ibid 87.

we will have a different automatic response than if we are asked if someone is unfriendly). The only remedy to S1's gullibility, on Kahneman's account, is to lean on the slow and deliberate workings of S2.

C. Explaining Divergent Stances on Intuitive Expertise by Reference to the Structure of the Environment

On the face of it, the contrast between the 'heuristics and bias' defiant stance towards the non-cognitive processes characteristic of S1, on one hand, and NDM studies' highlighting the centrality of those very same processes to the skills acquired by chess players and neonatal nurses, on the other, could not be starker. Whereas the former emphasises that reliance on S1 makes us vulnerable to all sorts of blunders, the latter demonstrates the extent to which purposefully side-lining those same processes can leave one with a poorer, less performant grasp of a situation. Without S1, the fireman won't sense that a building is about to collapse, and neonatal nurses may not detect very early signs of infection.

One may ponder what explains this divergent take. Helpfully, Kahneman and Klein[34] discuss both the shared understandings and the factors that are likely to have contributed to this divergence. Among these factors, Kahneman and Klein emphasise that the extent to which these intuitive, non-cognitive processes end up playing a constructive role in part hinges on the structure of the learning environment. Skilled intuitions are much more likely to develop (and prove reliable) in an environment of sufficient regularity which provides opportunity for systematic feedback, or what Hogarth refers to as a 'kind' environment:

> In kind learning structures, people receive good feedback, and the right lessons can be learned from experience. In wicked learning environments, feedback can be misleading, and the right lessons are not always learned.[35]

In a 'kind', fairly well-contained environment (such as a neonatal intensive care unit), the events occurring within it are more plausibly traceable to a set of causes with genuine predictive power, even if the latter is not yet explained from a theoretical perspective. This contrasts to the multitude of circumstances that may contribute to something like stock evaluations: in open-ended, shifting environments, an individual's attributing predictive power to particular factors is likely to be a misleading over-simplification.

[34] D Kahneman and G Klein, 'Conditions for intuitive expertise: A failure to disagree' (2009) 64 *American Psychologist* 515.

[35] Robin M Hogarth, *Educating Intuition* (University of Chicago Press 2001) 98. Hogarth and others later argue for a framework that identifies which environments are kind/wicked because of inferential errors and suggests that kind learning environments improve probabilisitc judgements in Robin M Hogarth, Tomás Lejarraga and Emre Soyer, 'The two settings of kind and wicked learning environments' (2015) 24 *Current Directions in Psychological Science* 379.

III. 'TACIT' LEARNING ATTITUDE(S)

While Kahneman and Klein's tracing the roots of their 'disagreement' to environmental structure differences rings true, their 'failure to disagree'[36] still presupposes a uni-directional understanding of the 'agent–environment' relationship. It also shows scant interest for the reasons why the same amount of exposure to a given environment can result in vastly different 'tacit learning' outcomes. Reference to varying degrees of cognitive prowess may be able to account for asymmetries within 'explicit learning' endeavours. Yet such prowess becomes less significant when it comes to what enables some to quickly develop – and maintain – an astute, intuitive grasp of a situation.

Among all the factors that are likely to impact upon the quality of the habits that structure experience-based learning processes, two are of particular relevance for our purposes: availability to conscious awareness and adaptability. Whereas the mechanisms that are meant to ensure a model's adaptability at a cognitive level are fairly familiar, argument-based processes, far less attention has been paid to our ongoing ability to adapt the mechanisms that condition our tacit learning – with habit prime among them.

This lack of attention proceeds in part from a widespread but mistaken assumption that habit is simply not or hardly adaptable. This might be true for Pavlovian automatisms and 'tics' – for ways of having a habit that are least available to conscious awareness. Yet this ignores ways of having a habit that are not only available to conscious awareness, but also highly goal-adaptable. This section reviews these two primary components – availability to conscious awareness (section III.A) and adaptability (section III.B)[37] – in a bid to gain a better understanding of the conditions under which habits support the learning processes that underpin our capacity for ethical agency (this ulterior motive will become clearer in chapter five).

A. Automaticity and Availability to Conscious Awareness

Despite it being the object of long-standing interest in psychology, there is currently no consensus about what automaticity means, or what it takes for a

[36] Kahneman and Klein, 'Conditions for intuitive expertise'.

[37] Highlighting the problems that stem from 'the inflexibility of [the experts'] information-processing system', Frensch and Sternberg have sought to present empirical evidence explaining why experts may at times be outperformed by non-experts: 'We claim that flexibility and expertise are inextricably linked. A problem solver's flexibility to adapt his or her reasoning when situational requirements change is affected by the size and structure of his or her knowledge organisation and by the extent to which the solution strategies have become proceduralised': Peter A Frensch and Robert J Sternberg, 'Expertise and intelligent thinking: When is it worse to know better' (1989) 5 *Advances in the Psychology of Human Intelligence* 157.

process to be deemed 'automatic'. Some have sought to isolate key features – from intentionality to controllability and conscious awareness – deemed to be indicative of automatic processes, whether they be considered necessary[38] or optional.[39] Such feature-based approaches, however, tend to suggest an unrealistic, mutually exclusive picture of automatic versus non-automatic processes. Gradual accounts, by contrast, make room for the fact that automatic processes more often than not operate *alongside* deliberative processes; the former displaying differing degrees[40] of sensitivity to the latter.[41]

Following Levy and Bayne, we may draw a spectrum that takes us from fully deliberative agency to automatic agency – the latter 'involves an absence (or at least a reduction) of the experience of doing'[42] – all the way to 'automatistic agency'. It is only in the latter case, particularly so when consciousness is 'globally disrupted' (Levy and Bayne refer to somnambulism, epileptic fugue, drug-related and trance states) that automaticity becomes impermeable to deliberative intervention. In all other cases, including that of 'automatic' (rather than 'automatistic') agency, automatic processes work alongside their deliberative counterparts, the latter taking over as soon as some disruption demands resumption of fully deliberative agency: 'When we meet with unexpected road conditions we switch from automatic to conscious agency, and are immediately conscious of what we are doing'.[43]

In fact, the extent to which automatic and intentional processes often mutually support each other – provided the underlying automaticity does remain 'within reach' of conscious awareness – can make any endeavour to disentangle them somewhat counter-productive. To illustrate the extent of such entanglement, the example of piano practice is often given. While piano practice must be

[38] Michael I Posner and Charles RR Snyder, 'Attention and cognitive control' in Robert L Solso (ed), *Information Processing and Cognition: The Loyola Symposium* (Erlbaum 1975).

[39] Bargh refers to 'efficient, unintentional, uncontrollable and unconscious' – all deemed to be optional features – as 'the four horsemen of automaticity': John A Bargh, 'The four horsemen of automacity: Awareness, intention, efficiency, and control in social cognition' in Robert S Wyer and Thomas K Srull (eds), *Handbook of Social Cognition*, vol 1 (Erlbaum 1994).

[40] The de-compositional account of automaticity distinguishes between different kinds of automaticity by appeal to the different combinations of features that characterise automatic processes: Agnes Moors and Jan De Houwer, 'Automaticity: a theoretical and conceptual analysis' (2006) 132 *Psychological Bulletin* 297; Agnes Moors and Jan De Houwer, 'What is automaticity? An analysis of its component features and their interrelations' (2007) *Social Psychology and the Unconscious: The Automaticity of Higher Mental Processes* 11.

[41] In their review of the literature on automaticity, Moors and De Houwer, 'Automaticity: A theoretical and conceptual analysis' express their ambivalence towards such a gradual approach, an ambivalence which might reflect their discipline's (psychology) methodological constraints: 'The good news is that a gradual approach is justified. The bad news is that we have no objective criterion to draw a line between the automatic and the nonautomatic member in each feature pair: every process is efficient, uncontrolled, unconscious, and fast to some extent'.

[42] Neil Levy and Tim Bayne, 'Doing without deliberation: automatism, automaticity, and moral accountability' (2004) 16 *International Review of Psychiatry* 209, 210.

[43] Ibid 214.

intentionally initiated, robust habits need to be developed in order for the agent to be able to express herself through that instrument (rather than laboriously pushing various piano keys). By automating a series of gestures and transitions, habit frees the agent's attention from the constraints of score reading and complex hand movements. This can and will lead to better piano practice in that the agent can actively engage with the piece she is playing and set new artistic goals. This empowering aspect of habit however fades away the moment the agent loses the ability to bring the automated patterns of behaviour back to conscious awareness.

B. Automaticity and Adaptability

Considered on its own, the concept of 'adaptability' of habit and its underlying automaticity is too vague to be helpful. What follows distinguishes between 'external, goal adaptability' and 'internal, understanding-of-self adaptability' reluctantly: while it has didactic value, this distinction artificially imposes a boundary when ideally there should be none. This will become apparent in chapter five.

i. External Goal Adaptability

The goals relevant to piano practice operate at many levels. Aside from the 'meta-goal' (ie playing the piano and perhaps developing some new mode of artistic expression), there will be lots of sub-goals that pertain to the particular piece being played, the type of tempo or nuance being sought, and so on. On the 'representational' account of action discussed in section I.A, each of those sub-goals would be said to be unconsciously activated when coming across an environmental cue that has been repeatedly associated with that particular goal.[44] That cue might be some annotation on the score or a particular chord being played, for instance.

Of course, these sub-goals need to be able to change for practice to continue to improve. This is where the adaptability condition comes in: the automaticity which underlies the habits supporting piano practice needs to have retained a degree of adaptability to goal changes if they are to empower (rather than hinder) piano practice. Such adaptability cannot be taken for granted.

[44] Note that Jerome Wakefield and Hubert Dreyfus, 'Intentionality and Phenomenology of Action' in Ernest Lepore and Robert Van Gulick (eds), *John Searle and his Critics* (Blackwell 1991) refer to the 'subsidiary acts' required by a skilled activity like playing the piano as examples of what they call 'Gestalt intentionality'. Unlike representation-mediated intentionality, such Gestalt intentionality does not, on their account, require that each subsidiary act in an activity like playing the piano be preceded by a representation of the act. Given that it is not feasible for all those subsidiary acts to be associated with a particular goal, it need not entail anything about goal-dependent automaticity *per se*.

Some, like Wood and Rünger[45] go as far[46] as to argue that one of '[t]wo defining features of habit automaticity' consists precisely in 'insensitivity to short-term changes in goals', even if they concede that habit may 'integrate[s] with more effortful goal pursuit [...] when necessary, as when habits prove unreliable in a given context or when people are especially motivated and able to tailor responses to particular circumstances'.[47]

This passing reference to 'special motivation' as a factor conditioning habit adaptability is important, and still frequently overlooked by contemporary accounts. One does not need to suffer from various forms of psychiatric disorders (such as Obsessive-Compulsive Disorder (OCD)[48]) to see one's responsiveness to affordances compromised. A mere 'lack of aspiration',[49] to use Annas' expression, can be just as disruptive. When it becomes contagious and/or perdures over time, such a lack of aspiration will modify those very affordances one initially failed to respond to. Rietveld and others' definition of 'affordance' as 'a relation between (a) an aspect of the (sociomaterial) environment and (b) an ability available in a "form of life"'[50] is particularly helpful in this respect.

Always in the making, a 'form of life' can nevertheless 'ossify' under the weight of social practices that have become so rigidified as to become mere routine. In their optimism about the extent to which all living beings remain dynamically responsive to states of disequilibrium in their relationship with their environment, phenomenological studies[51] have not paid as much attention as they might to the 'macro' factors that may compromise this cycle of dynamic responses. This will be the focus of the second part of this book.

[45] Wendy Wood and Dennis Rünger, 'Psychology of habit' (2016) 67 *Annual Review of Psychology* 289.

[46] For an alternative, 'auto-motive' account of goal-dependent action see John A Bargh, 'Auto-motives: Preconscious determinants of social interaction', *Handbook of Motivation and Cognition: Foundations of Social Behavior, Vol 2* (The Guilford Press 1990); John A Bargh, 'The automaticity of everyday life' in Robert S Wyer (ed), *The Automaticity of Everyday Life: Advances in Social Cognition, Vol 10* (Advances in social cognition, Vol 10, Lawrence Erlbaum Associates Publishers 1997); John A Bargh and Peter M Gollwitzer, 'Environmental control of goal-directed action: Automatic and strategic contingencies between situations and behavior' in *Integrative Views of Motivation, Cognition, and Emotion*, Nebraska symposium on motivation, Vol 41 (University of Nebraska Press 1994). On this view, an agent's goals can be activated by being elicited by environmental or contextual features.

[47] Wood and Rünger, 'Psychology of habit'.

[48] Rietveld and others refer to the changes experienced by 'OCD patients treated with DBS [deep brain stimulation]' and on that basis argue that 'These phenomenological changes can be understood as changes in their responsiveness to the field of affordances as a whole, not just to the social affordances encountered.' Erik Rietveld, Sanneke De Haan and Damiaan Denys, 'Social affordances in context: what is it that we are bodily responsive to' (2013) 36(4) *Behavioral and Brain Sciences* 436.

[49] Continued aspiration, for Annas, is what distinguishes intelligent habits from 'mere routine': Annas, *Intelligent Virtue* loc 221–22. This will be unpacked further in chapter three.

[50] Rietveld, Denys and Van Westen, 'Ecological-Enactive Cognition' 5. The term 'form of life' is of course borrowed from Wittgenstein.

[51] Led by Maurice Merleau-Ponty, *Nature: Course notes from the Collège de France* (Northwestern UP 2003).

ii. Adaptability of One's Self-understanding

To support the learning processes that underpin skills developed in response to normatively (or aesthetically) significant affordances, habits must not only be capable of adapting to teleological changes that stem from contextual constraints. They must also be able to adapt to endogenous goal changes. While this distinction between endogenous and exogenous goal changes is both artificial and somewhat misleading,[52] it has the merit of drawing attention to what Nanay refers to as the peril inherent in 'knowing yourself' a bit too confidently:

> 'Know thyself!', right? If we take the importance of change in our lives seriously, this just isn't an option. You might be able to know what you think of yourself in this moment. But what you think of yourself is very different from who you are and what you actually like […] Knowing thyself is an obstacle to acknowledging and making peace with constantly changing values. If you know thyself to be such-and-such a kind of person, this limits your freedom considerably […] As André Gide wrote in Autumn Leaves (1950): 'A caterpillar who seeks to know himself would never become a butterfly.'[53]

The metamorphoses we humans go through may not look as dramatic as caterpillars'. Yet the process of learning to live together with other humans does entail changes that can be profoundly destabilising: so destabilising, in fact, that we all develop various degrees of defence mechanisms. Just how robust these defence mechanisms are will greatly affect the extent to which we are capable of rising to ethical demands. Because these demands are never fixed in advance, emerging as they do from the particulars of every encounter, the skills that underpin ethical expertise not only presuppose attentiveness to 'the other'.[54] They also require 'an openness to an experience of self-doubt very different from that involved in becoming expert in other skills'.[55]

This experience of 'self-doubt' is distinct from that of a chess player who might, for instance, fail to notice her opponent's pin manoeuvre. Unlike the process of skill acquisition in domains like chess (or tennis), the gradual refinement of our ethical intuitions will demand that we be ready to question not just our habitual understanding of a given situation, but also our 'usual' understanding of our *selves* as persons 'who can knowledgeably cope'.[56] As Reed puts it:

> We need only be forced a little out of our moral 'comfort zone' in order for this to happen. Perhaps we inexplicably hurt someone's feelings, or we find ourselves in the

[52] Given what Varela thoughtfully refers to as the 'phylogenetic dialogue between an environment and the history of any active autonomous self': Francisco J Varela, *Ethical Know-How: Action, Wisdom, and Cognition* (Stanford UP 1992) 57.

[53] Bence Nanay, '"Know thyself" is not just silly advice: it's actively dangerous' *Aeon* (16 October 2017) aeon.co/ideas/know-thyself-is-not-just-silly-advice-its-actively-dangerous, accessed 15 December 2020.

[54] This is unpacked in chapter five.

[55] Robert C Reed, 'Euthyphro's elenchus experience: Ethical expertise and self-knowledge' (2013) 16 *Ethical Theory and Moral Practice* 245.

[56] Ibid 248.

> company of someone whose very different background throws into relief our own ignorance of certain aspects of life.[57]

In the morally loaded contexts inherent in most professional occupations, preserving (and continually developing) habitual skills that are sufficiently adaptable to exogenous constraints is hard enough. The endogenous, 'sense of self' adaptability presents an even greater challenge: the brutal constraints under which many professions operate lead to a frequent dissociation between one's private and professional persona. Understood as a coping mechanism, this dissociation has both ethical and personal costs. This is unpacked in the next chapter.

[57] Ibid 248.

3

Routine and Rigidified Habits

> [T]he horrible thing about all legal officials, even the best, about all judges, magistrates, barristers, detectives, and policemen, is not that they are wicked (some of them are good), not that they are stupid (several of them are quite intelligent), it is simply that they have got used to it. Strictly they do not see the prisoner in the dock; all they see is the usual man in the usual place. They do not see the awful court of judgment; they only see their own workshop.
>
> GK Chesterton, 'The twelve men'[1]

WE HAVE ALL been there: to fail to see beyond routine appearances and hence grasp the moral salience of a situation is easy. It is made easier still when that situation is structured around a normative framework that defines the roles of its protagonists, as is notably the case within the professions. To become a professional requires a process of habituation whereby one comes to internalise 'the way things are done'. Aside from its cognitive elements, this internalisation process typically encompasses a mix of intuitive understandings and both reflective and unreflective habits. These non-cognitive, deeply internalised aspects of expertise can be what distinguishes the merely competent from the truly brilliant: just as advanced chess players can 'see' their next move seemingly by merely looking at the board, some firemen seem able to sense when a building is about to collapse and must be evacuated. The examples reviewed in the previous chapter illustrate the heuristic value (and agency-enabling aspect) of 'habituation'. As a process that requires both immersion within a particular practice and internalisation of the norms that emanate from that practice, habituation conditions access to the unarticulated wisdom inherent in many occupations.

Yet habituation is double-edged. That very same process of immersion (and hence repeated exposure) can also be responsible for dulling the intensity of the emotional reactions that typically play a key role in flagging up a situation as demanding renewed ethical engagement. From that perspective, the opening quote from Chesterton has gotten it exactly right when it maintains that what most often stands in the way of a professional meeting her ethical responsibility is not so much stupidity (or character defects) but rather the deleterious aspect

[1] GK Chesterton, 'The twelve men' in GK Chesterton (ed), *Tremendous Trifles* (Sheed & Ward 1955).

of habituation. When a doctor or bleary-eyed legal official insists on following patently inadequate, routine proceedings in spite of significant clues calling for critical, renewed engagement on their part, they fall prey to the 'compromising' aspect of habit. This compromising aspect is concomitant with a degradation in the type of automaticity underlying the relevant habits: these habits become less adaptable, whether it be to contextual factors or to the need for endogenous, 'sense of self' transformations highlighted in the previous chapter.

This chapter seeks to throw light on habit rigidification in morally loaded contexts through the prism of professional responsibility. Because living up to such responsibility demands both technical skills and non-technical, ethical judgement, professional practice is a fruitful context in which to study what happens when the nature of the automaticity underlying habitual skills of moral significance degenerates.

Section I delves into the particular nature of the lay-professional encounter to highlight the high degree of teleological indeterminacy characteristic of most professional contexts. This teleological indeterminacy calls for a type of habit plasticity that needs to go hand in hand with what Socrates calls '*sophia*' – 'the art of knowing what you don't know'. This is unpacked in section II. Finally, section III considers the factors most likely to stand in the way of such 'wise' habit plasticity, ranging from the physiological and emotional costs of habit reversal to what William James would refer to as a 'rationalist', meta-theoretical understanding of one's work as a professional.

I. TELEOLOGICALLY INDETERMINATE PROFESSIONAL ENCOUNTERS

Some environments are artificially structured so as to minimise goal uncertainty: if I were to learn to play tennis in the middle of a busy playground, I would not only struggle to figure out which ball to hit, I would also need to navigate the need to avoid colliding with running children and potentially to settle some looming playground crisis. Outside the world of sports, one way of articulating what grounds the qualitative difference between professional responsibility and the responsibility of generic expert service providers is by delineating the different kinds of teleological indeterminacy at stake.

To understand this difference, it is useful to go back to the 'tennis in a playground' example. It would take me longer than in a standard 'tennis court' environment, but eventually I may become so attuned to the different kinds of balls being played, the playground's patterns of play and relationships between children that I may be able to preemptively settle a dispute in-between two serves while diverting non-tennis balls to their rightful recipient. I may be able to achieve all this without really thinking about it, just like a highly experienced hairdresser or car mechanic may be able to put at ease a waiting, distressed customer while giving instructions to an apprentice and putting the finishing touches to an amazing haircut or motor repair. In such cases, one may argue that what makes those highly experienced hairdressers or car mechanics brilliant at their job is their combining the required technical skills with a finely tuned situational awareness.[2] This awareness allows them to seamlessly address (or pre-empt) a variety of issues without letting the technical job at hand act as a barrier.

The same is true of a GP (ie a general medicine practitioner in the UK), criminal lawyer or educator, except for one important difference. The ease of discernment that the skilled intuitions mentioned above facilitate – sometimes referred to as giving rise to a situation of 'flow'[3] – is not enough. Or rather, it can prove too much: Railton's warning us of the dual edge inherent in such situations of 'flow' translates pretty smoothly from driving to professional contexts:

> although driving fluency permits better responsiveness to reasons and greater self-expression, it does not guarantee that one's driving will be rational. If anything, fluency can put one at risk of much more dangerous and irrational driving.[4]

Why would greater fluency put one at risk of 'more dangerous and irrational driving'? It might be unwarranted confidence triggering greater risk-taking. Or it might be that the delegation of the task of driving to an 'acquired habitus' compromises the extent to which the driver is prepared to look for and notice the unexpected. In the context of a car mechanic or hairdresser, this unavailability to factors that fall outside the well-oiled realm of waiting clients, apprentice needs and fringe cutting need not be ethically consequential. In a professional context, by contrast, such unavailability is much more likely to go hand in hand with a professional's incapacity to live up to her ethical responsibility. To unpack the latter thesis, section I.A delineates the situational vulnerability that is often concomitant with the need to resort to professional services. Section I.B traces the contours of the particular responsibility that stems from the need to address such vulnerability.

A. The Situational Vulnerability at the Heart of the Lay–Professional Encounter

Of those expert services whose safe delivery is in the public interest, healthcare,[5] some legal and financial services and education stand out because their

[2] Rietveld aptly describes this situational awareness in terms of 'an expert allow[ing] himself to be moved by the situation'. Rietveld also emphasises the importance of past experience in shaping this responsiveness: 'Our past experience determines which possibilities for action attract us. Thanks to this process the craftsman perceives a relevant affordance and is directly motivated to act. Perception underlies the expert's ability to be responsive to the situation and immediately make subtle discriminations': E Rietveld, 'Situated normativity: The normative aspect of embodied cognition in unreflective action' (2008) 117 *Mind* 973, 991.

[3] M Csikszentmihalyi, *Flow: The Psychology of Optimal Experience* (Harper and Row 1990).

[4] Peter Railton, 'Practical competence and fluent agency' in *Reasons for Action* (CUP 2009).

[5] Healthcare is meant to include all expert services aimed at supporting or improving our health (hence counsellors, psychologists, midwives, nurses, osteopaths etc are all included).

provision is often associated with a *situational* type of vulnerability. To understand the significance of the latter, one needs to grasp the way in which it differs from 'inherent'[6] forms of vulnerabilities: it is because we are fragile, enmattered[7] beings who need to rely on others' expertise to navigate today's world that we resort to expert services. These corporeal[8] and epistemic forms of vulnerability are inherent in that they can't be helped and are not context-dependent. They underpin the provision of a wide range of expert services, from car mechanics to healthcare providers, via mountain guides. Yet the services provided by a mountain guide do not typically bear on the continued development of those interests and concerns that are closest to our sense of self.

With educators, by contrast, the materials with which we develop a sense of self are collected and given shape. The vulnerability triggered by this phase of self-development can be either moderated or intensified, depending on the educator's professional stance, just as the vulnerability that stems from events such as prosecution, loss of employment, grave illness or divorce can. All these events have in common the fact that they can radically – sometimes overnight – transform one's social identity,[9] so that one is at risk of becoming 'the person accused of rape' or 'the person who has cancer' (or 'the person who is no good at school'). In that sense, such circumstances give rise to what Mackenzie would refer to as a 'situational' (rather than inherent) vulnerability:

> Situational vulnerability is context specific and is caused or exacerbated by social, political, economic, or environmental factors; it may be short term, intermittent, or enduring. For example, a person who has just lost his job is situationally vulnerable. This vulnerability may be short-lived if he has educational qualifications and skills that are in demand in the marketplace.[10]

If she is to challenge the profound transformation triggered by such events, the person resorting to professional services will need to retain the ability to

[6] MacKenzie defines 'inherent' sources of vulnerability as 'intrinsic to the human condition. These vulnerabilities arise from our embodiment, our inescapable human needs, and our inevitable dependence on others': Catriona Mackenzie, 'The importance of relational autonomy and capabilities for an ethics of vulnerability' in Catriona Mackenzie, Wendy Rogers and Susan Dodds (eds), *Vulnerability: New Essays in Ethics and Feminist Philosophy* (OUP 2014) 38.

[7] Martha Nussbaum, *Frontiers of Justice: Disability, Nationality, Species Membership* (Harvard UP 2006) 278.

[8] Fineman describes this corporeal, 'universal' vulnerability as the 'inevitable, enduring aspect of the human condition'. It carries with it the imminent or ever-present possibility of harm, injury, and misfortune: MA Fineman, 'The vulnerable subject: Anchoring equality in the human condition' (2008) 20 *Yale Journal of Law and Feminism* 1.

[9] In a related vein, Joel H Anderson and Axel Honneth, 'Autonomy, vulnerability, recognition, and justice' in John Christman and Joel Anderson (eds), *Autonomy and the Challenges to Liberalism: New Essays* (CUP 2005) 130 refer to 'social vulnerability' to emphasise 'the ways in which being able to lead one's own life is dependent on one's being supported by relations of recognition'. While the 'sense of self' vulnerability outlined here is clearly entangled with the 'affectively laden' attitudes they describe (in particular, self-trust, self-respect, and self-esteem), it is not reducible to any of these attitudes.

[10] Mackenzie, 'The importance of relational autonomy' 39.

meaningfully contribute to the way she projects her sense of self. To have such sense of self requires that there be, to a minimal degree, some movement of to and fro between the process of definition of our 'self' *from without* (natural events and human encounters) and *from within*[11] (the way we appropriate these events and encounters). This to and fro movement is never easy. In the circumstances described above, a professional's stance can have a considerable impact on how arduous it becomes. As such, the vulnerability at stake is both situational and relational: those lay–professional relationships that are concomitant with circumstances such as illness, prosecution, job dismissal and so on, can all too easily reinforce, rather than alleviate, the deep-rooted disconcertion that stems from such events.

Even when the knowledge asymmetry is made less considerable (thanks to internet resources and/or information sheets), the lay person may be left with little or no possibility to input into those events (both as they unfold, and in their aftermath). This isolation may be the result of routine adherence to formal procedures[12] or what Fricker describes as 'testimonial injustice': 'a speaker suffers testimonial injustice just if prejudice on the hearer's part causes him to give the speaker less credibility than he would otherwise have given'.[13] The negative stereotypes which the 'hearer's prejudice' stems from are commonly associated with certain illnesses or disabilities, but they can also be rooted in less tangible forms of social stigma.

Most importantly, the current delineation of professional obligations solely by reference to 'inherent' forms of vulnerability – such as the disclosure obligations meant to address our epistemic vulnerability – can have the insidious effect[14] of undermining the extent to which the lay person feels she has a voice that matters within a two-way consultation. These disclosure obligations can also act as an emotional shield for the professional, who need only see such disclosure as part of the many things she may master (and integrate into the situation of 'flow' described earlier). In all such cases, the lay person is precluded from meaningfully contributing to the delineation of the events or circumstances affecting her, thus making it particularly difficult to retain the minimal degree of to and fro movement described above.

Of course, the circumstances that prompt recourse to a professional need not be as tragic as those discussed above. Many of those circumstances will be

[11] Sangiovanni brilliantly argues that when the vulnerability inherent in this fragile process of sense-of-self redefinition is actively exploited, it becomes a form of social cruelty. On the latter and our commitment to moral equality, see Andrea Sangiovanni, *Humanity without Dignity: Moral Equality, Respect and Human Rights* (Havard UP 2017).

[12] These procedures can contribute to shielding the professional from the need to acknowledge the lay person, who appears merely as 'the usual person in the usual place': Chesterton, 'The twelve men'.

[13] Miranda Fricker, *Epistemic Injustice: Power and the Ethics of Knowing* (OUP 2007) 4.

[14] In that sense the current delineation of professional obligations – which can end up encouraging blanket disclosure practices – may be said to be 'pathogenic', to borrow MacKenzie's vocabulary: Mackenzie, 'The importance of relational autonomy'.

rather mundane and unlikely to ever imperil the continued construction of one's 'sense of self'. In such cases,[15] I have argued elsewhere[16] that the responsibility at stake is no different from that of other expert service providers.

B. The Particular Responsibility that Stems from Lay Situational Vulnerability

For our purposes, what matters is that those who do encounter such situational vulnerability face a particular challenge. Living up to the ethical demands entailed by such vulnerability demands a type of engagement that goes beyond the mere fulfilment of instrumental needs. It is not just a matter of figuring out the best way of addressing the concerns of one's client / patient / pupil. What is needed is the kind of awareness that is capable of challenging the unreflective workings of habituation and break through the 'mechanism' of second nature. To refer back to the previous chapter, the adequacy of the learning processes constitutive of such second nature may be said to not only depend on the type of participation afforded by a given environment; it also hinges upon the agent's responsiveness to affordances that have 'normative significance',[17] to use Rietveld's expression.

When the processes that enable a professional's intuitive grasp of a situation become less 'within reach' of conscious awareness and/or are less adaptable, this responsiveness is likely compromised (especially in unstable environments). While the availability to conscious awareness is rarely lost, an agent can much more easily lose her ability to adapt underlying habits in light of the demands of a particular situation.

In such instances of professional practice, the mechanistic reliance on increasingly rigid, deeply internalised patterns of behaviour (or thought) will compromise a professional's ability to continuously learn from such encounters. Importantly, it will also affect the extent to which she is capable of living up to the responsibility that stems from the layperson's situational vulnerability. To address the latter entails preserving one's 'responsiveness to the Other',[18] thus resisting any tendency to 'see the usual man in the usual place' (to refer to Chesterton's quote). Upholding such responsiveness[19] requires intentional action

[15] This includes phlebotomists or corporate lawyers for instance.

[16] S Delacroix, 'Professional Responsibility: Conceptual Rescue and Plea for Reform' [2022] 42 *Oxford Journal of Legal Studies* 1.

[17] Rietveld introduces this notion of affordances of 'normative significance' in Rietveld, 'Situated normativity'.

[18] When Levinas refers to the 'face of the Other' summoning each and every one of us, he offers a radical but eloquent phenomenological account of the ethical obligation that he deems concomitant with each 'encounter' with 'the Other': Emmanuel Levinas, *Totality and Infinity: An Essay on Exteriority* (Duquesne UP 1969) 51.

[19] 'Only by leaving myself open to self-questioning can my response to the other become appropriately responsive – that is, responsible. Thus, notwithstanding that Dreyfus and Dreyfus rightly

to be supported by a particular kind of automaticity, one that has retained a degree of what I call 'teleological plasticity'. In a professional context, this plasticity will manifest itself through a willingness to reconsider the pertinence of one's aims in light of the specificities of each lay–professional encounter.

II. HUMILITY AND '*SOPHIA*': PRE-CONDITIONS OF HABIT PLASTICITY?

Chapter two considered several examples of practices where habit can play a role that is not only compatible with, but actually supports intentional action.[20] What if, what is true of chess and tennis practice is also true of morally loaded practices? What if, in contrast to the frequent disparaging of the habitual within the moral sphere, one were to emphasise the extent to which the habitual can support our deliberate, moral selves? Annas' *Intelligent Virtue* takes on this 'what if' question by proposing an analogy between skills and 'virtue'.[21] This analogy is primarily aimed at delineating some middle way between overly behaviourist and overly intellectualist accounts of virtue. In her account, the automaticity characteristic of habitual processes is not only necessary to the development of moral judgement, it can also support it, provided one key condition is met. Just like tennis players, the moral agent must aspire for better practice.

The following proceeds in a spirit that is not dissimilar to Annas' in that its focus is on understanding the conditions under which the automaticity characteristic of habit is in a position to support and enable – rather than hinder – deliberative, professional practice. The aspiration condition highlighted by Annas is important, but it is not sufficient. One may strive towards impressive diagnostic accuracy or aim for very high advocacy success rates all the while failing to live up to one's specific responsibility. Without cultivating the 'art of knowing what one doesn't know', it is all too easy to shield oneself from ever having to question the pertinence of one's aims (whether it be through being taken aback by a lay–professional encounter or otherwise).

To maintain a spirit of Deweyan enquiry in the context of professional practice not only requires imagination[22] and creativity (insofar as the professional's goal is never settled in advance). It also requires humility – what Socrates would

emphasize the importance of staying "involved" and maintaining what Carol Gilligan calls a "care perspective" towards others (Dreyfus and Dreyfus 1990, p. 253), Levinas's work suggests that ethical expertise also entails a fundamental concern for what this involvement implies ethically for the agent – namely, an openness to gaining unexpected knowledge about oneself': Robert C Reed, 'Euthyphro's elenchus experience: Ethical expertise and self-knowledge' (2013) 16 *Ethical Theory And Moral Practice* 245, 250.

[20] For an account of habit that brilliantly outlines the Aristotelian alternative to the all too common understanding of habit as necessarily at odds with, or compromising autonomous, intentional action, see Clare Carlisle, *On Habit* (Routledge 2014).

[21] Julia Annas, *Intelligent Virtue* (Kindle Edition edn, OUP 2011).

[22] Zenon Bankowski and Maksymilian Del Mar, *The Moral Imagination and the Legal Life: Beyond Text in Legal Education* (Routledge 2016).

refer to as '*sophia*'. The latter is introduced in the context of a suggested analogy between virtue and *techne*: Socrates seems to inquire after virtue as if it were (or at least resembled) the expert knowledge of living well. But can virtue – and its messy world of ethical dilemmas – really be understood as a field one may master in the same way as one may master carpentry, seafaring or other '*techne*'? Significantly, Socrates uses the analogy in the context of the larger question of whether virtue can be taught.

Though Socrates oscillates on the issue,[23] he does express grave doubts about virtue's teachability, pointing at the fact that even those with the greatest reputation for virtue (Themistocles and Pericles) seem pretty bad at passing it on – even to their own sons (*M* 93a ff). In the *Meno*, Plato asks: '[I]s it plain to anyone that men cannot be taught anything but knowledge? [...] But if virtue is a kind of knowledge, it is clear that it could be taught' (*M* 87c). Just as expert knowledge wouldn't be 'expert' if it can't be taught, so should virtue be teachable (if the analogy between *techne* and virtue is valid).[24] Socrates' denial that he may be deemed a teacher in 'this kind of excellence'[25] can be taken as merely[26] disclaiming certain or 'expert' knowledge (*techne*) while acknowledging 'nonexpert' or 'human' wisdom (*anthrôpinè sophia*):

> What kind of wisdom? Human wisdom, perhaps. It may be that I really possess this, while those whom I mentioned just now are wise with a wisdom more than human; else I cannot explain it, for I certainly do not possess it, and whoever says I do is lying and trying to slander me. (*Apology*, 20d7–e3)

The 'it' which Socrates otherwise cannot explain is the Delphic oracle's response, according to which no man was wiser than Socrates. Socrates is puzzled by the oracle's claim because: 'I realize that I am wise concerning nothing great or small' (*Apology*, 21b4–5). Socrates resolves his puzzlement thus: what makes no one wiser than him is his appraisal of what he does not know.[27] The type

[23] In the *Protagoras*, Socrates reverses his earlier position (*Prot* 319a ff) and ends up arguing that virtue can be taught (*Prot* 361a–c).

[24] Note that in the *Protagoras*, Socrates reverses his earlier position (*Prot*319a ff) and ends up arguing that virtue can be taught (*Prot* 361a–c).

[25] 'Now since [your sons] are men, whom do you have in mind to supervise them? Who is an expert in this kind of excellence the human and social kind? [...] Is there such a person, or is there not?' [...] "His name, Socrates, is Evenus, he comes from Paros, and his fee is five minas." I thought Evenus a happy man, if he really possesses this art, and teaches for so moderate a fee. Certainly I would pride and preen myself if I had this knowledge, but I do not have it, gentlemen' (*Ap* 20b–c) see also *Ap* 23c–24b.

[26] Thrasymachus challenges Socrates' sincerity in the *Republic*: 'By Heracles [...] that's just Socrates' usual irony. I knew, and I said so to those people earlier, that you'd be unwilling to answer and that, if someone questioned *you*, you'd be ironical and do anything rather than give an answer' (*Rep* 337a4–7). For modern interpretations doubting Socrates' sincerity, see Norman Gulley, *The Philosophy of Socrates* (MacMillan 1968) and Henry Teloh, *The Development of Plato's Metaphysics* (Pennsylvania State UP 1981).

[27] 'What makes him the wisest of the Greeks – what he shares with no one he has yet met – is his recognition that he fails to know anything fine and good. Some of those he has met know things he does not know. But all of them think they know things fine and good, the most important things,

of knowledge at the heart of this appraisal is very different from the kind of knowledge one may miss in the context of seafaring or carpentry. At its root is 'the question posed by the Other'. This question 'is not one we are ever in a position to answer, no matter how much knowledge we possess and whatever its sources'.[28] On this account, to be wise is a matter of constantly (re)discovering how little one knows about others, and consequently about oneself too. This readiness to be called (or call oneself) into question goes hand in hand with habit plasticity, yet in practice it is not without costs. The next section explores these costs, which are still poorly understood.

III. OBSTACLES TO HABIT PLASTICITY IN PROFESSIONAL CONTEXTS

A. Case Study

Consider the following scenario, which has been used in an empirical study of medical judgement using immersive virtual reality (henceforth, 'VR'):[29] a patient comes in to see his GP. He has a complicated medical history (requires dialysis, etc) and suffers from aortic stenosis. He has been seen by two different heart specialists, one of whom recommends open-heart surgery, while the other suggests trans-catheter aortic valve implantation. While anxiously seeking advice from his GP, the patient behaves aggressively towards his young son, who is withdrawn during the consultation and visibly relaxes when his dad temporarily leaves to take a phone call.

I designed this scenario together with colleagues in pediatrics, general medicine, computer science and psychology in a bid to tease out methodological obstacles to the study of the non-cognitive underpinnings of professional judgement in VR. The end goal is to open the way to empirical studies of habit plasticity in morally loaded, ecologically valid scenarios. Since VR allows for any factors deemed likely to impact upon professional judgement to be controlled and replicated with a high degree of precision, reliance on VR has great potential. In this study, there were three factors that were deemed particularly likely to have an effect upon the GP's ability to address the signs of child-safeguarding concerns despite (or in parallel to) the need to grasp the patient's medical issue: (1) the GP's level of experience; (2) the salience of the signs of safeguarding concerns (this factor was called 'CUE'); and (3) the degree of complexity in the presentation of the medical issue (this factor was called 'LOAD', as in cognitive load).

when they do not. Socrates, alone of the Greeks, fails to have this false belief […] He alone realizes that "in truth he is worthless with respect to wisdom"': Hugh H Benson, *Socratic Wisdom: The Model of Knowledge in Plato's Early Dialogues* (OUP 2000) 172.

[28] Reed, 'Euthyphro's elenchus experience' 256.

[29] Xueni Pan and others, 'A study of professional awareness using immersive virtual reality: The responses of general practitioners to child safeguarding concerns' (2018) 5 *Frontiers in Robotics and AI* 1.

The experiment had a 2 × 2 between group design: in the high cognitive load version the two heart specialist letters were long and difficult to read; in the low cognitive load version they were brief, and structured around bullet points. As for the 'CUE' factor, the level of aggressiveness shown by the parent towards his son was made more or less[30] obvious (the son's behaviour remained identical). Sixty-four participants were divided into two groups (GP versus trainee GP) and within each group they were assigned to one of the four experimental conditions pseudo-randomly to ensure appropriate distribution between conditions.

The design of the scenario itself (based on a real-life case study) was chosen because the child-safeguarding cues predominantly required perceptual awareness rather than cognitive engagement on the part of the GP. Would a GP's level of experience translate into better perceptual awareness – what chapter one referred to as 'skilled intuitions'? If so, highly experienced GPs should find it easier to adequately address the signs of child-safeguarding concerns, even when the cues are subtle and the cognitive load higher.

The formulation of the theoretical grounds for this assumed resilience to cognitive load vary. Some would say that because of their efficient chunking of information and automation of certain procedures, expert knowledge structures place less demands on working memory, thus freeing resources for other tasks.[31] Under Kahneman's 'dual system' theory,[32] when cognitive load disrupts System 2's supervising role, the intuitions and emotions of System 1 are given free(er) rein: the more 'educated' or 'skilled' the latter, the better the outcome (and hence resilience to cognitive load). In this example, an experienced GP would have developed a way of intuitively apprehending this complex medical situation, which would enable her to quickly take into account issues that are not raised by the patient but that are no less important. In this scenario, some of these issues may not have anything to do with the patient's condition but relate to the patient's relationship with his son instead.[33]

In this instance, what we found was that a GP's ability to pick up signs of child-safeguarding concerns – hence adapting to a widening of the pertinent features calling upon her attention – was significantly correlated with particular psychological traits / stress levels, but not with a GP's level of experience (or degree of cognitive load[34]). GPs who were less stressed, less neurotic, more

[30] Even in the 'subtle' cue conditions, one of the co-authors (Caroline Fertleman, paediatrician who is also the senior co-author of *The Child Protection Practice Manual* Hann and Fertleman (OUP 2016)) made sure that the cues were obvious enough, in that experts in this area were deemed very likely to identify potential problems from the beginning.

[31] Paul J Feltovich, Michael J Prietula and K Anders Ericsson, 'Studies of expertise from psychological perspectives' (2006) *The Cambridge Handbook of Expertise and Expert Performance* 41, 23.

[32] Daniel Kahneman, *Thinking, Fast and Slow* (Macmillan 2011).

[33] In the UK, GPs are entrusted with the responsibility to identify potential child abuse issues: as the primary contact point for families with healthcare concerns, they have to flag up any concerns they may have.

[34] It is worth noting that even though they fell some way short of significance, the load manipulation results were consistent with the established literature. Had the effect of the difference between the two cognitive loads – high and low – been less subtle, the study may not have been underpowered: Pan and others, 'A study of professional awareness'.

agreeable and extroverted tended to be better at raising potential child abuse issues in their notes (as judged by a panel of 10, who assessed the degree to which those notes translated adequate awareness on a scale of 1 to 10). While it was a surprise finding,[35] this result can be interpreted in a way that supports the next sections' emphasis on the emotional and physiological costs of habit reversal on one hand, and habit plasticity on the other. In the above scenario, the habit in question would be that of focusing on the technical, medical issue at stake, at the expense of seemingly peripheral ethical (and in this case, legal) demands.

B. The Emotional and Physiological Costs of Habit Reversal

While the process of habit formation often eludes conscious awareness from the start, in the vast majority of cases a habit can be reversed by raising it to awareness.[36] The more deeply ingrained the habit, the more effort is required to reverse it. This effort often has a negative emotional valence.[37] The physical and/or psychological anguish that is frequently associated with habit reversal in humans reflects the role of somatic markers in the process of habit acquisition.

According to Damasio's theory,[38] for each action that is in the process of becoming habitual, the brain accumulates information about the somatic outcomes (what bodily sensations are associated with that action). That information is then encapsulated within an intuitive 'marker' that is subsequently activated (and steers behaviour) in any context relevant to that action. Even those who challenge Damasio's somatic marker theory readily concede the essential role played by bodily sensations in the formation – and reversal – of habits. The habit reversal process can sometimes be painful (smoking cessation is the easiest example) and/or utterly disorienting. Proust for instance compares the effect of certain novels to 'temporary bereavements, abolishing habit [of thought, in this case]'.[39]

[35] The pre-immersion psychological questionnaire was included on the advice of colleagues in psychology.

[36] Some habitual patterns can remain persistently out of reach of conscious awareness. Neil Levy and Tim Bayne, 'Doing without deliberation: Automatism, automaticity, and moral accountability' (2004) 16 *International Review of Psychiatry* 209 highlight the continuum that leads from 'automatistic' processes all the way to automatic action that is informed by and controlled by deliberative agency.

[37] This negative valence largely depends on the agent's attitude or 'mood', to borrow Bennett's expression: 'The mood I'm calling enchantment involves, in the first instance, a surprising encounter, a meeting with something that you did not expect and are not fully prepared to engage. Contained within this surprise state are (1) a pleasurable feeling of being charmed by the novel and as yet unprocessed encounter and (2) a more unheimlich (uncanny) feeling of being disrupted or torn out of one's default sensory-psychic-intellectual disposition. The overall effect of enchantment is a mood of fullness, plenitude, or liveliness.' Jane Bennett, *The Enchantment of Modern Life: Attachments, Crossings, and Ethics* (Princeton UP 2016) 5.

[38] Antonio Damasio, *Descartes' Error: Emotion, Reason and the Human Brain* (Random House 2008).

[39] Marcel Proust, *In Search of Lost Time*, vol 5 (Vintage 1996) 642.

Habit reversal can also prove impossible. This is most obviously the case when a habit answers a physiological or biological need. Just like we may have developed a habit of walking close to walls or hedges as a way of coping with dramatic gushes of wind, a plant may have a habit of growing on a particular side of the house, no matter how sunny the other side might be, or how much pruning that plant endures on its favoured side of the house. To reverse the habit of that plant would necessitate the modification of this plant's biological needs and vulnerabilities – in short, it would require a different plant. While humans have habits of that sort too (think breathing, sleeping, but also environment-specific adaptations), most of our habits *can* be reversed, albeit at a psychological and/or physiological cost that reflects the extent to which a habit has been internalised.[40]

Much of what we know about the latter costs is drawn from studies that focus on addiction.[41] For our purposes, this emphasis on addiction is unfortunate, since it has drawn attention away from the mechanisms that underlie habit *plasticity*, to concentrate mostly on reversal instead. The next section reviews some of the known trade-offs when it comes to the need for habit plasticity within learning processes. It also considers the extent to which some meta-theoretical stands can skew the balance in favour of model stability (with undesirable ethical consequences).

C. Balancing Model Stability and Habit Plasticity within the Learning Process

Preserving one's learning capacity requires a balance to be found between the plasticity necessary to being able to draw upon new knowledge-generating experiences and the stability without which learned memories get forgotten.[42]

[40] This relationship between a habit's degree of internalisation and the 'cost' of its reversal turns out to be central to what is best described as the unavoidable asymmetry between humans and 'algorithmic machines' when it comes to the mechanisms underlying socio-moral changes. Unlike the reversal of human habits, the cost of reversing algorithmic habits comes down to mere efficiency losses. In the absence of somatic markers associated with the internalisation process, algorithmic systems are unlikely to ever experience the process necessary to habit reversal in a 'bereavement-like' fashion. For more developments, see Sylvie Delacroix, 'Automated systems and the need for change' in Christopher Markou and Simon Deakin (eds), *Is Law Computable?* (Hart Publishing 2020).

[41] Barry J Everitt and Trevor W Robbins, 'Neural systems of reinforcement for drug addiction: from actions to habits to compulsion' (2005) 8 *Nature Neuroscience* 1481; Barry J Everitt and Trevor W Robbins, 'Drug addiction: Updating actions to habits to compulsions ten years on' (2016) 67 *Annual Review of Psychology* 23; David O'Tousa and Nicholas Grahame, 'Habit formation: Implications for alcoholism research' (2014) 48 *Alcohol* 327; Wendy Wood and Dennis Rünger, 'Psychology of habit' (2016) 67 *Annual Review of Psychology*.

[42] This insight is far from new. Yet its re-discovery within the field of machine learning is invigorating surprise-focused research, see Myron Tribus, *Thermodynamics and Thermostatics: An Introduction to Energy, Information and States of Matter, with Engineering Applications* (D Van Nostrand 1961) 64–66; Mohammadjavad Faraji, 'Learning with surprise: Theory and applications' (PhD thesis, École Polytechnique Fédérale de Lausanne 2016); Mohammad Javad Faraji, Kerstin Preuschoff and Wulfram Gerstner, 'Balancing new against old information: The role of puzzlement surprise in learning' (2018) 30(1) *Neural Computation* 34.

In a professional context, this balance will necessarily reflect both cognitive and emotional constraints. These are briefly outlined for now, since much of what follows anticipates arguments developed in chapter five.

From a cognitive perspective, the ongoing refinement of one's model proceeds 'at sea' (as with 'Neurath's boat'). To successfully revise one's understanding of professional excellence requires that at least some of its components remain 'afloat'. The balance between the need for habit plasticity on one hand, and model stability on the other will also reflect emotional constraints. A professional's ability to adequately engage[43] with each 'lay' encounter requires that empathy[44] be 'put in its proper place'.[45] Chapter five notably articulates the distinction between empathy and 'the work of attention': the latter can but need not leverage empathy as a prompt.

Aside from these inevitable, agent-specific cognitive and emotional factors, some meta-theoretical stands about the relationship between theory and practice within professional ethics can artificially tip the balance in favour of model stability. Even if it is uncommon for a professional to explicitly dismiss the significance of environmental features on meta-theoretical grounds, a theoretically anchored, over-confident understanding of what professional excellence requires does not leave much room for encounter-based learning processes. Because each encounter appears settled by an overarching understanding of what counts as good practice, the professional is conveniently shielded from the emotional labour demanded by genuine engagement. Behind the façade of 'verbal niceties',[46] what is missing, as a result of any 'rationalist' stand[47] is a spirit of 'enquiry' (*à la Dewey*):

> We must be uncomfortable, troubled, pained or disturbed by the current state of affairs in order to truly inquire. […] One who practises ethics gains skill and

[43] Montgomery rightly emphasises the importance of this aspect of professionalism when referring to 'the detachment required to replace the personal subjectivity of a merely sympathetic emotional reaction with an objective response based on empathy, evidence and careful deliberation': Jonathan Montgomery, 'The virtues and vices of professionalism' in Dinesh Bhugra and Amit Malik (eds), *Professionalism in Mental Healthcare: Experts, Expertise and Expectations* (CUP 2011) 18.

[44] Empathy has been named an 'essential learning objective' by the American Association of Medical Colleges, and there is a special focus on empathy training in US medical schools.

[45] Paul Bloom, *Against Empathy: The Case for Rational Compassion* (Random House 2017) 208 (loc). In the legal sphere, studies of magistrates' 'emotional labour' have also contributed to the recent re-assessment of the role of empathy within legal practice: Sharyn Roach Anleu and Kathy Mack, 'Magistrates' everyday work and emotional labour' (2005) 32 *Journal of Law and Society* 590. Similarly, for solicitors: Chalen Westaby, '"Feeling like a sponge": The emotional labour produced by solicitors in their interactions with clients seeking asylum' (2010) 17 *International Journal of the Legal Profession* 153; Chalen Westaby and Emma Jones, 'Empathy: An essential element of legal practice or "never the twain shall meet"?' (2018) 25 *International Journal of the Legal Profession* 107.

[46] Schiff highlights the perilous, shielding effect of 'verbal niceties'. 'Such verbal niceties "surrounded" Eichmann with 'the most reliable of all safeguards against the words and the presence of others, and hence against reality as such': Jacob Schiff, 'The varieties of thoughtlessness and the limits of thinking' (2012) 12 *European Journal of Political Theory* 99, 102.

[47] William James, 'Pragmatism: A new name for some old ways of thinking' in *Pragmatism and Other Writings* (Penguin Classics 2000).

> knowledge such that she has a larger arsenal at her disposal when confronting a new quandary, but the practitioner will not be 'especially good' at responding to these quandaries. The more one knows, the more one is aware of how very tenuous and limited one's knowledge is.[48]

Formulated as a (partial) answer to the need to foster plastic habits of evaluation, the Socratic skepticism towards any claim to 'know *a priori*' what constitutes excellence in the domain of virtue is at the heart of what is sometimes called the 'anti-theory' movement in ethics.[49] Its underlying, contextual understanding of ethics[50] is united against any understanding of moral judgements that 'can be thought of as consequences of applying abstract principles to moral problems in an almost computational way, giving a procedure for deducing the morally correct answer in any given circumstances'.[51]

Not only is there an interesting link between one's temperament and such an anti-theoretical stance (a link most notably highlighted by James[52]), such a stance also goes hand in hand with what might be called an 'ethics of attention'. Connecting the classical pragmatists such as James and Dewey to figures as diverse as the late Wittgenstein,[53] Løgstrup or Levinas, this 'ethics of attention' is unpacked in chapter five. It is of particular relevance because of its potential as an answer to the challenge that stems from a naturalist commitment: what, if anything, enables us to stand back from the habitual, if all we have at our disposal to trigger this movement of critical scrutiny are our thoroughly 'habituated', socio-cultural sensitivities?

[48] Kim Garchar, 'Imperfection, practice and humility in clinical ethics' (2012) 18 *Journal of Evaluation in Clinical Practice* 1051.

[49] Wittgenstein may be one of the fiercest proponents of this 'anti-theory' movement. 'If I could explain the essence of the ethical only by means of a theory – [Wittgenstein] observed during a conversation annoyed by Waismann (1979, 117) – then what is ethical would be of no value whatsoever': quote taken from Anna Boncompagni, *Wittgenstein and Pragmatism: On Certainty in the Light of Peirce and James* (Palgrave Macmillan 2016) 6.

[50] This contextual understanding of ethics has also been defined as 'a new metaethical stance according to which "the ethical" is inherently open and interwoven with numerous aspects of human life in such a way that it cannot be exhaustively captured theoretically': Hans Fink, 'Against ethical exceptionalism – through critical reflection on the history of use of the terms "ethics" and "morals" in philosophy' (2020) 21 *SATS* 85.

[51] Stanley G Clarke and Evan Simpson, *Anti-theory in Ethics and Moral Conservatism* (SUNY Press 1989) 2.

[52] In the first of his *Pragmatism* lectures, James links the history of philosophy to a confrontation between different temperaments, tracing their respective prevalence to different philosophical moments: James, 'Pragmatism'.

[53] Along this line, Boncompagni identifies 'a convergence' between James' 'concern with understanding the other, […] the other's point of view as potentially expressive of a whole way of being' and 'the Wittgensteinian use of the notion of forms of life […] which helps us to focus not only on the way we live but also on the way we and others might live': Boncompagni, *Wittgenstein and Pragmatism*.

4

Growing Out *of the Habitual*

> [E]thics strives to legislate a world in which the good is done fluidly, as a matter of habituation, if not fact, even as it is recognized that the very thing ethics can never be is an acting that is merely habit or matter of fact. Even as ethics seeks to become familiar, it insists on rendering the world unfamiliar. The emergence of ethical obligation both insists on regularity in one's conduct and resists that regularity.
>
> James Hatley, Janice McLane and Christian Diehm (eds), *Interrogating Ethics*[1]

FIRST HIGHLIGHTED BY Aristotle, the role of habituation within the processes by which we come to acquire our pre-reflective 'ethical know-how'[2] continues to be the focus of a large – mostly Aristotelian – strand of moral philosophy.[3] The no-less important capacity to break free of habit, by contrast, gets far less attention. Yet living an ethical life demands that we sometimes stand at odds with the usual. Hatley's quote (above) vividly captures this double edge of habituation: while habits condition the possibility of ethical agency, they can also compromise it.[4] This double edge is echoed in the two chapters you have (hopefully) just read.

On the empowering side, chapter two highlighted the primordial role played by the experience-based, skilled intuitions that positively structure so many parts of our lives, including the ethical. The compromising side was explored through the prism of professional responsibility, as a context whose inherent teleological indeterminacy demands highly plastic habits. Many factors can contribute to endangering this plasticity. Agent-based factors include 'thoughtlessness', lack of aspiration (or humility), stress, fear and so on. Environmental factors include systems designed to exploit our habitual selves (as is the case of many apps

[1] James Hatley, Janice McLane and Christian Diehm (eds), *Interrogating Ethics: Embodying the Good in Merleau-Ponty* (Duquesne UP 2006) 3.

[2] Nigel DeSouza, 'Pre-reflective ethical know-how' (2013) 16 *Ethical Theory and Moral Practice* 279.

[3] And to a lesser extent psychological studies, for habit arguably remains a 'blind spot' in empirical studies of moral judgement. For an empirical study focusing on the process of habit formation, see Phillippa Lally and others, 'How are habits formed: Modelling habit formation in the real world' (2010) 40 *European Journal of Social Psychology* 998.

[4] Habituation only becomes a threat to ethical agency when such agency has lost its plasticity, whether it became rigidified by embracing some religious or ideological framework, through emotional trauma or otherwise.

and online tools) or to grant us potentially endless 'normative holidays'. These systemic hazards will be reviewed in chapters six and seven.

The challenge that occupies us in this chapter can be formulated thus: what if habit plasticity is not enough when ethical agency is concerned? Perhaps the problem with the many who find themselves supporting ideologies that back the 'legitimate' extermination – or mutilation – of fellow human beings can be phrased in terms of excessively plastic habits of thought? If ethical agency is to mean anything, it must have at its core an account of exactly what it is about us, human beings, that endows us with the capacity to stand back from and challenge habitual, accepted norms rather than blindly adapt to them. How would a habit-centred account of ethical agency provide such an account?

This chapter throws light on the logic that underpins the continued dominance of negative answers to the above question: for a wide strand of philosophy (dominated by Kantian accounts), ethical agency is all about the mechanisms that allow us to grow *out* of the habitual.

I. GROWING OUT OF THE HABITUAL: HABIT VERSUS REASON

Habits constrain us. Because their compelling force typically eludes us,[5] they may be seen as a moral menace, surreptitiously compromising our autonomy. In her seminal work on habit,[6] Clare Carlisle traces a philosophical thread that links Kant to Kierkegaard and Bergson, via less well-known authors such as Maine de Biran and his ambivalent appraisal of what he called the 'double law' of habit. The latter is deemed to be the 'general cause of our progress on the one hand, of our blindness on the other'.[7] Because habit can eclipse reflective thought – and because reflective thought is deemed (by those authors within the Kantian thread) to condition the exercise of our freedom – habit belongs firmly to the messy, causal space of desires, inclinations and the like.

While this defiant stance towards habit is probably as old as philosophy itself (see Parmenides' quote in the introduction), its Western popularity grew markedly after the Second World War, given the challenge posed by the widespread,

[5] '[O]f all enemies, habit is perhaps the most cunning, and above all it is cunning enough never to let itself be seen, because the person who sees the habit is saved from the habit': Søren Kierkegaard, *Works of Love* (Princeton UP 1995) 36.

[6] Clare Carlisle, 'Creatures of habit: The problem and the practice of liberation' (2006) 38 *Continental Philosophy Review* 19; Clare Carlisle, 'Between freedom and necessity: Felix Ravaisson on habit and the moral life' (2010) 53 *Inquiry* 123; Clare Carlisle, *On Habit* (Routledge 2014).

[7] For Carlisle, it is precisely De Biran's ambivalence that makes his account of habit particularly interesting, as this ambivalence is born out of the tensions underlying his metaphysics' dualist presuppositions. 'Biran's whole account of habit is characterised by tensions and inconsistencies that testify to a kind of struggle between reason and habit: on the one hand, there is the insistence on a dualistic psychology, and on the other hand the acknowledged failure clearly to separate activity and passivity, perception and sensation, the voluntary and the involuntary': Carlisle, 'Between freedom and necessity' 129.

obedient contribution to Nazi crimes. Pamela Radcliff[8] estimates that between 100,000 to 500,000 people were direct participants in the planning and execution of such crimes, with every single branch of the bureaucracy involved. 'That most of the perpetrators of the genocide were normal people, who will freely flow through any known psychiatric sieve — however dense'[9] – is not only 'morally disturbing'. It also does much to explain the post-war distancing from an understanding of moral judgements according to which they are but expressions of attitudes devoid of any claim to objectivity:

> The Viennese positivists' dismissal of ethical and religious discourse as unverifiable, and therefore merely expressive, was an exciting novelty when the enemy was the ancien régime of clergymen and courtiers. The war changed everything. What had seemed tough-minded and revolutionary now seemed merely complacent.[10]

Unless one built an account of ethics and moral values that had room for objectively better or worse ways of answering the 'how should I / we live?' question, one couldn't help but feel dangerously ill-equipped when it came to addressing the Eichmanns of this world. Neither exceptionally evil nor apparently insane, Eichmann, like so many of his compatriots, was content to follow mass-extermination orders. Who was he to challenge the judgements that informed his superiors' orders? Why should he know better? An understanding of moral judgements as 'mere' expressions of attitudes would rather not have to answer any such questions – indeed it may have thrived on the basis of a silent (and, it turns out, demonstrably false) assumption that, to use Murdoch's words:

> '[W]hatever anybody's likely to think about morals is going to be more or less okay. I mean, one might say it's a sort of pre-Hitler view. It's a view which goes with our sort of 19th-century optimism and a feeling of progress and a feeling that people are fundamentally decent chaps, a view which after recent history [...] one cannot in general take'.[11]

Yet instead of encouraging further reflection about the kind of creatures we are – and what this entails when it comes to better (or worse) ways of answering the ethical question – post-World War II moral philosophy was dominated by a push for the very 'absolutes' which early twentieth century pragmatism had sought to discredit. Some philosophers[12] who otherwise harboured pragmatist

[8] Pamela Beth Radcliff, *Interpreting the 20th Century: The Struggle Over Democracy* (Teaching Company 2004).

[9] Zygmunt Bauman, *Modernity and the Holocaust* (Cornell UP 1989) 19.

[10] Nakul Krishna, 'Is goodness natural?' *Aeon* (28 November 2017).

[11] Documentary interview, Michael Chanan, 'The Idea of Freedom' (*Solus Enterprises, Chanan Films*, 1972), available at www.youtube.com/watch?v=zJHIwnr3UlI accessed 10 February 2021, quoted by Krishna, 'Is goodness natural?'

[12] Lon Fuller's early, sympathetic stance towards a certain kind of 'romantic' (legal) pragmatism is unpacked in Charles L Barzun, 'Jerome Frank, Lon Fuller, and a romantic pragmatism' (2017) 29 *Yale Journal of Law & the Humanities* 129.

inclinations felt compelled[13] to give 'Kantian moorings' to a concept of human dignity that seemed too vulnerable to political and socio-cultural perversions.

As a prominent example, Habermas is said to have:

> struggled for years with the problem of how to maintain a Kantian bent toward universality in questions of justice, which entails maintaining a distinction between justice and the habits of ethical life, while at the same time questioning traditional Kantian transcendentalism.[14]

The roots of Habermas' effort to distance himself from the metaphysical presuppositions of transcendental philosophy[15] while nevertheless holding on to the need for those 'Kantian moorings' to counter 'irrationalism' (a word closely associated with Habermas' experience of fascism) are candidly acknowledged in the following:

> I once asked Habermas in a public forum what was the most difficult aspect of his philosophy to defend. He didn't hesitate to answer: quasi-transcendentalism. And when I asked why he thought that he had to defend it [...] his answer was straightforward: the Holocaust.[16]

The tensions that pervade the work of Habermas' late friend, Lawrence Kohlberg – whose theory of stages of moral development is often deemed to exemplify the rationalist approach to moral judgement – have similar roots. Typically used as an old foil by contemporary intuitionist perspectives, Kohlberg's claim that 'action is not a moral action unless it is generated by moral reasoning and motives'[17] is often quoted without any regard for the circumstances that led Kohlberg to embrace such a strong Kantian stand.

Interestingly for our purposes, Kohlberg's repeated emphasis on the purity of motives as constitutive of moral action suggests that his Kantian stand has a lot to do with its presupposing a clear break between the messy world of habits and instincts on one hand and the world of reasons on the other. It is possible, in other words, that Kohlberg endorsed a defiant stance towards habit because it seemed to him to be the only way of warding off the peril inherent in the

[13] As Arthur Cohen noted about those seeking reason, 'It is not obscene for human beings to try to retain their sanity before an event which boggles sanity': Arthur Allen Cohen, *The Tremendum: a Theological Interpretation of the Holocaust* (Continuum Publishing Co 1993).

[14] Mitchell Aboulafia, 'Introduction' in Mitchell Aboulafia (ed), *Habermas and Pragmatism* (Routledge 2002) 4.

[15] Unlike Apel (Karl-Otto Apel, 'Regarding the relationship of morality, law and democracy: On Habermas's Philosophy of Law (1992) from a transcendental-pragmatic point of view' in Mitchell Aboulafia, Myra Bookman and Catherine Kemp (eds), *Habermas and Pragmatism* (Taylor & Francis Group 2002) 19) Habermas argues that even the necessary presuppositions of argumentation are fallible, a move that testifies to Habermas' pragmatist inclinations.

[16] Aboulafia, 'Introduction' 4.

[17] Lawrence Kohlberg, *The Meaning and Measurement of Moral Development*, The Heinz Werner lectures (Clark UP 1981).

'socialisation' model's[18] overemphasis on adequate adjustment to society: 'to identify morality with conformity is to be forced to take the position that a loyal Nazi was behaving morally'.[19] As a result, Kohlberg defined moral maturity by reference to the individual's capacity to 'differentiat[e] his self from the rules and expectations of others and defin[e] his values in terms of self-chosen principles'.[20] This can be seen as a direct attempt to address the question mentioned in the introduction to this chapter: 'What if the problem lies in over-plastic habits of thought?'.

Kohlberg is not alone in having felt the need to resort to a Kantian framework to fend off the Holocaust's calamitous implications. Yet the tension it introduced at the heart of his theory is nowhere as blatant. Aside from a poor fit with the descriptive core of his theory,[21] this Kantian framework is resolutely at odds with his declared preference for a naturalist stance.[22] Was there an alternative? The short answer is yes, there was. Before chapter five outlines the role played by an 'ethics of attention' in structuring the capacity we all share to question

[18] At least a caricatured version of this socialisation view – 'society is prior to the individual, both chronologically and morally. It is the source of all values, which are eventually reflected in the individual' Melford Spiro, 'Culture and personality: The natural history of a false dichotomy' (1951) 14 *Psychiatry* 19, 20. Both sides of the debates have been harmed by over-simplification: Martin Hoffman's theory for instance points out the influence of the developing child's activity (which includes cognitive activity) in socialisation.

[19] Lawrence Kohlberg, 'Moral stages and moralization' in Thomas Lickona (ed), *Moral Development and Behavior: Theory, Research, and Social Issues* (Holt, Rinehart and Winston 1976) 3.

[20] Kohlberg (ibid 33) further refined the definition of his post-conventional level as based on a 'theory-defining level of discourse,' that is, 'defining a moral theory and justifying basic moral terms or principles from a standpoint outside that of a member of a constituted society': Lawrence Kohlberg, 'Continuities in childhood and adult moral development revisited' in Paul Baltes and K Warner Schaie (eds), *Life-Span Developmental Psychology: Personality and Socialization* (Academic Press 1973) 192.

[21] At a descriptive level, one may interpret his first four moral stages as explicitly acknowledging that emotions are essential to everyday moral judgements (empirical studies concede that very few people ever reach the emotionally detached fifth and sixth stages of development). In the first and second stages, people are successively driven by fear of punishment and the prospect of hedonic gains, while in the third they are led by their desire to be liked by others. As for the fourth stage – the type of moral reasoning that is dominant in industrialised societies – Jesse Prinz successfully argues that even the appeal to law and order 'may have an emotional undertone': Jesse J Prinz, *The Emotional Construction of Morals* (OUP 2007).

[22] Kohlberg had an otherwise defiant attitude towards what he called 'the Grand Canyon of modern philosophy' – the gap between is and ought: Dwight Boyd and Lawrence Kohlberg, 'The is-ought problem: A developmental perspective' (1973) 8 *Zygon®* 358, 358. 'By asserting that any conception of what moral judgment ought to be must rest on an adequate conception of what it is' (Lawrence Kohlberg, 'Kohlberg on moral development and moral education' in Brenda Munsey (ed), *Moral Development, Moral Education, and Kohlberg: Basic Issues in Philosophy, Psychology, Religion, and Education* (Religious Education Press 1980) 67), Kohlberg seeks to call on the spirit of a pragmatist tradition to which he is clearly attracted (see among others, Lawrence Kohlberg and Rochelle Mayer, 'Development as the aim of education' (1972) 42 *Harvard Educational Review* 449) yet belies by structuring his model of ethical development on the basis of a strictly Kantian normative stand.

accepted norms, the next section highlights a different way of apprehending the events – and human faults – that facilitated the mass extermination of Jews. What if past and present atrocities have less to do with a lack of principled reasoning, and more to do with well-oiled arguments (or routines) conveniently shielding[23] us from what would otherwise be powerful, ethical intuitions standing in the way of such atrocities?

II. WHEN 'REASON' SHIELDS US FROM NORMATIVE SIGNIFICANCE

While in political and moral philosophy Nazism has become the epitome of 'that which is pretty well universally execrated',[24] few of those philosophical theories have delved into the social and psychological processes that enabled those crimes. Given the risk of any such investigation slipping into seemingly justifying or normalising the enormity of those atrocities, one may argue that this is a good thing. Yet I suspect that those misgivings also have something to do with the fact that such inquiry would present us with a mirror throwing an awkward light onto our own social practices. The Weimar Republic may have had a better education system than any of our present ones, advanced technology and a flourishing cultural scene.[25] No other Nation could boast quite so many world-famous philosophers (and scientists), nor – one suspects – quite as many citizens able to quote Kant.

Thus far the post-World War II debate in Anglo-Saxon jurisprudence has been dominated by an overarching, normative concern: to prevent blind obedience to law. This is the key consideration behind the 1958 Fuller–Hart debate, which structured much of late twentieth century jurisprudence.[26] Hart's defence of legal positivism by reference to the need to avoid any conflation of what law is and what law ought to be suggests that principled reflection on the latter

[23] In a different context (studying expert craftsmen' responsiveness to pertinent features of a situation), Rietveld emphasises the extent to which a switch to a reflective stance (rather than the non-reflective, 'skillful coping' stance reviewed in chapter one) can affect a craftsman's responsiveness: 'Responsiveness can be blocked by adopting an attitude of detachment or disengagement. In such an attitude "one is set for not acting", which blocks the normal direct embodied impact of events on emotion and action (Frijda 2007, p. 111). As soon as action becomes reflective in a disengaged way, this immediate motivating character of the object disappears': Erik Rietveld, 'Situated normativity: The normative aspect of embodied cognition in unreflective action' (2008) 117 *Mind* 973, 994.

[24] GEM Anscombe, *Intention* (2nd edn, Harvard UP 2000) 72.

[25] '[I]n Germany, genocide was the central feature of the official ideology; it was stated publicly and explicitly and required the full power of the society's highly-developed technological and organizational capabilities. This was not random terror, or government oppression, or coercion as a means of staying in power, but was death as science and administration. It is often pointed out how strange it is that this occurred in a country that saw itself as the most advanced artistically, philosophically, and technologically': Charles Maier, 'The unmasterable past: History, Holocaust, and German national identity' (1992) 21 *Theory and Society* 290, 293.

[26] HLA Hart, 'Positivism and the separation of law and morals' (1958) 71 *Harvard Law Review* 593; Lon Fuller, 'Positivism and fidelity to law: A reply to Professor Hart' (1958) 71 *Harvard Law Review* 630.

(implicitly seen as deficient in the Nazi example) is the best way to safeguard the integrity of the former.

That at least some of those who did obey Nazi law and committed atrocities in its name did so with eyes wide opened is not much discussed. Eichmann's quoting the categorical imperative to explain his principled refusal to make exceptions[27] for particular Jews with influential sponsors is rarely dwelled upon. Yet it instantiates precisely the way in which principled reflection (perverted as it can be by its socio-cultural environment) can not only license but facilitate barbarity, for it can become 'the most reliable of all safeguards against the words and the presence of others'.[28]

Building upon Arendt's analysis of Eichmann's Germany as 'an inverted moral order, a social environment in which the categories of legality and illegality, morality and immorality, were not only blurred but upside down',[29] Pauer-Studer and Velleman open the diaries of several 'lower-level perpetrators' in an attempt to understand how 'so many individuals could lose their moral bearings'.[30]

Thus, we hear of the quandary faced by Kretschmer, a German pharmacist who joined the Nazi party in 1939[31] and served in a *Sonderkommando* that took part in mass executions:

> As I said, I am in a very gloomy mood. I must pull myself out of it. The sight of the dead (including women and children) is not very cheering. But we are fighting this war for the survival or non-survival of our people. [...] We have to eat and drink well because of the nature of our work, as I have described to you in detail. Otherwise we would crack up. [...] If it weren't for the stupid thoughts about what we are doing in this country, the Einsatz here would be wonderful, since it has put me in a position where I can support you all very well. Since, as I already wrote to you, I consider the last Einsatz to be justified and indeed approve of the consequences it had, the phrase: 'stupid thoughts' is not strictly accurate. Rather it is a weakness not to be able to stand the sight of dead people; the best way of overcoming it is to do it more often. Then it becomes a habit.[32]

[27] 'This uncompromising attitude toward the performance of his murderous duties damned him in the eyes of the judges more than anything else, which was comprehensible, but in his own eyes it was precisely what justified him, as it had once silenced whatever conscience he might have had left. No exceptions – this was the proof that he had always acted against his "inclinations," whether they were sentimental or inspired by interest, that he had always done his "duty."': Hannah Arendt, *Eichmann In Jerusalem: A report on the Banality of Evil* (Penguin 1994) 137.

[28] Ibid.

[29] Herlinde Pauer-Studer and J David Velleman, 'Distortions of normativity' (2011) 14 *Ethical Theory and Moral Practice* 329.

[30] 'The philosophical significance of the Nazi crimes must be obscured when they are used as toy examples of immorality; for if their immorality had been as obvious to the perpetrators as it is today, the crimes might never have occurred. [...] explaining how so many individuals could lose their moral bearings is one of the main philosophical challenges of the Nazi crimes – a challenge that goes unacknowledged when those crimes are treated simplistically': ibid.

[31] Kretschmer was rejected by the SS for 'failure to satisfy requirements during a course on ideology' (Ernst Klee, Willi Dressen and Volker Riess, *'The Good Old Days': The Holocaust as Seen by Its Perpetrators and Bystanders* (Konecky & Konecky 1991) 296, quoted in ibid 348).

[32] Ibid.

The need to overcome spontaneous moral sentiments – denigrated as 'weaknesses' – is one of the key themes appearing in each of the diary entries considered by Pauer-Studer. In every case, 'principled' reflection is used to assuage intense emotional reactions:

> At noon was present at a special action in the women's camp ... – the most horrible of all horrors. Hschf. Thilo, military surgeon, was right when he said to me today that we are located here in the anus mundi [anus of the world].[33]

This quote is from a then 58-year-old physician with a doctorate in philosophy who served at Auschwitz and noted his reaction upon first attending gas chambers mass murders. He also attended 'medical' killings by phenol injection in order to collect samples for the purpose of medical research. His tone is that of a detached professional:

> The SS physician primarily designated for liquidation [by injection] those prisoners whose diagnosis was Allgemeine Körperschwäche [general bodily exhaustion]. I used to observe such prisoners and if one of them aroused my interest, owing to his advanced state of emaciation, I asked the orderly to reserve the given patient for me and let me know when he would be killed with an injection. [...] The patient was placed on the dissecting table while he was still alive. I then approached the table and put several questions to the man as to such details which pertained to my research.[34]

Whether they be delineated professionally (see above) or ideologically ('we are fighting this war for the survival or non-survival of our people'[35]) the roles used by the perpetrators define the type of reasoning that is used to sanction the abhorrent. While one can hardly draw any general conclusion from the small number of diaries sampled in Pauer-Studer's paper, political and legal theory's general disregard for those sources reporting the impact of emotional disengagement is nevertheless perplexing.

If the atrocities that played such a big role in shaping many post-World War II political, moral and legal philosophies had less to do with a lack of principled reflection, and more to do with such reflection acting as a shield from otherwise powerful emotions and intuitions, the assumed need for 'absolutes' is turned on its head. From a theoretical perspective, we need more – rather than less – of the naturalist premises that informed early twentieth-century pragmatism. From a practical perspective, instead of counting on some punctual 'deliberative rescue' from the threat of ethical and political perversion, greater emphasis needs to be placed on our capacity for pre-reflective discernment. This capacity goes hand in hand with an attentive way of developing and sustaining habits, which is outlined in the next chapter.

[33] Ibid.
[34] Ibid 343.
[35] Ibid.

5

Growing within *the Habitual*

Consistent pragmatists must base even their most radical critiques not on transcendent grounds but practical affairs; but these affairs are, in some instances at least, precisely what calls for criticism.

Vincent Colapietro, 'Doing – and undoing – the done thing'[1]

THE SUCCESS OF the 'liberal' naturalism developed in chapter one – its ability to construct a narrative that takes us from human beings with needs and desires to internalised standards of right and wrong – hinges upon a key ambiguity inherent in the concept of habit. In its most depleted understanding, habit is reducible to behavioural tics that will never support or intersect with the reflective aspects of our lives. Pollard contrasts this 'way of having a habit' – 'which is available to pre-rational humans and other non-rational animals'[2] – with that which is 'available to humans once they have acquired the capacity to act for reasons'.[3]

This peculiarly human way of having a habit is sometimes described as involving the capacity to 'contemplate alternatives; [and] step back from the natural impulse and direct critical scrutiny at it'.[4] The aim of this chapter is to unpack what makes this 'human way of having a habit' possible in the first place in a bid to understand what, if anything, might compromise it. Chapter four outlined the still dominant, intellectualist way of answering that question. For a large strand of philosophy (dominated by Kantian ethics), what enables us to 'step back from the natural impulse' is our noumenal nature as self-determining, free beings.[5]

A naturalist stance forbids any reference to such an Archimedean vantage point (this vantage point need not be formulated along transcendental, Kantian lines, and may include Platonic forms, 'natural' values or *a priori* principles).

[1] Vincent Colapietro, 'Doing – and undoing – the done thing: dewey and bourdieu on habituation, agency, and transformation' (2004) 1 *Contemporary Pragmatism* 65, 75.

[2] Bill Pollard, 'Naturalizing the space of reasons' (2005) 13 *International Journal of Philosophical Studies* 69, 76.

[3] Ibid.

[4] John McDowell, 'Two sorts of naturalism' in John McDowell, *Mind, Value and Reality* (Harvard UP 1998).

[5] Jürgen Habermas, *The Future of Human Nature* (Polity 2003); Susan Wolf, *Freedom Within Reason* (OUP 1990).

When it comes to explaining our capacity to step back from the habitual, all the naturalist has at its disposal are socially conditioned emotions, practices and habits of evaluation. Under what conditions can the latter trigger the movement of critical scrutiny without which the 'peculiarly human' way of having a habit becomes out of reach? The scarcity of answers to this question cannot be blamed only on the continued dominance of non-naturalist accounts of ethical agency. Aristotelian types of naturalism have placed so much emphasis on the gradual construction of our ethical sensibilities through a process of habituation that their accounts of what, if anything, enables us to suspend habituated modes of thought to consider the need for change are either meagre or overly reliant on some abstract 'responsiveness to reasons'.

Section I highlights the gaps left by this traditional reliance on 'responsiveness to reasons' to explain our capacity to challenge the usual. To fill these gaps, this chapter critically considers the role played by 'responsiveness to the other'. The always unsettled, relational effort that underlies this pre-reflective form of situational discernment is deemed central to ethical agency, thus closing the loop started in chapter two. Can the pre-reflective 'intelligence' inherent in our ethically relevant habits be captured in a way that accounts for our capacity to initiate change in the practices that shape our ethical sensitivity? Section II and III argue that it can, provided one delineates the conditions under which we are capable of 'attentively' developing and maintaining the relevant habits.

Rather than being conceived as a 'meta-habit' (or an emotional capacity that sits alongside those habits), the kind of attention required is best conceived as a *way of having* a habit. The extent to which such a way of having a habit remains adequately responsive to 'the other' can be compromised by both exogenous, environmental factors and endogenous, rigidification-of-self factors. This chapter concludes by highlighting the extent to which compromised 'other-responsiveness' can go hand in hand with some increasingly illusory 'reason-responsiveness'. The latter becomes illusory when our behaviours, attitudes and frames of thought keep being structured around norms 'cotton-woolled' in abstract reasoning. The resulting insulation from any situation-prompted critique[6] means those norms become out of touch with the normative demands emerging from our evolving forms of life.

I. RESPONSIVENESS TO REASONS

If all we have at our disposal, when it comes to explaining our ability to step back from the habitual, are our socially conditioned emotions and habits of

[6] This scope and ambition of this situation-prompted critique need not be limited to the particular context at hand: as it is delineated in this chapter, our 'responsiveness to the other' is best delineated as an – often neglected – springboard for the exercise of our critical, normative agency.

evaluation, then to nevertheless postulate the capacity to 'contemplate alternatives' to the habitual[7] as key to our 'second nature' may sound optimistic. What would trigger such contemplation? Emotions? Not if they are themselves dulled by habit:

> If habit causes feelings to decline, presumably to the point of expiration, then how is the role of emotional response – whether as a character trait; as the pleasure and pain accompanying virtuous and vicious acts; or as a motivational factor in action – to be accommodated?[8]

A. Why 'Reasons'?

An Aristotelian account of excellence in the moral sphere would stress that situation-specific discernment is all you need. A lot hangs on exactly how one characterises such discernment. McDowell's emphasis on the extent to which such discernment participat[es] in the 'space of reasons' is emblematic of a deeply-rooted, dominant strand within moral philosophy. This emphasis is tied to what McDowell openly refers to as the need to find a middle ground between 'reflective thought' and 'conformity to Galilean law'.[9] The concern, in other words, is to construct an account of pre-reflective discernment that establishes its (relative) independence from purely causal processes. The assumption is that this can only be achieved if there is a minimal degree of reasons-responsiveness.

This assumption is problematic on more than one count. It is problematic, first, because it often goes hand in hand with an apprehensive dismissal of what is bundled as 'situational factors'. From pizza boxes[10] to ambient smells,[11] countless studies highlight the extent to which we are prone to being influenced by factors that should not have any bearing on our moral judgement. These empirical results are sometimes referred to as the 'situationist threat'.[12] For many theorists, this 'threat' corroborates their conviction that we only 'truly' remain 'the agents of the things we do'[13] if we retain our responsiveness to impersonal, situation-independent reasons.

[7] As per McDowell's quote, above.

[8] Clare Carlisle, 'Between freedom and necessity: Felix Ravaisson on habit and the moral life' (2010) 53 *Inquiry* 123.

[9] John McDowell, 'Responses' in Nicholas H Smith (ed), *Reading McDowell: On Mind and World* (Routledge 2002) referring to Charles Taylor, 'Foundationalism and the inner-outer distinction' in Smith (ibid).

[10] Simone Schnall and others, 'Disgust as embodied moral judgment' (2008) 34 *Personality and Social Psychology Bulletin* 1096.

[11] Yoel Inbar, David Pizarro and Paul Bloom, 'Disgusting smells cause decreased liking of gay men' (2012) 12 *Emotion* 23.

[12] Carolina Sartorio, 'Situations and responsiveness to reasons' (2018) 52 *Noûs* 796.

[13] J David Velleman, 'The voice of conscience' (1999) 99 *Proceedings of the Aristotelian Society* 57, 57–76.

What if, instead of reiterating the importance of 'reasons-responsiveness', the same theorists had endeavoured to understand what circumstances we do need to be sensitive to in order to be responsive to apt reasons[14] – not just 'established norms of rational receptivity',[15] to borrow Lovibond's phrase? Considered from this perspective, the more abstract our 'reasons receptiveness' becomes, the more it risks perpetuating collective habits of thought. These collective habits are liable to conceal ethically salient features of a situation. The vigilance these habits require to keep them in check cannot take refuge in purely rational reflection, safely removed from the 'situationist threat' of smelly rooms and pizza boxes-littered desks.

> [T]he shortcomings of which [this attitude of vigilance] stands ready to accuse itself are different. They relate not to our possible failure to be all that other (decent, morally upright) people in our social milieu expect us to be, but rather to a possible failure to subject these very social expectations to the scrutiny they deserve.[16]

Within a non-reductive, 'liberal' understanding of ethical agency,[17] what is at stake in delineating some adequately responsive, pre-reflective discernment is not so much its escaping purely causal conformity to 'Galilean law'. What adequate pre-reflective discernment needs to escape, if anything, is 'unchecked' exposure to 'social and ideological determination'.[18] An account of the difficulty inherent in preserving such critical distanciation remains under-developed even within the work of authors who, like Dreyfus, are particularly attentive to the resources inherent in pre-reflective forms of intelligence:

> McDowell concludes that, [...] thanks to our inculcation into our culture, we become sensitive to reasons, which then influence our 'habits of thought and action'. One can easily accept that in learning to be wise we learn to follow general reasons as guides to acting appropriately. But it does not follow that, once we have gotten past the learning phase, these reasons in the form of habits still influence our wise actions.[19]

Replace the 'it does not follow that' sentence in the above with 'it does not follow that these reasons will always remain adequate guides to acting appropriately', and you get a better characterisation of the question left open by McDowell's 'reasons responsiveness' account. At the heart of this question is the fallibility of the reasons yielded by our socio-cultural practices. This fallibility entails that

[14] That question demands a mix of normative and empirical analysis. In contrast, see: 'Are we really sensitive to the various aspects of the actual circumstances that we need to be sensitive to in order to be sufficiently responsive to reasons? At the end of the day, this is an empirical question, so the most I can offer here is an educated guess': Sartorio, 'Situations and responsiveness to reasons'.

[15] Sabina Lovibond, *Ethical Formation* (Harvard University Press 2002).

[16] Ibid.

[17] See chapter one.

[18] Lovibond, *Ethical Formation.*

[19] Hubert L Dreyfus, *Overcoming the Myth of the Mental: How Philosophers Can Profit from the Phenomenology of Everyday Expertise* (American Philosophical Association 2005) 50.

there will often be a gap between those reasons and the normatively significant features of a situation.

B. The Gap between 'Reasons' and Normative Significance

Sometimes to remain responsive to reasons demands a willingness to break from existing reasons' influence. In other words, one can't be too much in the business of 'following' reasons if one is to remain adequately responsive to them. If this sounds confusing, it is because of the reasons-based characterization of the problem, which is too abstract to grasp what is at stake. What conditions the peculiarly human way of having a habit is our responsiveness to situations that are always infused with normative significance. This responsiveness can be compromised by merely following a set of given reasons.

For most of us (the *phronimos* excluded), our habits of thought and action will be apt at generating their own self-sustaining reasons. How does one build into one's account of adequate unreflective action the necessary capacity to challenge such self-sustaining reasons and maintain adequate 'discernment' (ie availability to the ethical demands that may emerge from novel situations)? Pollard emphasises the importance of the agent's 'capacity to opt out [of habit] for reasons' but, just like McDowell, does not delve into exactly what underlies this capacity.[20] Pollard's focus is on delineating that subset of habitual actions which can be deemed 'rational': '[t]hat subset will consist of those habitual actions which cohere with the agent's worldview'.[21]

> And that in turn will be enough to rule out nail-biting and cigarette smoking when they are against the agent's better judgement. These actions are not justifiable in the right sense.[22]

But will it be enough to rule out habits generated by frequent repetition of abhorrent or simply inadequate practices? An agent's worldview is likely to be malleable enough to accommodate – and in some cases encourage – habits that one would struggle to deem rational. While Pollard's 'rational coherentist' answer to what underlies our capacity 'to opt out of habit' has the merit of not conjuring some rationalist trick from the outside, it also exposes the limits of any solely reasons-based account of habit suspension, whether that account has us reaching out for the 'right' reasons or not. To be plausible, any understanding of the requisite responsiveness will have to go down a notch in its level of abstraction.

[20] In Pollard's case this is thanks to what may be dubbed a 'coherentist' bypassing strategy.

[21] '[T]his world view will consist of her beliefs, interests, projects and preferences, any other items which disclose how the world is for her': Pollard, 'Naturalizing the space of reasons'.

[22] Ibid.

The next section unpacks the resources inherent in the 'work of attention': as a quotidian, low-key endeavour, the 'work of attention' aims to uncover the often-unarticulated norms that structure the practices within which we are embedded. The reasons which such work allows us to remain responsive to are never given in advance. In this sense they are unlike the reasons that inform both internal criticism (based on already articulated, shared norms) and external criticism (based on norms whose validity or 'truth' is deemed established or self-evident). This will be further unpacked in section III.

II. HABIT AND THE WORK OF ATTENTION

> If we ignore the prior work of attention and notice only the emptiness of the moment of choice we are likely to identify freedom with the outward movement since there is nothing else to identify it with. But if we consider what the work of attention is like, how continuously it goes on, and how imperceptibly it builds up structures of value round about us, we shall not be surprised that at crucial moments of choice most of the business of choosing is already over.[23]

The contrast drawn by Murdoch between 'the continuous work of attention' and the 'moment of choice' not only criticises any fixation on the 'moment of choice' (whether it is presented in a fatalistic or 'radically unprecedented' fashion). It also takes aim at 'our British philosophers [who] are of course very interested in reasons'.[24] The problem is not the interest in reasons *per se*, but rather the idea that 'the production of such reasons [...] does not in any way connect or tie the agent to the world or to special personal contexts within the world'.[25] The problem, in other words, lies with what makes a reasons-based apprehension of a given situation attractive to many: its being structured along impersonal lines.

On this view, reasons-based analysis reflects our ability to abstract ourselves from the particulars that stem from a given situation – and the personal habits and dispositions we bring to that situation.[26] In short, it reflects our capacity to be free, responsible moral agents. Little wonder, in that context, if relatively

[23] Iris Murdoch, *The Sovereignty of Good* (Routledge 2013) 36.
[24] Ibid.
[25] Ibid.
[26] This is related to the 'rule following' discussion in chapter three, section III: when Bridges (Jason Bridges, 'Rule-following skepticism, properly so called' in James Conant and Andrea Kern (eds), *Varieties of Skepticism: Essays after Kant, Wittgenstein, and Cavell* (De Gruyter 2014)) asks for a 'diagnosis of why the idea of the special mental process should be so tempting in the context of philosophical reflection', I think the temptation has something to do with our emotionally felt need to assert our freedom – and concomitant responsibility. For many, to think of ourselves as ships stirred by a mix of habitual undercurrents and emotional winds won't do. Hence the need for what Blackburn refers to as a 'Kantian captain': Simon Blackburn, *Ruling Passions* (Clarendon Press 1998).

little heed is paid to the continuous work that takes place in the background, as we learn to find our way around our life with others. To refer to this background work as 'the work of attention' is helpful for our purposes since it highlights the complex relationship between habit and attention.

It is all too easy to think of habit and attention as two forces working against each other: if one assumes that attention can only be 'paid' deliberately, as a manifestation of our intentional selves, habits are kept in check if and only if we pay attention. When I end up at the usual school pick up point, albeit kilometres from where I was actually supposed to pick up my son on that day, I pay for my lack of attention. In contrast to this narrow, 'intentional self' understanding of attention, chapter two highlighted the tacit learning attitude that underpins the development of countless skills and capabilities. In that case, our intentional self is liable to compromise our ability to pay the kind of attention that conditions the acquisition of the intuitive intelligence leveraged by neonatal nurses and firemen (to refer only to the examples developed in chapter two). That same intentional self can also compromise skilful, habituated performance: this performance-sapping effect is best documented within sports practice.[27]

The contrast between intentional and pre-reflective attention is not the only one relevant for our purposes. Of significance, too, is the difference between punctual and diachronic attention, third versus first and second-person attention, humble versus model-driven attention etc. When it comes to understanding the roots of our ability to challenge habitual, ethically significant modes of thought or behaviour, the importance of the quality of one's attention is best grasped through examples. While the first two are taken from the realm of professional ethics, the third focuses on quotidian encounters, and the extent to which these encounters can help us 'see past' habitual salience.

A. GP Consultation with Seemingly 'Peripheral' Child Safeguarding Concerns

Here it helps to recall the virtual reality GP consultation experiment depicted in chapter three (section III). One of the hypotheses that structured that experiment was that highly experienced GPs would find it easier to adequately address the signs of child-safeguarding concerns, even when the cues are subtle and the

[27] In sports, the extent to which conscious, deliberate thought can be detrimental to skilful performance is well documented. See for instance: 'Everything went wrong with my batting … You can't change a habit instinctively. When you're playing well you don't think about anything and run-making comes naturally. When you're out of form you're conscious of needing to do things right, so you have to think first and act second. To make runs under those conditions is mighty difficult': Barrington (as told to Pilley) in Ken Barrington and Phil Pilley, *Playing it Straight* (S Paul 1968) 97–98. Cited in John Sutton, 'Batting, habit and memory: The embodied mind and the nature of skill' (2007) 10 *Sport in Society* 763, 765.

cognitive load higher. That hypothesis was not supported by the experiment's results. These results showed instead that a GP's ability to pick up signs of child-safeguarding concerns (hence adapting to a widening of the pertinent features calling upon her attention) was significantly correlated with particular psychological traits and stress levels. GPs who were less stressed, less neurotic, more agreeable and more extroverted tended to be better at raising potential child abuse issues in their notes.[28]

The formulation of the above hypothesis was partly informed by a 'positive' understanding of professional habituation, whereby years of practice can instil an intuitive ability to 'see' solutions – or diagnoses – in a way that is comparable to a chess master's ability to 'see' dynamic chess formations. The intelligent habits at the heart of such non-cognitive expertise were outlined in chapter two, along with the so-called 'dual system theory'. According to such a theory, this ability to bypass slow, burdensome cognitive processes allows for a much quicker apprehension of the problem at stake. This bypassing process can also free the professional's attentional resources in a way that increases her ability to pick up what might otherwise be dismissed as peripheral or irrelevant considerations.

That the VR experiment's results did not support the 'more experienced GPs will be better at picking up child-safeguarding concerns' hypothesis does not necessarily invalidate the above, positive understanding of professional habituation. Many factors can compromise the extent to which an experienced professional is in a position to capitalise on those freed attentional resources (in a way that increases situational awareness). To grasp the full range of those factors, one needs to distinguish between merely punctual or synchronic versus diachronic attention.

Because the overwhelming focus of the experiments'[29] underlying 'dual system theory' has been on synchronic, environmental distractions[30] that affect the subject's cognitive judgement – or perceptual awareness – at time 't', the impact of longer term, diachronic factors has been under-studied. Yet perceptual awareness is shaped and cultivated over time. The factors that can compromise this continued honing process are more difficult to pin down. Some are likely to fall under what Julia Annas refers to as a broad 'lack of aspiration'.[31]

This 'lack of aspiration' can stem from a variety of personal attitudes. Some of these attitudes are driven by character traits, others by rigidified theoretical

[28] Xueni Pan and others, 'A study of professional awareness using immersive virtual reality: The responses of general practitioners to child safeguarding concerns' (2018) 5 *Frontiers in Robotics and AI* 1.

[29] Steven J Kass, Kerstan S Cole and Claudia J Stanny, 'Effects of distraction and experience on situation awareness and simulated driving' (2007) 10 *Transportation Research Part F: Traffic Psychology and Behaviour* 321; Juliana Burges Sbicigo, Gerson Américo Janczura and Jerusa Fumagalli de Salles, 'The role of attention in perceptual and conceptual priming' (2017) 10 *Psychology & Neuroscience* 117.

[30] The virtual reality experimental setting would count as one of those distractions.

[31] Julia Annas, *Intelligent Virtue* (Kindle Edition edn, OUP 2011).

stances: the level of theoretical certainty with which a professional approaches her task will have a big impact on the extent to which she looks beyond the features that habitually draw her attention. Motivation to see past 'the usual person in the usual place'[32] (in this case, the patient) is indeed likelier if one retains some degree of inquisitiveness[33] and uncertainty. Far from a punctual, intentional intervention needed to keep habits on track, the work of attention necessary to maintain a spirit of Deweyan enquiry is an *effort* that needs to become habitual in order to support *from within* a multitude of intelligent habits.

B. Imposing a Mental Defence in Criminal Law

There are times when the work of attention throws an uncomfortable light on habits that are constitutive of important social (and, in this case, legal) practices. To understand the pre-reflective roots of the process that sometimes leads from modified perceptual awareness to social and/or legal change endeavours, the following example is helpful.

Kaczynski was a mathematician who, convinced that technological society was destroying society, fashioned his own 'mail bombs' to murder (or maim) a variety of people. These people all had in common the fact that their activities were deemed by Kaczynski to be particularly detrimental. Kaczynski became known as the Unabomber.[34] He was arrested years later, when his brother guessed Kaczynski was the author of a 35,000 word manifesto 'Industrial Society and its Future', which had been published by major newspapers in return for a promise to halt the bombings.

Against Kaczynski's articulate and vehement opposition, his defence lawyers wanted to put on a mental defence. Confronted with relentless pressure and convinced that this defence would not be used for the purpose of establishing his guilt, Kaczynski reluctantly agreed to speak to a psychiatrist. When he was double-crossed, and this mental defence was used to spare him the death penalty, Kaczynski wrote to the judge (before attempting suicide):

> It is humiliating to have one's mind probed. [My lawyers] calculatedly deceived me in order to get me to reveal my private thoughts, and then without warning they

[32] GK Chesterton, 'The twelve men' in GK Chesterton (ed), *Tremendous Trifles* (Sheed & Ward 1955).

[33] Empathy can also play a role, even if, in a scenario like this virtual GP consultation, responsiveness to the child's vulnerability may be compromised by excessive empathy with the father's (loud) predicament. The reasons-based responsiveness of 'high-functioning autistic adults' who are said to have to 'compensate' for their empathy deficit by 'discover[ing] moral rules and principles of conduct for themselves by reasoning, as they would in other matters, on the basis of patient explicit enquiry', may fare better as a result: Jeanette Kennett, 'Autism, empathy and moral agency' (2002) 52 *The Philosophical Quarterly* 340.

[34] Michael Mello, 'The non-trial of the century: Representations of the Unabomber' (1999) 24 *Vermont Law Review* 417, 421.

> made accessible to the public the cold and heartless assessments of their experts [...] [T]o me this was a stunning blow [...] [and] the worst experience I ever underwent in my life [...] I would rather die, or suffer prolonged physical torture, than have the [mental] defense imposed on me in this way by my present attorneys.[35]

Despite its eloquence, Kaczynski's request to represent himself was rejected by the judge. Kaczynski was sentenced to life without parole (he pleaded guilty rather than put forward a mental defence). From his cell, Kaczynski wrote:

> Perhaps I ought to hate my attorneys for what they have done to me, but I do not. Their motives were in no way malicious. They are essentially conventional people who are blind to some of the implications of this case, and they acted as they did because they subscribe to certain professional principles that they believe left them no alternative. These principles may seem rigid and even ruthless to a non-lawyer, but there is no doubt my attorneys believe in them.[36]

What Kaczynski's attorneys did (with the best of intentions) was to '[make] nonsense of his deepest commitments, of what mattered to him and made him who he was [...] The mental defence would discredit what he regarded as his life's principal contribution to human welfare, the manifesto that he had killed to get into print'.[37]

Striking as this case is you might wonder what, if anything, it has to do with the background work of attention that is meant to challenge ethically relevant habits. It's not as if Kaczynski's predicament escaped the attention of either his attorneys or the judge denying his request to represent himself. His attorneys may well have agonised over the extent to which they should heed his eloquent, articulate plea not to rely on a mental defence. Their decision not to does not necessarily suggest a lack of either synchronic or diachronic attention: aside from the fact that they probably did engage with that case to the best of their abilities (synchronic attention), they may also have cultivated some exemplary perceptual awareness over the span of their professional career.

The relevance of this case does not consist in what it might (or might not) tell us about the extent to which the judge's and attorney's habits of thought were kept plastic enough thanks to a high degree of perceptual awareness. Of particular interest instead is what it tells us about the weight of the implicit norms that structure public-facing, expert discourses. One of the things that makes this case striking is Kaczynski's articulate grounds for rejecting psychiatry's claim to be in a position to legitimately label someone as 'sick':

> 'Our society tends to regard as a "sickness" any mode of thought or behavior that is inconvenient for the system, and this is plausible because when an individual

[35] William Finnegan, 'Defending the Unabomber' *New Yorker* (16 March 1998) www.newyorker.com/magazine/1998/03/16/defending-the-unabomber, 1123 accessed 21 February 2022, quoted by David Luban, 'Lawyers as upholders of human dignity (when they aren't busy assaulting it)' (2005) *University of Illinois Law Review* 815, 828.

[36] Mello, 'The non-trial of the century' 502.

[37] Luban, 'Lawyers as upholders of human dignity' 829–30.

doesn't fit into the system it causes pain to the individual as well as problems for the system'.[38]

Few of those unfortunate enough to be diagnosed with mental health issues will reject as eloquently the very grounds of their diagnosis. Yet many are in a position where that mental health diagnosis will be lived as some way of 'cutting the grass from under their own feet' so to speak: the voice they had is taken away and becomes the voice of a 'mentally ill' person. In some cases, the very integrity of the projects that structured their life up to that diagnosis is under threat: where they might have felt misunderstood before, they now feel excluded from those worthy of the kind of engagement necessary to any degree of reciprocal sense-making.

C. Seeing Past Habitual Salience and the Role of Personal Encounters

The unease one may feel when reading about the Kaczynski case may have less to do with Kaczynski himself[39] and more with our society's readiness to 'bow' to mental health expertise. Are we, as a society, asking enough questions? Are we challenging the epistemic grounds of this body of expertise rigorously enough? Is the widespread, unarticulated fear of 'madness' making us more complacent than we should be when it comes to the conditions under which this scientific discourse is allowed to have such profound implications for the lives of those affected?

The above are difficult questions. There is little doubt that they need to be asked, again and again. Few things are as dangerous as our habitually bowing to convention or the authority of experts, especially when the expertise in question is taken to warrant interventions that impact upon a person's continued ability to deploy their sense of self. In a related context, Janna Van Grunsven explores the way in which current scientific discourses foster a two-way 'perceptual breakdown' between 'typically developed cognitive agents' and autistic people.[40] Whereas autistic people's perceptual difficulties when it comes to social cognition are well-documented, the extent to which autistic people's own 'sense-making' endeavours remains 'perceptually opaque to neurotypicals' is far less discussed.

> Take 'stimming' or 'self-stimulatory behavior,' which many autistics engage in and which can take on a variety of forms: humming, grunting, rocking, flapping, spinning, finger flipping, etc. Stimming is often seen as merely pathological stereotypical

[38] Theodore Kaczynski, 'The Unabomber's manifesto: Industrial society and its future' (1995) para 155 besser.tsoa.nyu.edu/howard/Anarchism/Unabom/manifesto2.html, accessed 30 June 2021.

[39] This unease is distinct from the outrage or shock that stems from the fact that Kaczynski is a person who was willing to murder to get his views across.

[40] Janna Van Grunsven, 'Enactivism and the paradox of moral perception' (2021) *Topoi*.

> behavior – behavior that isn't communicative, expressive, or thoughtful. But if we look at personal testimonies and recent community based participatory research, what emerges is a much richer perspective on stimming. [...] Attentive neurotypicals can perceive and be responsive to the meanings expressed through stimming as a form of sense-making if 'due care' is taken, such that a person's 'specific style of emotional expression' isn't reliably misperceived.[41]

Aside from the effort involved to develop and maintain the level of attention that might make an autistic person's 'sense-making' endeavours less opaque, Van Grunsven convincingly argues that scientific discourses such as the 'Theory of Mind Deficit' view[42] have a lot to answer for when it comes to neurotypicals' lack of perceptual engagement with autistic people. The harm caused by this engagement deficit arguably takes its roots in a 'sense of self vulnerability' that is very similar in kind to that outlined in chapter three in the context of professional practices. That chapter articulated the extent to which educators, some lawyers and a wide range of medical specialties (from geriatrics to oncology) will frequently find themselves in a position where the quality of their engagement may either alleviate or aggravate their patient, client or pupil's sense of self vulnerability.

The ensuing responsibility cannot be theirs only. For the work of attention to critically support our habitual deference to a range of experts, that work needs to constantly challenge what those experts deem worthy of attention.[43] As for the experts themselves (and each and every one of us[44]), that same work

[41] Ibid, quoting Trip Glazer, 'Epistemic violence and emotional misperception' (2019) 34 *Hypatia* 59 at 61.

[42] 'According to [the Theory of Mind Deficit], the minds of autistic people are marked by an allegedly damaged or absent Theory of Mind mechanism, which is thought to enable people to understand their own behavior as well as the behavior of others as caused by mental states such as beliefs, desires, intentions, emotions (Baron-Cohen 1995; Frith & Happé 1999). [...] By naturalizing autistic persons as marked by a deficient Theory of Mind and maintaining that they are as a matter of scientific fact "dead souls in a living body," we reliably fail to see autistic persons as the "the center of an open life," as a sense-making "meaningful life" tout court': Van Grunsven, 'Enactivism and the paradox of moral perception'.

[43] The potential contestation aspect inherent in the work of attention is sometimes missing from those accounts that seek to show how habit and attention can work together. See for instance: 'We can think of attentiveness as single-mindedness. To pay attention to what one is doing is to "centre oneself in one's activity", increasing one's attunement to those possibilities for action that are relevant to it, so that they stand out for one more strongly. Attentiveness decreases one's attunement to those competing possibilities. In this way, paying attention to what one is doing helps to keep one's activity on track': Komarine Romdenh-Romluc, 'Merleau-Ponty: Actions, habits, and skilled expertise' in Daniel Dahlstrom, Andreas Elpidorou and Walter Hopp (eds), *Philosophy of Mind and Phenomenology: Conceptual and Empirical Approaches* (Routledge 2015).

[44] In the realm of ethics, expertise may be said to be either universal or non-existent. On this debate, see Christopher Cowley, 'A new rejection of moral expertise' (2005) 8 *Medicine, Health Care, and Philosophy* 273; Christopher Cowley, 'Expertise, wisdom and moral philosophers: A response to Gesang. Jul 2012' (2012) 26 *Bioethics* 337; JAN Crosthwaite, 'Moral expertise: A problem in the professional ethics of professional ethicists' (1995) 9 *Bioethics* 361; Itiel E Dror, 'The paradox of human expertise: Why experts get it wrong' in Narinder Kapur (ed), *The Paradoxical Brain* (CUP 2011); Bernward Gesang, 'Are moral philosophers moral experts?' (2010) 24 *Bioethics* 153.

is essential if receptivity to situational features other than those made salient by habitual stances is to be preserved.

To counteract the way in which habits make certain aspects of our perceived environment stand out – these aspects seem to *invite* the habitual action[45] – is not easy. While one can adopt intentional, deliberate strategies – such as my repeatedly bringing to mind the new school pickup point as I cycle to collect my son – these strategies are resource-intensive. Not only can they backfire as a result,[46] they are also unlikely to succeed in a situation where I am less aware of the habits that structure my apprehension of a given situation. As an example, I may not realise that I am silently discounting the gravity of the lived experiences shared by my neighbour because of my awareness of her mental health issues. I might have developed that discounting habit because of what I read, or what I might have heard from mental health experts. And those experts themselves might have developed what has become a habitual discounting stance on the basis of what they believe to be robust scientific grounds.

In contrast to deliberate strategies, the development of a disposition to apprehend each and every human encounter with the kind of humility that was associated with Socratic wisdom in chapter three is more likely to bear fruit. The development of such a disposition does not happen overnight. Nor does it respond well to some wilful (and proud) 'stiffening of muscles'. Weil refers to the latter image to illustrate the superiority of attention over will when it comes to self-improvement:

> Inner supplication is the only reasonable way, for it avoids stiffening muscles which have nothing to do with the matter. What could be more stupid than to tighten up our muscles and set our jaws about virtue, or poetry, or the solution of a problem. Attention is something quite different.
>
> Pride is a tightening up of this kind. There is a lack of grace (we can give the word its double meaning here) in the proud man. It is the result of a mistake.[47]

Of course, the work of attention is not always about self-improvement. That first-person-singular work can turn first-person-plural when it hooks upon features of our collective habitat (to refer back to Williams' image). When the work of attention touches upon inter-personal habits, its highlighting aspects of our environment that would have paled in comparison to those we are habitually drawn to is but a first step. Some form of contestation needs to follow if

[45] Referring to the work of Merleau-Ponty, and his emphasis on the way in which 'the perceived environment is able to bring about action without the need for any thought', Romdenh-Romluc emphasises: '[W]hen one develops a habit, one both acquires a pattern of behaviour, and a way of perceiving the world – one comes to perceive relevant parts of the world as offering opportunities to perform the habitual actions': K Romdenh-Romluc, 'Habit and attention' in Rasmus Thybo Jensen and Dermot Moran (eds), *The Phenomenology of Embodied Subjectivity* (Springer 2014) 13 and 18.

[46] I may be so focused on making sure I get to the correct pick-up point instead of the habitual one that I fail to notice calls for help from a neighbour I pass along the way.

[47] Simone Weil, *Gravity and Grace* (University of Nebraska Press 1997) 116.

that work of attention is to bring about change in the structure of our shared axiological habitat.

Simone Weil's resolution to travel to Germany (in 1932) to work in a factory is a good example of that transition. As a factory worker, she experienced first-hand the contrast between the 'dehumanizing and deadening' form of labour and the dreams of a workers' revolution. The 'vitriolic' reaction of her French colleagues to her sober and pessimistic assessment of the Soviet government 'reveals how determined the leaders of the labor movement [were] to remain wrapped in illusion'.[48] That reaction is also a reminder of the extent to which the work of attention is liable to boil down to nothing if it remains wrapped under theoretical blankets.[49] This has interesting implications for the way in which ethics is taught in various professional schools.

The still largely untapped potential of immersive virtual reality (IVR) in the context of professional ethics education stems from that frequently unacknowledged gap between ethical theorising and actual, non-reflective reactions to ethically significant situations. Because IVR has been shown to mobilise the more primitive parts of our brains before we have had time to 'reason' that the environment is simulated,[50] it is possible to confront students with live ethical dilemmas in a way that solicits their non-reflective responses. These responses are often accompanied with the physiological signs associated with pressure (such as sweating or increased heartbeat). Of particular interest are the post-immersion classroom debates.

In a pilot 'law and ethics' class I developed during the 2016/17 academic year in UCL, students were confronted with a modified IVR version of the trolley dilemma.[51] This immersion experience took place after having theoretically debated and stated their preferred solution to that dilemma. In the seminar that followed, 'students were encouraged to triangulate between their abstract stances, the actual action they took, and to explain and reason through this'.[52] Bolstered by the fact that most students acted in a way that was incompatible with their abstract, theoretical stance, that seminar conversation anchored a

[48] Mark Shiffman, 'Review of *Simone Weil: Attention to the Real*', ndpr.nd.edu/reviews/simone-weil-attention-to-the-real, accessed 22 June 2021.

[49] The dramatic effect of such 'blankets' was illustrated in chapter four – see Kretschmer's letter to his family in Ernst Klee, Willi Dressen and Volker Riess, '*The Good Old Days*': *The Holocaust as Seen by Its Perpetrators and Bystanders* (Konecky & Konecky 1991) 171. 'It is a weakness not to be able to stand the sight of dead people'.

[50] See eg Xueni Pan and Mel Slater, 'Confronting a moral dilemma in virtual reality: A pilot study' (Proceedings of the 25th BCS Conference on Human-Computer Interaction): Mel Slater and others, 'A virtual reprise of the Stanley Milgram obedience experiments' (2006) 1 PLOS ONE e39; Aitor Rovira and others, 'The use of virtual reality in the study of people's responses to violent incidents' (2009) 3 *Frontiers in Behavioral Neuroscience* 59.

[51] The details of this pilot law and ethics class, together with assessment of pedagogical value, student reactions etc are reported in Sylvie Delacroix and Catrina Denvir, 'Virtually teaching ethics' in Catrina Denvir (ed), *Modernizing Legal Education* (CUP 2020).

[52] Ibid.

student-led inquiry into the role played by emotional, intuitive reactions. This inquiry ran through the rest of the course. Crucially, for some this inquiry was not merely theoretical: at the end of the academic year, some students relayed the extent to which that immersive experience contributed to their apprehending their law clinic and other work experiences differently. For those students, the virtual, otherwise sanitised encounter with some avatar(s) constituted what Bennett would refer to as a 'hook' that enabled a 'more extended form of engagement'[53] with the real-world experiences that followed. In that sense, these virtual immersions did contribute to what Del Mar would refer to as an 'education of attention and encounter', without which 'the legal life can all too quickly become a hotbed for moral blindness'.[54]

Of course, this 'education of attention' would be doomed if such virtual encounters were all it had to go by. At their best, such virtual encounters will help jolt us out of patterns of habitual salience: as we internalise ways of apprehending the world that are strongly influenced by our various roles (and education), we will become attuned to some features of our environment, often at the expense of others. In that way IVR experiences can help us see what we don't habitually see, 'in the moral sense of "see" which implies that clear vision is a result of moral imagination and moral effort'.[55] Yet aside from their helping us to see 'past' habitual salience, such experiences are no substitute for 'responsiveness through the physicality of encounter'.[56]

The next section highlights the mutual dependence between the possibility of ongoing immanent critique of a form of life's institutions on one hand and responsiveness to 'the other' on the other hand. It is because this responsiveness, as a capability, can be compromised by the very institutions it is meant to renew that chapters six and seven focus on the institutional contexts most likely to affect this way of having habits.

III. RESPONSIVENESS TO THE OTHER: A FORGOTTEN CAPABILITY?

As it is envisaged here, 'responsiveness to the other' is a capability.[57] Neither reason-based nor empathy-based, attention-based responsiveness, combines

[53] Jill Bennett, *Empathic Vision: Affect, Trauma, and Contemporary Art* (Stanford UP 2005) 65.

[54] Maksymilian Del Mar, 'The education of attention and encounter in the legal academy' in Zenon Bankowski and Maksymilian Del Mar (eds), *The Moral Imagination and the Legal Life: Beyond Text in Legal Education* (Routledge 2016) 36.

[55] Murdoch, *The Sovereignty of Good*.

[56] Marett Leiboff, *Towards a Theatrical Jurisprudence* (Routledge 2019) 90.

[57] While Nussbaum, following Aristotle, draws a list of capabilities deemed central to human flourishing, Sen goes 'list-free' and emphasises the need for groups to settle axiological choices and be 'active participant[s] in change': Martha Nussbaum, *Frontiers of Justice: Disability, Nationality, Species Membership* (Harvard UP 2006); Amartya Sen, *Development as Freedom* (Oxford Paperbacks 2001).

an emphasis on the kind of humility associated with Socratic wisdom[58] with a proactive concern to understand 'the other's point of view as potentially expressive of a whole way of being'.[59] As such, the 'ethics of attention'[60] at the heart of this responsiveness aims to develop the capacity at the same time to see details, and to grasp the overall sense, the 'point' in the lives of those around us.

The pragmatism inherent in such an 'ethics of attention' not only differentiates it from the idealist elements inherent in what Habermas may refer to as our 'obligation to take the perspective of the other'.[61] It also distinguishes it from the sort of encounter described in radical terms by Levinas[62] when he refers to the 'face of the Other' summoning each and every one of us.[63] While an ethics of attention will share Levinas' emphasis on the centrality of empathetic imagination, its remedy to what Arendt deplored as 'thoughtlessness'[64] does not necessarily entail 'learning from every new human face'.[65] What it does entail is a degree of civic vigilance that is increasingly discouraged by current forms of life.

[58] See chapter three.

[59] Boncompagni draws a parallel between what she sees as an under-developed 'ethics of attention in James' and 'the Wittgensteinian use of the notion of forms of life [...] which helps us to focus not only on the way we live but also on the way we and others might live': Anna Boncompagni, *Wittgenstein and Pragmatism: On Certainty in the Light of Peirce and James* (Palgrave Macmillan 2016).

[60] From an intellectual pedigree perspective, such an 'ethics of attention' connects the classical pragmatists such as James and Dewey to figures as diverse as the late Wittgenstein, Løgstrup or Levinas.

[61] Under Habermas' delineation of the pragmatic presuppositions underlying any inclusive and non-coercive rational discourse, everyone is *required* to take the perspective of everyone else. An extended 'we-perspective' is meant to emerge from this interlocking of perspectives, from which all can test in common whether they wish to make a controversial norm the basis of their shared practice: Jürgen Habermas, 'Reconciliation through the public use of reason' in Ciaran Cronin (ed), *The Inclusion of the Other: Studies in Political Theory* (Polity 1999) 58.

[62] 'To approach the Other in conversation is to welcome his expression, in which at each instant he overflows the idea a thought would carry away from it. It is therefore to receive from the Other beyond the capacity of the I, which means exactly: to have the idea of infinity. But this also means: to be taught. The relation with the Other, or Conversation, is a non-allergic relation, an ethical relation; but inasmuch as it is welcomed this conversation is a teaching. Teaching is not reducible to maieutics; it comes from the exterior and brings me more than I contain. In its non-violent transitivity the very epiphany of the face is produced': Emmanuel Levinas, *Totality and Infinity: An Essay on Exteriority* (Duquesne UP 1969).

[63] When it comes to awakening us from habits, such encounters may be metaphorical. It may be facilitated by a piece of art, or the reading of a great novel.

[64] Arendt's response to everyday thoughtlessness is a turn to stories. Arendt says that thinking arises when 'I, having watched an incident in the street or having become implicated in some occurrence, now start considering what has happened, telling it to myself as a kind of story, preparing it in this way for its subsequent communication to others': Hannah Arendt, *Responsibility and Judgment* (Schocken Books 2003) 93.

[65] Kearney defines empathetic imagination as the ability to be receptive to the other: 'can we be responsible for the other if we are not first receptive to the other? ... if we can't hear its call, if we cannot empathize?': Richard Kearney, *Poetics of Imagining: Modern to Post-Modern* (Fordham UP 1998) 232.

As a capability, responsiveness to the other conditions the possibility of what Sen calls 'critical agency'.[66] To foster such 'critical agency', '[w]hat is needed is not merely freedom and power to act, but also freedom and power to question and reassess the prevailing norms and values'.[67]

A. Selective Responsiveness and the Possibility of Immanent Critique

We cannot be responsive to all, at all times. Absolute and constant other-responsiveness is neither possible nor desirable. Determining who one should be responsive to – and in what circumstances – hinges on a variety of factors: in an elevator, it might be a matter of social etiquette; in a crowded running peloton a matter of prudential interest. As a capability, our responsiveness to the Other can and should be exercised selectively. Just how selectively will depend in part on our character, way of growing up and social mores.

It also depends on the content of our obligations. In some cases, we have a moral obligation to respond to a particular person. In other cases, we have a legal obligation. In the *Ethical Project*, Kitcher traces the emergence of distinctive, ethical standards to the need to remedy 'altruism failures'.[68] On that account, it is because we have learned the limits of our sympathetic instincts that we have developed increasingly sophisticated systems of norms. When 'mere' etiquette or the stigma associated with immorality is not enough to produce the desired social outcomes, legal norms backed by sanctions step in.[69]

Insightful as it is, Kitcher's narrative has less to say about the mechanisms that underlie our continued ability to challenge – and modify when needed – the moral and legal norms that remedy our 'altruism failures'. What, if anything, anchors the critical stance necessary to triggering such normative changes? While a purely internal stance won't do (since it cannot be anchored in precisely the norms to be challenged), any critique based on some Archimedean point safely removed from particular forms of life is incompatible with Kitcher's (and

[66] Aware of the variety of meanings associated with the term 'agency', Sen uses it 'in its older – and 'grander' – sense as someone who acts and brings about change, and whose achievements can be judged in terms of her own values and objectives': Amartya Sen, *Development as Freedom* (Oxford Paperbacks 2001).

[67] Jean Dreze and Amartya Sen, *India: Development and Participation* (OUP on Demand 2002) 258.

[68] Philip Kitcher, *The Ethical Project* (Harvard UP 2011).

[69] The legal obligation to render assistance is a case in point: in most civil law countries, this is a statutory obligation. If you witness a traffic accident, you have a legal obligation to take reasonable steps to help the injured (or ascertain that help is on the way) without regard to possible personal reasons not to help (such as lack of time). These regulatory interventions will in turn have down-stream effects on our responsiveness: these effects are analysed in chapter six.

this book's) naturalist commitment.[70] In this respect, what Jaeggi refers to as 'immanent criticism'[71] proves particularly helpful.

> 'Whereas internal criticism looks for its critical standard in norms (values or ideals) that it understands as shared, more or less explicit basic beliefs of a community, immanent criticism starts from a different understanding of norms and their relation to reality. Specifically, it assumes that social reality is always normatively constituted, and it renders these norms inherent in reality explicit, even where they are not articulated [...] Here norms are sought out in the social interactions, practices, or institutions themselves, not only in the articulated self-understanding of a community or an individual'[72]

The process of 'seeking out' those norms that implicitly structure the practices within which the critic herself is always already embedded needs to start from somewhere. What prompts that critical process? Jaeggi emphasises the importance of the 'theoretical effort' inherent in that process: 'to put it very simply, with a "good eye" we might be able to see when people are suffering, but we need a theory to decipher this suffering as something caused by exploitation or alienation in Marx's sense'.[73]

The concern at the heart of this book is less with the 'deciphering' part, and more with the extent to which the degradation of our ability to attentively inhabit ways of perceiving the world might compromise the 'good eye' Jaeggi refers to. As a capability, our responsiveness to the 'other' is but one manifestation of the work of attention, but it is a critical one in the context of ethically significant practices. The 'other' stands for all those whom we have not learned to identify as demanding engagement from us, whether that learning process was rooted in explicit or implicit norms. Crucially, the kind of engagement at stake cannot be settled in advance of each encounter. In that way, to be responsive to 'the other' demands a readiness to suspend learned patterns of interaction, to consider anew the norms that structure each relationship.

This suspension process will only occasionally be triggered by deliberation. The rest of the time, the possibility of such suspension depends on the quality of our pre-reflective ethical agency,[74] which itself hinges on 'how those who are

[70] This is unpacked in chapter one.

[71] '[C]riticism of forms of life must do without a meta-language game, without a neutral "Archimedean point" removed from all particular forms of life; at the same time, however, criticism must not remain purely internal if it is to thematize forms of life as such. This dilemma can be resolved by a strong version of what is called, following Hegel, "immanent criticism"': Rahel Jaeggi, *Critique of Forms of Life* (Harvard UP 2018) 174.

[72] Ibid 199.

[73] Ibid 207.

[74] Sympathy and empathy are but some of the feelings that can prompt the relevant responsiveness on our part. One can be responsive to someone without being sympathetic. To refer back to the virtual reality scenario surveyed in chapter three: the GP not only acknowledging the presence of her patient's child, but letting that presence potentially change her understanding of her duties as a professional need not involve any sympathy. It does presuppose a degree of responsiveness that can be – and often is – lacking, whether because of our focusing on a particular task or – more depressingly – because of some general 'aloofness'.

involved in a form of life can conduct themselves towards it or relate to it'.[75] To put it differently: the quality of our pre-reflective agency largely depends on the quality of the habitat afforded by a form of life. In the carefully curated and optimised environments described in chapter seven, opportunities for the continuous honing of our pre-reflective dispositions are scarce. Why? Because such honing presupposes the possibility of failure and experimentation. Any genuine trial and error process is impossible in an environment that leaves no room for true 'inhabitation': the uncertainty inherent in the way some habitat will shape me needs to be reciprocal. In any genuine 'habitat', the way I shall transform it is normally uncertain too. Not so in the environments described in chapter seven.

The halting of experimentation that is facilitated by such environments is easily missed in an account of ethical agency exclusively premised upon some abstract 'responsiveness to reasons'. An account that complements the latter with our 'responsiveness to the other', by contrast, is meant to highlight the necessarily open-ended and relational nature of the effort needed to foster our pre-reflective, ethical intelligence.

B. A Pervasive – Yet Optimistic – 'Mode of Being Ethical'?

In *Ethical Know-How*, Varela brings to the fore the 'pervasiveness' of our pre-reflective, non-propositional 'mode of being ethical' with the following example:

> Consider a normal day in the street. You are walking down the sidewalk thinking about what you need to say in an upcoming meeting and you hear the noise of an accident. You immediately see if you can help. You are in your office. The conversation is lively and a topic comes up that embarrasses your secretary. You immediately perceive that embarrassment and turn the conversation away from the topic with a humorous remark.[76]

The above quote is meant to draw our attention to the extent to which the actions described 'do not spring from judgment and reasoning, but from an immediate coping with what is confronting us'.[77] The extent to which such 'immediate coping' has been traditionally neglected by philosophers, who are typically drawn to the more visible, deliberative aspects of ethical agency, was highlighted in chapter two. Phenomenological studies have done much to counterbalance this intellectualist trend. Yet their optimism about the extent to which all living beings remain dynamically responsive to what Rietveld refers to as

[75] Jaeggi, *Critique of Forms of Life* 218.
[76] Francisco J Varela, *Ethical Know-How: Action, Wisdom, and Cognition* (Stanford UP 1992).
[77] Ibid.

'states of disequilibrium'[78] is not necessarily warranted. What if the above is not 'a normal day in the street' anymore?

Varela's cheery scenario may not only reflect his own generous character. It may also be illustrative of times gone-by. Few passers-by had mobile phones 30 years ago (Varela's book was published in 1992). What if these ubiquitous connection devices have compromised our physical availability to 'the noise of an accident' (think earpods)? What if the feeling of hyper – yet virtual – connectedness leaves us numb to actual events occurring outside our connected circles? If we are becoming more responsive to events (including accidents) reported on social media than to those happening under our nose, what impact does this have on the 'pervasive mode of being ethical' reported above? The importance of this pre-reflective type of ethical agency has not diminished; our ability to live up to it might have.

C. Compromised 'Forms of Life'

> A form of life can merit ethical critique in multiple ways. It can, for instance, be criticised as unsuccessful if it does not take care of basic human needs and vulnerabilities. If it does not provide us with something fine to live up to. If it creates suffering and blocks for human flourishing.[79]

To conceptualise our responsiveness to the other as an endangered capability paves the way for a type of critique that not only takes on board the importance of what Varela refers to as a 'pervasive mode of being ethical'. This type of critique is also in a position to question the optimistic stance embodied in Varela's 'normal day in the street' scenario. Consider this alternative:

> Consider a normal day in the street. You are walking down the sidewalk thinking about what you need to say in an upcoming meeting, taking care to avoid threading on a pair of feet protruding from a covered passageway. It is freezing. You adjust your scarf while considering the flowery pattern on the blanket you glimpsed next to those feet. The umbrella bearer ahead of you gets stopped by police officers. It's a routine stop and search, yet it causes some commotion. The umbrella bearer – tall, bearded, dark complexion – complains he is going to be late for a job interview, swinging his umbrella in the process, which causes a couple of other umbrella bearers to turn to identify the source of disturbance. Soon the whole sidewalk is obstructed. A tiny schoolgirl is stuck between you and a lady shouting at her phone. You try to make space for her. You are promptly questioned about your relationship to this girl. Luckily the obstruction clears at that precise moment. You apologise and promptly move on.

[78] Erik Rietveld, Damiaan Denys and Maarten Van Westen, 'Ecological-Enactive Cognition as engaging with a field of relevant affordances' in *The Oxford Handbook of 4E Cognition* (OUP 2018).

[79] Cecilie Eriksen, *Moral Change: Dynamics, Structure, and Normativity* (Springer 2020) 146.

While you may have 'freedom and power to act' in the above scenario, do you also have what Sen refers to as 'freedom and power to question and reassess the prevailing norms and values'?[80] In theory, you do. In practice, while you remember feeling concerned when you first witnessed a 'stop and search' all those years ago, these have now become such a normal part of your daily commute that you have become skilled at avoiding the frequent sidewalk bottlenecks that result from such occurrences. You used to take pride in always looking out for smaller, potentially vulnerable fellow side-walkers until the recent schoolgirl interpellation incident prompted a rethink. You have enthusiastically opted in to the 'solidarity tax' introduced by your municipality to support services for the homeless and been annoyed at the ineffectiveness of such services.

In the above scenario, what compromises your ability to 'question and reassess the prevailing norms' is not stupidity nor character defects. Having gotten used to the homeless sleeping on the sidewalk, you see 'the usual man in the usual place',[81] to refer back to the quote from Chesterton at the start of chapter three. The bottlenecks triggered by stop and search police interventions are similarly perceived as a routine occurrence. The habits of thought and action developed in reaction to those occurrences may enable more skilful navigation of the sidewalk, yet they also numb the intensity of the emotional reactions that may have led you to question such targeted 'stop and search' practices.

We all need a degree of habit-enabled emotional numbing. Some, such as members of the medical and legal profession who are exposed to acute distress or suffering, do so more than others. Yet relying on such numbing effect without constructing some discussion forum for the articulation[82] of 'imperfectly rationalised intuitions'[83] is to deprive ourselves from a potentially vital mechanism for societal change. In the medical domain, those cross-disciplinary discussion fora have been in place for some time.[84] They play a major role in the bottom-up,

[80] Dreze and Sen, *India: Development and Participation*.

[81] '[T]he horrible thing about all legal officials, even the best, about all judges, magistrates, barristers, detectives, and policemen, is not that they are wicked (some of them are good), not that they are stupid (several of them are quite intelligent), it is simply that they have got used to it. Strictly they do not see the prisoner in the dock; all they see is the usual man in the usual place. They do not see the awful court of judgment; they only see their own workshop': GK Chesterton, 'The twelve men'.

[82] Instead of 'imperfectly rationalised intuitions, van den Herik and Rietveld refer to 'situated appreciations of particular situations': 'Language thus enables individuals to engage a situation together, by drawing attention to certain aspects of the sociomaterial practices we care about and exploring different ways of going on together. Moreover, sharing a verbal expression of situated appreciation enables people to determine whether and how their appreciations of the same situation are similar or different, and, in the case in which they are different, a consensus can be negotiated': Jasper C van den Herik and Erik Rietveld, 'Reflective Situated Normativity' (2021) *Philosophical Studies*.

[83] Bernard Williams, 'Conflicts of value' in *Moral Luck: Philosophical Papers* (CUP 1981).

[84] Hillel D Braude, *Intuition in Medicine: A Philosophical Defense of Clinical Reasoning* (University of Chicago Press 2012); Mark Quirk, *Intuition and Metacognition in Medical Education: Keys to Developing Expertise* (Springer 2006); Amanda Woolley and Olga Kostopoulou, 'Clinical intuition in family medicine: More than first impressions' (2013) 11 *The Annals of Family Medicine* 60.

continued re-articulation of the normative landscape that structures rapidly transforming medical practices.

Beyond the medical context, this process of bottom-up (re)-articulation of the norms structuring our practices presupposes a movement of to and fro between 'imperfectly rationalised intuitions' – often formed on the back of our encounters with 'the other' – and the reasons or principles we associate with our practices. It is when the re-articulation of those reasons is allowed to proceed in the abstract only that they risk losing touch with the demands emerging from our evolving forms of life. The resulting rigidification of the relevant frames of thought may be perceived as a necessity, given the emotional labour involved in engaging with the demands of 'the other'.[85] To support – and appropriately relay – this form of labour demands 'in-between' spaces: small-scale fora that allow the often tentative transition from privately held intuitions to reasons-backed arguments 'apt for the public sphere'.[86]

Such fora are also a vital tool when it comes to balancing the need for emotional defence mechanisms on one hand and a minimal degree of openness to an experience of self-doubt on the other. The need for such defence mechanisms stems from the same roots as those which make us reliant on habit in the first place. In the never-ending process of self-(re)construction, we need 'a structure weak enough to yield to an influence, but strong enough not to yield all at once'.[87] As precisely such structures, habits cannot remain such and be systematically open to change all at once:

> If we were simply receptive to change, without limit, then we would be incapable of habit. Each new action or experience would transform us, so that we would have no character or integrity to call our own. We would be empty, entirely subject to circumstance, blown hither and thither by the winds of change.[88]

It is that fear of being 'blown about' by the contingent circumstances life throws at us that underlies the appeal that some overarching religious, ideological or moral discourses have for many of us. Because they bypass the need to articulate what it is about us, constantly evolving human beings, that calls for doing things in a particular way, such discourses afford a fixed framework that defines the self's relationship to others. The dangers inherent in the resulting, ideological rigidification of habits of thought and action have been known for some time.[89]

[85] Arlie Russell Hochschild, *The Managed Heart* (University of California Press 2012).
[86] Williams, 'Conflicts of Value'.
[87] William James, *Psychology: Briefer Course* (Harvard UP 1984) 126.
[88] Clare Carlisle, *On Habit* (Routledge 2014).
[89] The most studied aspect of those risks is arguably what some see as the increasing political polarisation phenomenon (the empirical determinants of which are contested): Marc J Hetherington, 'Putting polarization in perspective' (2009) 39 *British Journal of Political Science* 413; Charles Pattie and Ron Johnston, 'Talking with one voice? Conversation networks and political polarisation' (2016) 18 *The British Journal of Politics and International Relations* 482; Andres Reiljan, '"Fear and loathing across party lines" (also) in Europe: Affective polarisation in European party systems' (2020) 59 *European Journal of Political Research* 376.

What is less familiar is the hazard inherent in the process of habit rigidification fostered by our increased reliance on profile-based optimisation tools. This will be explored in chapter seven.

For now it is worth noting the two-way relationship between the extent to which our idea of self is allowed to go unchallenged, and the extent to which the words – or mere presence – of others become out of reach. Anticipating the social uniformisation that stems from impaired responsiveness to the other, de Tocqueville described almost two centuries ago a democracy engendering:

> [a] crowd of men, all alike and equal, turned in upon themselves in a restless search for those petty, vulgar pleasures with which they fill their souls. Each of them, living apart, is almost unaware of the destiny of all the rest. His children and personal friends are for him the whole of the human race; as for the remainder of his fellow citizens, he stands alongside them but does not see them; he touches them without feeling them; he exists only in himself and for himself.[90]

De Tocqueville's prescient account of democratic individualism has given rise to countless analyses of its corrosive political and sociological effects. Less common are those that attempt to grasp the implications of such atomisation phenomenon when it comes to our continued ability to question accepted values and norms. Since this trend toward atomisation is arguably accelerated by our increased reliance on the optimisation tools mentioned earlier, the need to consider what 'counter-measures', if any, may mitigate the progressive erosion of our capability for 'other responsiveness' has never been more pressing. These measures are considered from a collective, institution and system-building perspective in the next two chapters.

[90] Alexis de Tocqueville, *Democracy in America* (Penguin 2003) 805.

Part II

Collective Habits and Moral Transformations

> Moral change and moral achievement are slow; we are not free in the sense of being able suddenly to alter ourselves since we cannot suddenly alter what we can see and ergo what we desire and are compelled by.
>
> Iris Murdoch, *The Sovereignty of Good*[1]

ANYONE WHO HAS ever been drawn into surveying various instances of 'look at how wrong we managed to get things then' is likely to have witnessed the sense of unease that often comes with the realisation that one does not need to go very far into the past to find examples of morally embarrassing practices. As one moves on from accounts of slavery and witches drowning to consider the relatively recent decriminalisation of homosexuality, the following question surfaces: which of our own practices will our descendants be consternated by? Given that there is no reason to think that we are any less fallible in our collective moral stances today than we were yesterday, the question triggered by this acknowledgment of moral fallibility is often phrased in terms of moral change.[2]

Do we have what it takes to perceive the need for moral change and act on it? Because the word 'change' presupposes some identifiable 'before' and 'after', this way of phrasing the question reinforces the traditional emphasis on individual deliberation that sits at the heart of many understandings of ethics. Unlike the 'minor gestures'[3] – the non-deliberative meanderings that feed processes of moral transformation – the deliberate actions of 'heroic' individuals can more easily be identified as a break with the 'before'. Focusing on the possibility of *change* thus leads us to look for deliberate interventions that may be said to have set in motion a process of 'major' moral change. Never mind the fact that actual examples of individuals whose heroic deliberations single-handedly led

[1] Iris Murdoch, *The Sovereignty of Good* (Routledge 2013).

[2] Cecilie Eriksen brilliantly delves into the normative and meta-ethical challenges that stem from considering the need for moral change from a fallibility perspective in Cecilie Eriksen, *Moral Change: Dynamics, Structure, and Normativity* (Springer 2020).

[3] Erin Manning, *The Minor Gesture* (Duke UP 2016).

to significant moral changes are few and far between: we cling on to this heroic, deliberative narrative for fear that without it, we are but pawns.

What follows considers a different way of phrasing the question that stems from our moral fallibility. Once we take on board the role played by the non-deliberative 'work of attention' within social and moral dynamics, the individual and her moral perspicacity are but one side of the equation. At least as important are the institutional structures that shape the kind of habits we cultivate. Considered from that perspective, the question shifts to the extent to which some institutional structures are more likely than others to contribute to rigidified, rather than malleable habits. Chapter six focuses on legal institutions, while chapter seven considers the effect of our increased reliance on algorithmic tools meant to optimise aspects of our daily existence.

6

Law and Habits

A bit like unstable isotopes, political institutions have standard patterns of decay that are explained by the nature of the thing that is decaying.

Leslie Green, 'Positivism and the inseparability of law and morals'[1]

When law develops organically, in a highly homogeneous, tight-knit community, we may answer questions about the grounds of law in a way that is rather similar to that outlined in chapter one in the context of ethics: 'this is what we do' may be the rock-bottom answer. Far from inviting some 'anything goes' approach to the way we structure our living together, this reference to what we do can come with the strongest degree of conviction – it may be deemed 'primitively appropriate', to refer back to Ginsborg's expression.[2] That a given community is not able to point to any rule or edict that grounds its condemnation of murder, incest etc does not make the condemnation any less stringent. In that context, one may query what, if anything, leads us to delineate such condemnations as instances of 'law' rather than some shared ethics?

Hart's answer was to designate the above, organically evolved set of norms as 'pre-legal'. Section I outlines Hart's account of this so-called 'step from the pre-legal to the legal' for two reasons. First, negatively, because Hart's account coincidentally contributed to anything having to do with habit being excluded from the scope of legal theory. Positively, Hart's account – especially those elements inspired by Durkheim and Weber – provides key building blocks for the depiction of the two-way movement that leads from collective patterns of behaviour to law and back. The former part – collective patterns of behaviour giving rise to law – is described in section II, while the return movement – leading from law to different kinds of habit – is accounted for in section III. That return movement is crucial to understanding the extent to which law's institutional structures can end up fostering habits that are no longer 'inhabited' with the kind of attention described in chapter five. In contrast to the latter chapter's focus on individual ethical lives, the consequences of the resulting rigidification

[1] Leslie Green, 'Positivism and the inseparability of law and morals' (2008) 83 *NYUL Rev* 1035, 1057.

[2] See chapter one. Hannah Ginsborg, 'Primitive normativity and skepticism about rules' (2011) 108 *The Journal of Philosophy* 227.

are considered from the perspective of our capacity to engage in collective norm-generating practices.

I. THE NARROW VIEW: THE STEP FROM 'THE PRE-LEGAL TO THE LEGAL'

> When mores are sufficient, laws are unnecessary; when mores are insufficient, laws are unenforceable
>
> Émile Durkheim[3]

A. Organically Grown Customs versus 'Constitutive' Practices

Because of the ambiguity inherent in the term 'mores', the above quote is easily misunderstood. Instead of conceiving law as the source of social order, one of Durkheim's key contributions was to draw attention to the significance of informal practices that can be said to bring about structured social realities. These practices differ from organically grown, traditional customs in that their emergence does not presuppose customs' high degree of social conformity. What these practices do presuppose however is some shared endeavour: this may stretch from the creation of an intellectually challenging game (such as chess) to efforts to find better ways of living together, via the occupational and scientific practices Durkheim initially focused on.[4] In all cases, the practices can be said to be 'constitutive'[5] in that they bring about a social reality. Participants to such practices mutually coordinate the sense they make for one another by reference to that social reality: the British art of queuing is a simple but effective example. Crucially, participation in such practices is not conditional upon being a member of a particular community or sharing a particular set of beliefs, unlike customary practices.

The potential inherent in this delineation of 'constitutive' social practices versus customs was not lost on legal theory, even if it took a while: it came to play a key role in the second half of the twentieth century. One of the key challenges for legal theory – at that time just like at any other time – is to account for law's normative dimension. As a social artefact, whence does law draw its power to bind us? Once answers structured around a purported correspondence with

[3] This quote is attributed to Durkheim by JA Eisenach, AS Hanser and N Gingrich, *Readings in Renewing American Civilization* (McGraw-Hill 1993) 54.

[4] Developed in Durkheim's doctoral dissertation – *The Division of Labour in Society* (first published in 1893) – Durkheim's analysis of constitutive practices in the context of science appears in Book III, Chapters 1 and 2, while reference to constitutive practices in occupations appears in the Second Preface of 1902: Emile Durkheim, *The Division of Labor in Society* (Simon and Schuster 2014).

[5] Anne Warfield Rawls, 'Durkheim's theory of modernity: Self-regulating practices as constitutive orders of social and moral facts' (2012) 12 *Journal of Classical Sociology* 479.

'Nature' or 'God's will' are discredited, legal theory is left in need of an alternative narrative.[6] An account of law's normative force by reference to accepted, customary practices will only work in the most tight-knit communities.[7] In contrast to the 'mechanical' form of solidarity[8] that characterises the latter communities, the 'organic' solidarity found in societies[9] characterised by increasing degrees of social and functional differentiation[10] means that even the business of 'accepting' the law becomes specialised. Only a sub-group of that society need 'accept' the law, and generally deal with matters of legal identification, implementation and revision.

B. Addressing a 'Defective' Form of Social Control Through 'Official' Rules

Durkheim's analysis of the transition from 'mechanical' to 'organic' forms of solidarity plays a central role[11] in Hart's construction of the 'step from the pre-legal to the legal'. Hart's account isolates the needs and deficiencies that a legal system, as a specific form of social control, may be deemed to answer. 'Granted a few of the most obvious truisms about human nature and the world we live in',[12] a pre-legal community will be structured around a set of rules fundamental to the smooth running of society. These rules are likely to restrict the free use of violence, theft, and deception (to refer to the examples mentioned by Hart), but there will be no way of 'authoritatively' identifying the body of rules governing that society. Similarly, a pre-legal society will lack the resources

[6] This need for an alternative narrative, and the challenges it gave rise to, are outlined in Sylvie Delacroix, *Legal Norms and Normativity: An Essay in Genealogy* (Hart Publishing 2006).

[7] '[T]he society is formed by similar segments, and these in turn enclose only homogeneous elements': Durkheim, *The Division of Labor in Society* D 152: 128.

[8] Ibid.

[9] '[These societies] are constituted, not by the repetition of similar and homogeneous segments, but by a system of different organs each of which has a special role, and which are in turn formed by different parts. The social elements are not either juxtaposed to one another like the rings of an earthworm, nor enclosed within one another, but coordinated and subordinated vis-à-vis one another around a central organ which performs a moderating action toward the rest of the organism': ibid D 157; 132.

[10] Poggi helpfully emphasises the inter-dependence that results from this social differentiation: 'the component parts are differentiated from one another, that is, they engage in activities which vary, sometimes markedly, from one part to another, but are to a considerable extent complementary to one another, for each activity can be carried out in a sustained manner only by drawing on the results of other activities': Gianfranco Poggi, *Durkheim* (OUP 2000) 39. In contrast, there is 'little dissimilarity (and thus possible complementarity) both *between* and *within*' the parallel 'segments' found in societies characterised by 'mechanical' forms of solidarity. 'The population as a whole, to use a typical ecological expression which Durkheim does not employ, has found its niche in the environment; but that niche is tight, allows very little variation between units and over time, and basically compels the human population to adapt to the environment's natural givens (and their own patterns of change, if any) rather than shifting and modifying them through technology': ibid 40

[11] Hart criticised Durkheim in Herbert LA Hart, 'Social solidarity and the enforcement of morality' (1967) 35 *The University of Chicago Law Review* 1.

[12] HLA Hart, *The Concept of Law* (2nd edn, Clarendon Press 1994) 89.

necessary to being able to adapt the rules to changing circumstances, and to being able to authoritatively acknowledge and punish the violation of its rules.

> It is plain that only a small community closely knit by ties of kinship, common sentiment, and belief, and placed in a stable environment, could live successfully by such a regime of unofficial rules. In any other conditions such a simple form of social control must prove defective and will require supplementation in different ways.[13]

Hart's so-called 'officials' – the sub-group of people who are in the business of legal identification, revision and adjudication – are key to this 'supplementation'. Coming hand-in-hand with these officials are meta rules. Deemed the smallest common denominator that allows for the emergence of law, this 'rule about rules' – the 'rule of recognition' – presides over the authoritative identification of the rules regulating a society. It also provides for the possibility of adapting those existing rules to changing circumstances and authoritatively settling disputes.

> The introduction of the remedy for each defect might, in itself, be considered a step from the pre-legal into the legal world; since each remedy brings with it many elements that permeate law: certainly all three remedies together are enough to convert the regime of primary rules into what is indisputably a legal system.[14]

C. Accounting for the Emergence of Law as a Normative Phenomenon

Hart's explicit focus on law's existence conditions via those three 'remedies' introduces an important split: Hart's 'step from the pre-legal to the legal' narrative is not meant to explain law's normative dimension.[15] Hart is not the first to introduce such a methodological split. At the end of the sixteenth century, Montaigne's critique of the natural law model leads him to uncover such a precarious, 'tiny spring'[16] at the origins of law that he is faced with the task of 'reconstructing' law's authority in spite of the weakness of its empirical origins ('laws are often made by fools, and even more often by men who fail in equity because they hate equality: but always by men, vain authorities who can resolve

[13] Ibid 92.

[14] Ibid 94.

[15] As Coleman notes, 'the internal point of view is an existence condition of a social rule, and it marks the fact that people treat the rule as reason-giving. It does not explain why or how the rule does so': Jules Coleman, 'Incorporationism, conventionality, and the practical difference thesis' in Jules Coleman (ed), *Hart's Postscript, Essays on the Postscript to the Concept of Law* (OUP 2001) 119.

[16] '[L]aws gain their authority from actual possession and custom: *it is perilous to go back to their origins*; laws, like our rivers, get greater and nobler as they roll along: follow them back upstream to their sources and all you find is a tiny spring, hardly recognizable; as time goes by it swells with pride and grows in strength': Michel de Montaigne, *The Complete Essays* (Penguin Classics 1991) (emphasis mine).

nothing'[17]). For Montaigne, the matter is first and foremost to see to it that the law does not only amount to the product of its historical birth, or at least that its authority is not seen as flowing from there. The 'law of pure obedience'[18] posited by Montaigne inaugurates a long-standing trend within legal positivism.

While Kelsen endeavours to ground the normativity of law on law alone (thus excluding any consideration of political or moral legitimacy) via the Basic Norm,[19] Hart's adoption of a hermeneutical method avoids the issue altogether. Hart's emphasis on the need to '[portray] rule-governed behavior as it appears to its participants'[20] does not commit him to explaining what it is about law, or about the context of interaction in which it is embedded, that gives rise to its normative status. Hart underlines 'the crucial difference between merely convergent habitual behaviour in a social group and the existence of a rule of which the words "must", "should", and "ought to" are often a sign'.[21] Beyond the mere predictability of punishment, Hart emphasises the internal aspect of rules, which implies that some people at least 'must look upon the behaviour in question [to which the rule refers] as a general standard to be followed by the group as a whole'.[22] For Hart, the normative statement 'it is a rule' can only make sense in the context of regular behaviour combined with a reflective critical attitude shared by at least part of the population: the officials, who 'accept' and hold the 'internal point of view' towards the Rule of Recognition. This leaves open two questions.

The first one has to do with the reasons underlying officials' 'acceptance'. Here Hart rightly points out that this acceptance might stem from all sorts of prudential or moral reasons, as well as 'an unreflecting inherited or traditional attitude, or the mere wish to do as others do'.[23] The second question has to do with what allows the Rule of Recognition to emerge in the first place. Hart's specifying in the 'Postscript' that the Rule of Recognition should be understood

[17] Ibid 1216.

[18] 'The first commandment which God ever gave to Man [...] the law of pure obedience. It was a bare and simple order, leaving man no room for knowing or arguing': ibid II 12, 543. The point of this law of pure obedience would above all consist in being ultimate, thus avoiding an infinite – and dangerous – regress in its motives. To that extent, the quasi-tautological character of its formulation (obedience to the law would be justified by a law of pure obedience) would merely confirm the necessity of avoiding developing any interest in this last and ultimate law. Montaigne's concern is indeed – let's repeat it – to spare us the peril that the disgusting appearance of the origins of law could constitute. On this basis, Montaigne's law of pure obedience probably amounts to the best way of stopping inquiry into the sources of law at a "safe" point, a point referring to law alone, thus excluding the precariousness of power and the origins it represents'. This is further unpacked in Sylvie Delacroix, 'Montaigne's inquiry into the sources of normativity' (2003) 16 *Canadian Journal of Law and Jurisprudence* 271.

[19] Hans Kelsen, *General Theory of Law and State* (Harvard UP 1949); Hans Kelsen, *Pure Theory of Law* (University of California Press 1967).

[20] HLA. Hart, *Essays in jurisprudence and philosophy* (Clarendon Press 1983) 13.

[21] Hart, *The Concept of Law* 10.

[22] Ibid 56.

[23] Ibid 202.

as a *conventional* rule[24] may be regarded as pointing at one possible answer. As a purported narrative for the emergence of law as a normative phenomenon, however, this conventionalist framework raises more questions than it answers.

According to the 'mainstream' account provided by Lewis,[25] conventions are solutions to recurrent coordination problems, which emerge not in consequence of an agreement, but as a convenient alternative to such agreement. So far so good. Yet as a situation in which it is instrumentally rational to coordinate one's action with those of others, and in which it is more important that we coordinate than how or why we do so,[26] coordination problems do not have much in common with the contexts of social interactions that call for the emergence of law. The political choices at stake are not only 'far more complex and manifold than the basic structure of a coordination problem'.[27] From the perspective of those whose lives will be governed by the legal system in place, the choice between alternative modes of governance is also very unlike the options that structure a coordination problem. In the latter instance agents 'would like to abide by whichever option secures uniformity of action among them'.[28]

As an alternative to the mainstream, 'game-theoretic' model, Marmor puts forward 'constitutive conventions', whose point is not to solve a coordination problem but to constitute a distinct and partly autonomous practice (such as, for instance, chess, opera or law). The social practices constituted by such conventions are said to be 'autonomous' in that the point of engaging in them is not fully determined by any value that is external to the conventions constituting the practice (such as for instance solving a coordination problem). Some constitutive conventions will be less autonomous than others: law is less autonomous than chess, for instance, as its development is clearly related to moral and political concerns.[29]

These moral and political concerns do not spring out of nowhere: they will be tied to organically grown dispositions and aspirations. Whereas one might conceive of a game created on the basis of mathematically delineated objectives,

[24] 'But the theory remains as a faithful account of conventional social rules which include, besides ordinary social customs (which may or may not be recognised as having legal force), certain important legal rules including the rule of recognition': ibid 256.

[25] David K Lewis, *Convention: A Philosophical Study* (Harvard UP 1963).

[26] As a result, theorists centred on this concept of a coordination problem need not pay much attention to the motives or concerns driving the agents involved in the convention, concentrating rather on the structural conditions leading to its emergence. Among these conditions figures a certain kind of exchange of information allowing the participants to the convention to be aware of their mutual preferences and to recognise salience.

[27] Andrei Marmor, 'Legal conventionalism' in Jules Coleman (ed), *Hart's Postscript, Essays on the Postscript to the Concept of Law* (OUP 2001) 202.

[28] Ibid 201.

[29] Once constituted, law (as well as, chess, or opera) nevertheless establishes values of its own, in whose function people might be drawn to engage in that practice. The main feature which, according to Marmor, distinguishes coordination conventions from constitutive conventions consists in our inability to explain the people's reasons for engaging in the latter (constitutive) kind of convention just by reference to the desirability of conformity of action. As Marmor observes: 'it is normally the values inherent in the practice that explain people's reasons for engaging in it': ibid 211.

the aspirations that preside over the emergence of law as a 'constitutive' practice are unlikely to be insulated from the habits and dispositions we develop as we learn to live together. Hart's insistence on analysing the 'step into the legal world' by reference to the notion of 'acceptance' has done much to ward off the need to build an account of legal normativity that is not artificially insulated from non-deliberative agency. The next section unpacks what a genealogy of legal normativity that does not shy away from those non-deliberative roots might look like.

II. NON-DELIBERATIVE COMPONENTS WITHIN A GENEALOGY OF LEGAL NORMATIVITY

A genealogy of legal normativity has the merit of looking in the right direction. Unlike Hart's account, which only considers the way in which law's normative dimension manifests itself (through the 'critical reflective attitude' adopted by the 'officials'), a genealogical account questions what conditions the possibility of law as a normative phenomenon. Its ambition is not, however, to find the starting point of legal normativity. A genealogy by definition proceeds from the awareness of the impossibility of finding the origin of the object it studies. Its goal is to trace the social and cultural factors that have contributed to bringing about the phenomenon in question. In doing so, its hope is not to discover some founding principle that would provide some definite grounding for that phenomenon, but to cast a new, challenging light upon it.[30] This limit, essential to the genealogical project, makes it particularly suited to the study of legal normativity. As one will struggle to isolate a situation that is not in some way preceded by some form of normativity (whether it counts as legal or not is in itself contentious), its 'origin' will always vanish to some further, inaccessible point.

The other major asset of genealogy as a method is its commitment to debunking any form of realist metaphysics. The challenge underlying an account of law that brings together its social and normative dimensions in one continuous explanation (unlike the accounts surveyed in section I.C) is to face up to the implications of social and historical[31] contingency for our understanding

[30] For a brilliant and recent outline of genealogy as a philosophical method see Matthieu Queloz, *The Practical Origins of Ideas: Genealogy as Conceptual Reverse-Engineering* (OUP 2021).

[31] The full power of a genealogy typically reveals itself when it is directed at institutions whose self-understanding requires concealing the impact of these historical processes. The stronger their claim to authority, the more reluctant these institutions are to reveal their historical variability and contingency, 'both in the sense that they are what they are rather than some others, and also in the sense that the historical changes that brought them about are not obviously related in a grounding or epistemically favourable way to the ethical [or legal etc.] ideas they encouraged': Bernard Williams, 'Naturalism and genealogy' in Edward Harcourt (ed), *Morality, Reflection and Ideology* (OUP 2000) 155.

of normativity. Much of my *Legal Norms and Normativity: An Essay in Genealogy*[32] was devoted to delineating a constructivist alternative to both classical natural law models and those 'positivist' accounts that 'elide the gesture that institutes normativity'.[33] Yet this constructivist focus suffered from a lack of attention to the non-deliberative components of that 'gesture'. What follows may be seen as an endeavour to remedy this.

A. Habit Hostility

Ever since Hart's swift critique of Austin (this critique introduced the 'internal point of view' to distinguish rules from mere habits), legal theory has mostly proceeded on the basis of the assumption that any account of the normativity of law must be deliberative all the way through. To let habits impinge upon such an account would sabotage the lot since, as Shapiro puts it bluntly, 'habits are not normative activities'.[34] Given 'the normative nature of legal activity', asserting any form of conceptual link between the latter and habits would fall foul of 'Hume's challenge', supposedly forbidding any 'derivation of an ought from an is'.[35]

This meta-ethical assumption is concomitant with a one-sided view of habit: in its negative (rather than enabling) aspect, habit is what can stand in the way of our living up to our responsibility as normative animals. This responsibility would stem from the characteristically human capacity to occupy the 'space of reasons', which in turn enables us to make normative claims that will guide our moral or political agenda. This capacity to 'reach for reasons' would be what conditions the very possibility of our normative freedom – no less.

On a non-reductive naturalist understanding of ethical agency, accounting for our normative freedom (and responsibility) is no less important. Chapter one outlined the extent to which the challenge concomitant with such an explanation is arguably greater, since we cannot count on any Archimedean point

[32] Sylvie Delacroix, *Legal Norms and Normativity: An Essay in Genealogy* (Hart Publishing 2006).

[33] To borrow the vocabulary used by Schmitt in his critique of 'normativist' accounts *à la Kelsen*. This critique is unpacked in Sylvie Delacroix, 'Schmitt's critique of Kelsenian normativism' (2005) 18 *Ratio Juris* 30.

[34] Scott J Shapiro, *Legality* (Harvard UP 2011). See also: 'Because the planning model replaces habits with plans, it has no problem explaining the normative nature of legal activity. When a judge applies the law, he is following a plan directing him to do so. He takes the plan as settling for him how he ought to proceed' (ibid).

[35] Ibid. In contrast, see: 'The logical positivist fact/ value dichotomy was defended on the basis of a narrowly scientistic picture of what a "fact" might be, just as the Humean ancestor of that distinction was defended upon the basis of a narrow empiricist psychology of ideas' and impressions'. The realisation that so much of our descriptive language is a living counterexample to *both* (classical empiricist and logical positivist) pictures of the realm of 'fact' ought to shake the confidence of anyone who supposes that there is a notion of *fact* that contrasts neatly and absolutely with the notion of 'value' supposedly invoked in talk of the nature of all 'value judgments': Hilary Putnam, *The Collapse of the Fact / Value Dichotoomy and Other Essays* (Harvard UP 2002) 26.

of reference to explain what enables us to step back and confront commonly accepted practices to declare them wanting. To understand what conditions the possibility of such reflexive scrutiny, attention must be paid to what typically hampers it: habits, and the different ways of having a habit.

B. Habit Ambivalence

While considerable work has already been devoted to delineating the ways in which 'practices' (conventional or otherwise[36]) may give rise to legal norms, far less attention has so far been paid to the patterns of repeated behaviour – habits – that feed such practices. As seen above, some legal theorists will tell you there's a good reason for such scant developments, for 'habits are not the right sort of things that can impose obligations'.[37] Hart was not among those theorists. Far from assuming that habits are not worthy of philosophical inquiry, Hart notes in a book review published in 1952:

> What makes behavior intelligent (or stupid) is its relation to the agent's needs or purpose. [...] For the purpose of his analysis Mr. Holloway [...] exhibits the intelligent response not as a sharp break from habit but as a development and refinement of it. Few philosophers, I think, could fail to benefit from this examination of the intelligent versus stupid dichotomy and of the connection between human intelligence, too often portrayed in absolute and splendid isolation, and habit equipment.[38]

The Concept of Law's scant developments on habit may have proceeded in part from didactic concerns: to admit that habits can be had with some degree of reflexivity might have muddled the otherwise neat distinction between rule and habit thanks to the internal point of view. It may also have had a lot to do with Hart's efforts to dispel Austin's 'habit of obedience' framework and 'free the concept of a rule from confusion with the concepts of a *command* or a *habit*'.[39] Beyond (and behind) these factors, Hart was in the grip of a meta-ethical dilemma[40] that did not allow for an account of normativity that goes from human beings with needs, desires, and most importantly habits, to a fully fledged normative framework. Had Hart allowed himself to delve further into the relationship between the practices that are constitutive of social norms

[36] Marmor, 'Legal conventionalism'; Gerald J Postema, 'Coordination and convention at the foundations of law' (1982) 11 *Journal of Legal Studies* 165; Gerald J Postema, 'Norms, reasons and law' (1998) 51 *Current Legal Problems* 149; Michael E Bratman, 'Shared cooperative activity' (1992) 101 *The Philosophical Review* 327.

[37] 'Fortunately, plans are the right sort of things': Scott J Shapiro, 'Law, plans, and practical reason' (2002) 8 *Legal Theory* 387, 438.

[38] HLA Hart, 'Signs and Words' (1952) 2 *The Philosophical Quarterly* 59, 59.

[39] HLA Hart, 'Analytical Jurisprudence in Mid-Twentieth Century: A Reply to Professor Bodenheimer' (1956) 105 *University of Pennsylvania Law Review* 953, 958.

[40] For a full account of Hart's meta-ethical dilemma (leading to his agnostic position), see Sylvie Delacroix, 'Meta-ethical agnosticism in legal theory: Mapping a way out' (2010) 1 *Jurisprudence* 225.

and the habits that necessarily underlie them, he might have leaned towards the kind of non-reductive naturalism outlined in chapter one. There were at least two familiar intellectual paths available to him.

i. The Wittgensteinian Take on 'Custom'

Given his explicit reliance on Wittgenstein's *Philosophical Investigations*, Hart could have chosen to expand upon the latter's reference to 'custom' as a way of explaining how the causal processes constitutive of habit get to acquire the significance they do when they evolve into rule-following practices:

> "Then can whatever I do be brought into accord with the rule?" – Let me ask this: what has the expression of a rule – say a sign-post – got to do with my actions? What sort of connection is there here? Well, perhaps this one: I have been trained to react to this sign in a particular way, and now I do so react.
>
> But this is only to give a causal connexion, only to explain how it has come about that we now go by the sign-post; not what this going-by-the-sign really consists in. On the contrary, I have further indicated that a person goes by a signpost only in so far as there exists a regular use of sign-posts, a custom.[41]

Wittgenstein's focus is to show that rule-following's 'bedrock' is 'simply what we do': 'if I have exhausted the justifications I have reached bedrock, and my spade is turned. Then I am inclined to say: "This is simply what I do"'.[42] This upstream focus, going from rule-following practices back to causal connections, means that Wittgenstein is not particularly preoccupied with the factors that enable *changes* in rule-following practices. As seen in chapter one, that is arguably the trickiest aspect of naturalist accounts of rule-following. Such accounts need to articulate the degree of reflexivity[43] needed for such changes, without betraying the key naturalist insight: that any such reflexivity is necessarily embedded in, and conditioned by, the 'bedrock' of causal connections that are constitutive of 'custom'. This is nicely captured in Bourdieu's analysis of the 'habitus'[44] characteristic of highly homogeneous, traditional societies:

> the stabler the objective structures and the more fully they reproduce themselves in the agents' dispositions, the greater the extent of the field of doxa, of that which is taken for granted. When, owing to the quasi-perfect fit between the objective structures and

[41] Wittgenstein, *Philosophical Investigations*.

[42] Ibid.

[43] In his 'Wittgenstein on rules: the phantom menace', Scott Hershovitz reminds us that 'Wittgenstein does not show that all rule-following is unreflective, just that some cases are, cases like the ones he highlights where reasons run out': Scott Hershovitz, 'Wittgenstein on rules: The phantom menace' (2002) 22 *Oxford Journal of Legal Studies* 619, 630.

[44] '... focusing [...] on the degree to which different habitus equip agents with the capacity to swivel on the history that has made them by reflexively monitoring and adjusting its force': Tony Bennett and others, 'Habit and habituation: Governance and the social' (2013) 19 *Body & Society* 3, 11.

the internalized structures which results from the logic of simple reproduction, the established cosmological and political order is perceived not as arbitrary, i.e. as one possible order among others, but as a self-evident and natural order which goes without saying and therefore goes unquestioned, the agents' aspirations have the same limits as the objective conditions of which they are the product.[45]

ii. The Weberian Narrative

Alternatively, Hart could have developed a narrative along Weberian lines (even if he denied it, we know that Hart carefully read Weber's *Economy and Society*[46]). The key challenge would then consist in articulating a narrative that builds upon Weber's typology of social relationships. Such a narrative would set forth a continuum from forms of social relationship based on 'usage' (*Brauch*) and 'custom' (*Sitte*),[47] via what Weber calls 'conventions', all the way to a legal order, as a convention backed by a group of people deemed to have the duty (and legitimacy) to apply sanctions against those who transgress the law. A distinctive feature of the latter consists in the fact that 'the subjective attitudes of the participating individuals are directed towards the belief in a *legitimate order*'.[48] With striking similarities to Hart's internal point of view, Weber illustrates the latter attitudes with the following example:

> [W]hen a civil servant appears in his office daily at a fixed time, he does not act only on the basis of custom or self-interest which he could disregard if he wanted to; as a rule, his action is also determined by the validity of an order (viz., the civil service rules), which he fulfils partly because disobedience would be disadvantageous to him but also because its violation would be abhorrent to his sense of duty (of course, in varying degrees).[49]

[45] Pierre Bourdieu, *Outline of a Theory of Practice* (CUP 1977) 166.

[46] In her biography of HLA Hart, Nicola Lacey highlights Hart's apparent (but unacknowledged) indebtedness to Weber's sociology: 'Yet there is an interesting question here about the influence of sociological thought on Herbert's work. On one occasion, John Finnis consulted one of Herbert's volumes of Max Weber and found it heavily annotated (as was the case with most of the books which Herbert read closely). Finnis later asked him on two separate occasions about Weber's influence on his account of the "internal aspect of rules". Herbert denied that any such influence existed, ascribing the origins of the idea instead to Peter Winch's *The Idea of a Social Science*. Finnis felt unable to respond to his denial by saying that he had seen the counter-evidence in his copy. The volume which Finnis saw, *Max Weber on Law in Economy and Society*, is now in the library of Hebrew University in Jerusalem, to which Herbert left his library of over 900 books. Herbert's annotations suggest strongly that there was a Weberian undertow in *The Concept of Law*': Nicola Lacey, *The Nightmare and the Noble Dream: A Life of HLA Hart* (OUP 2004).

[47] A uniformity in social action is a usage 'in so far as the probability of its existence within a group is based on nothing but actual practice': Max Weber, *Economy and Society: An Outline of Interpretive Sociology* (University of California Press 1978) vol 1. A custom is a usage which has been established for a long time.

[48] Anthony Giddens, *Capitalism and Modern Social Theory: An Analysis of the Writings of Marx, Durkheim and Max Weber* (CUP 1971) 154.

[49] Weber, *Economy and Society*.

Far from a one-way evolutionary story that would identify forms of social order based on usage or custom as 'primitive', such a narrative would remain true to Weber's insights only if it managed to articulate the dynamic relationship between each form of social order.[50] In particular, Giddens highlights the fact that a legal order not only builds upon usage and custom, but also facilitates the emergence of new forms of usage and custom:

> There is no clear empirical line between usage and custom, and what Weber calls "convention". Conformity is not, in this case, a matter of the voluntary disposition of the individual. [...] The empirical relationship between custom, convention and law is an intimate one. Even the hold of sheer usage may be very strong. Those who frame laws to cover conduct which was formerly merely 'usual' frequently discover that very little additional conformity to the prescription in question is attained. However, usage and custom do in most cases provide the origin of rules which become laws. The reverse also occurs, although less frequently: the introduction of a new law may eventuate in new modes of habitual conduct.[51]

Section III focuses on this 'reverse' movement, to consider the extent to which the division of normative labour enabled by law's institutional structure can facilitate the development of habits that are of a very different kind than those in which a legal system originates: the latter habits are unpacked below.

C. From Collective Patterns of Behaviour to Legal Norms

The figure outlines a continuum that stretches from collective patterns of behaviour all the way to legal norms, via habits and practices. There is an overlap between some 'practices' and our most reflective habits. Just like reflective habits, practices stem from collective patterns of behaviour, and they presuppose a reflective awareness of the needs or purposes served by that pattern of behaviour (with a concomitant ability to change that pattern in light of those needs or purposes[52]). While some practices are born out of a deliberate commitment to do something together (vector 3 in the figure), other practices originate in habitual patterns of behaviour that gradually acquire a reflective dimension.[53]

[50] In most empirical cases, elements from each form of social order will not only co-exist but 'dynamically' facilitate (or hinder) their respective development.

[51] Giddens, *Capitalism and Modern Social Theory*.

[52] 'The reason that these automatic, habitual actions are performed is to serve the agent's chronically accessible goals. Thus, habitual, automatized goal-dependent actions are purposive. The agent's reason for acting – to serve a chronic goal – is not present to her consciousness at the time of acting. Nevertheless, it is operative in her psychological economy. It is a motivating factor that explains her actions': Neil Levy and Tim Bayne, 'Doing without deliberation: Automatism, automaticity, and moral accountability' (2004) 16 *International Review of Psychiatry* 209.

[53] Example 2 provides an example of a practice born out of habituated modes of behaviour which gradually take on normative significance. These habituated behaviours hence give rise to expectations of conformity / standards that are referred not only to coordinate but also to criticise deviance.

Figure The two way movement from patterns of behaviour to legal norms, and back

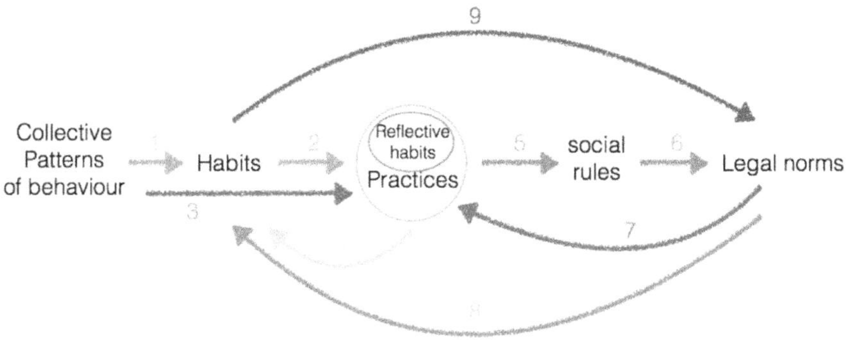

Aside from highlighting the return movement from legal norms to habits and practices, this graph debunks the assumption that the social practices giving rise to law must presuppose deliberative agency[54] all the way through (or vector 3). Not only are these types of social practices unlikely to account for most of the social processes giving rise to law, legal theory's overwhelming focus on such deliberate practices also hinders our chances to construct a rich understanding of legal normativity.

Most legal philosophers who have sought to capture the way in which the foundations of law are social practices have been influenced by either Bratman's[55] 'shared cooperative activity' model,[56] or by Lewis'[57] 'coordination convention' model.[58] These 'hypercommital'[59] models either mask or underplay

[54] 'We exercise deliberative agency when we deliberate or reflect on what we ought to do, attempting to evaluate our reasons for action in the light of our values, convictions, and beliefs about the world. This kind of agency has rightly impressed philosophers – largely, we suspect, because deliberative agency seems to be uniquely human – but in fact only a small proportion of our actions involve much in the way of deliberation or reflection': Levy and Bayne, 'Doing without deliberation'.

[55] Bratman, 'Shared cooperative activity'.

[56] Jules Coleman, *The Practice of Principle: In Defence of a Pragmatist Approach to Legal Theory* (OUP 2001); Shapiro, 'Law, plans, and practical reason'.

[57] Lewis, *Convention.*

[58] Postema, 'Coordination and convention'. Postema has since distanced himself from a strict Lewisean model of conventions, whose function is to solve a recurrent coordination problem: see notably Gerald J Postema, 'Morality in the first person plural' (1995) 14 *Law and Philosophy* 35. Postema's later work on custom comes closest to the type of account defended here, even if the discursive (and hence reflective) side is still emphasised at the expense of the non-reflective elements: Gerald J Postema, 'Custom, normative practice, and the law' (2012) 62 *Duke Law Journal* 707.

[59] Matthew Smith criticises these accounts for requiring both 'commitment to conceptual and epistemic agreement' and 'strong practical commitment' ('[N]amely a commitment by each party to engage in the activity with the other parties and (if a shared cooperative activity) to being mutually supportive in the activity'), thereby raising important doubts about the extent to which such

the degree of passivity inherent in many (if not most) of the social practices giving rise to law. Unlike a shared commitment to go on a park run every week (or to sing a duet every night), we tend to find ourselves already immersed in many of the social practices giving rise to law. Our role as participants in these practices is rarely one of initiation. More often than not, it is our uncovering the implicit norms that structure such practices – rather than the formulation of new explicit norms – that conditions our ability to transform these practices. This passive dimension is not the only aspect that distinguishes the bulk of legal practices from newly formed practices based on explicit, deliberate commitments.

The uncertainty inherent in the constant reformulation of the goals that structure law as a set of normative practices also stands in sharp contrast to the relatively unambiguous and well delineated nature of the fitness goal that drives a weekly park run practice. Often going hand in hand with this degree of goal uncertainty is the extent to which a practice entails ongoing 'learning how'. In a set of practices like law, learning how legal rules and principles apply to a given reality[60] (not just 'that' they apply) demands a critical grasp of both the explicit and implicit norms that structure such practices. Since these implicit norms are never settled, legal practices have an inherently didactic element: one has never finished learning how to interpret the law, in a way that is not necessarily true of the park run practice.

It is because the elements that are critical to this 'learning how' cannot be formalised in advance, dependent as they are on our ongoing endeavours to develop better ways of living together, that one cannot grasp the full significance of this didactic element with an exclusive focus on deliberately generated legal practices. Just as the implicit normativity that structures our ongoing 'learning how' must remain open to challenges that stem from the kind of encounters described in chapter five, there must be a constant movement of to and fro between law's explicit and implicit norms. A legal system that looses touch with the dynamics underlying this implicit normativity is a legal system that is unlikely to be able to sustain the kind of practices capable of generating the norms necessary to its successful evolution.

Only by building (reflective) habits into the continuum that leads from patterns of behaviour to legal norms can we account for the role played by law's institutional structure in fostering the return movements described in vectors 7 and 8 in the figure (as well as the normative implications flowing from vector 9). Before unpacking the 'moral risks' inherent in these return movements in section III,

'hypercommital' models are apt at conceptualising the bulk of social practices at the root of law's institutional structure: Matthew Noah Smith, 'The law as a social practice: Are shared activities at the foundations of law?' (2006) 12 *Legal Theory* 265, 283.

[60] Samuel Chilovi and George Pavlakos, 'The explanatory demands of grounding in law' (2021) *Pacific Philosophical Quarterly*.

defining vectors 1 to 7 provides an opportunity for a neat summary of our discussion so far:

Figure The two way movement from patterns of behaviour to legal norms, and back

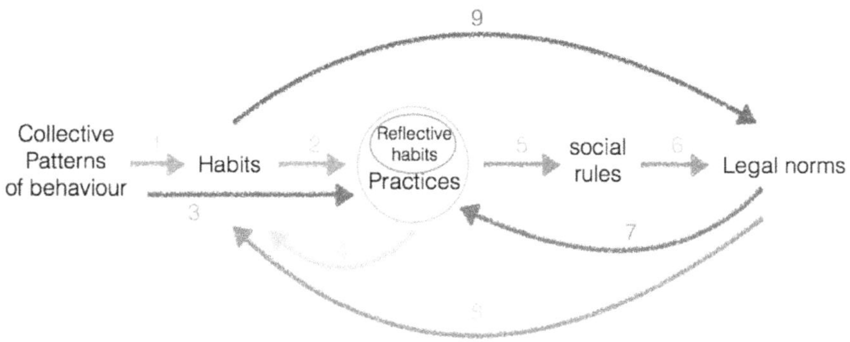

1. The repetition of a particular pattern of behaviour leads to it becoming automatic on the part of those in whom a habit has taken hold. Such automaticity is concomitant with a reduction in the experience of behaving in that particular way.[61]

   Example: All the members of a particular family may be referred to by a particular name. When some members of that family move out to live independently, they continue being referred to by that name.

2. A reflective habit requires some critical distanciation from the internalised pattern of behaviour, which is evaluated in the light of the needs or purposes of the agent(s).

   Example: Events such as a family falling out, or growing to include children born out of concomitant relationships, may lead a community to reflect upon the needs or purposes served by their naming habit. They may adapt the latter so that names follow a strict patriarchal or matriarchal line, for instance.

3. A practice can emerge out of a shared commitment or endeavour to do something together, without having to involve any degree of automatic agency[62] (unlike habits). Bratman's 'shared cooperative activity' model and Lewis' coordination convention model have been the most influential among legal philosophers.

[61] 'The paradigm of such behaviour is the over-learned action. One is usually (fully) conscious when performing an over-learned action, but one is not conscious of the over-learned action itself': Levy and Bayne, 'Doing without deliberation'.

[62] Levy and Bayne helpfully distinguish between automatic agency ('Automatic agency involves an absence – or at least a reduction – of the experience of doing') and automatistic agency, within which they distinguish between global automatisms and local automatisms: 'Global automatisms involve a global disruption of consciousness; they occur in the context of somnambulism [etc.] Individuals in these states perform fairly complex actions in a "robotic" manner. Their environmental awareness is limited [...] What we call "local automatisms", by contrast, involve only a disruption of consciousness and control over a particular kind of action. A person with a local automatism is fully conscious, but they experience no sense of agency over a particular complex and apparently voluntary action': ibid.

Example: A community may resolve to get together to mark the naming of a child.

4. With repetition, a practice may come to be internalised in a way that gives rise to the type of automatic agency characteristic of habit (marked by diminished awareness of the pattern of behaviour underlying it), yet without the goal-oriented adaptability and critical distanciation associated with reflective habits.

   Example: A community gets together every time a child is born, without necessarily remembering why.

5. The values associated with some practice lead to peer pressure to conform and widespread social condemnation of any deviation from that practice, thus marking the emergence of a social rule.

   Example: A family's failure to name a child (and to mark that occasion publicly) is condemned by the community.

6. An institutional structure is built to support the continuous adaptation, implementation and adjudication of such social rules.

   Example: A child's name needs to be registered with a public institution for that child to be recognised legally.

7. Some legal norms or institutions give rise to novel practices, some of which may disrupt a community's habits of thought (or behaviour).

   Example: The legalisation of gay marriage is prompting wider shifts (in comparison to those that triggered that legalisation) in a community's habitual understanding of marriage, family and parenthood.

The next section unpacks the moral risk inherent in the development of law's institutional structure by referring to the return movement encapsulated in vector 8 (in contrast to vector 7) and vector 9, as well as the type of alienation that may result from it.

III. THE TYPES OF HABITS LAW MAY FOSTER

> [T]he horrible thing about all legal officials, even the best, about all judges, magistrates, barristers, detectives, and policemen, is not that they are wicked (some of them are good), not that they are stupid (several of them are quite intelligent), it is simply that they have got used to it. Strictly they do not see the prisoner in the dock; all they see is the usual man in the usual place. They do not see the awful court of judgment; they only see their own workshop.
>
> GK Chesterton, 'The twelve men'[63]

The above quote has appeared more than once throughout this book, largely because it has inspired much of the research underlying it. This section throws

[63] GK Chesterton GK, 'The twelve men' in GK Chesterton (ed), *Tremendous Trifles* (Sheed & Ward 1955).

light on the qualitative difference (section III.A) between the habits that are capable of generating the practices at the heart of a legal system and some of the habits that this system's 'division of normative labour' (section III.B) is conducive to. Why? Because unlike the goal-oriented (hence adaptable) habits that give rise to legal practice,[64] the habits that may be formed on the back of a legal system's institutionalised adaptation to change can contribute to a pernicious kind of alienation (section III.C).

A. Qualitatively Different Habits

In a 'pre-legal' world, to borrow Hart's vocabulary, people are regulated by norms that 'have no particular origin in the enactment of an individual or an institution':[65] they find their origin in a pattern of collective behaviour which acquires particular significance in light of the purpose it has come to be associated with. While it is habitual in nature, that pattern of behaviour cannot give rise to the kind of practice[66] constitutive of a legal system unless it is capable of adapting to changing aspirations (vector 2 in the figure). In the absence of a 'rule about rules' establishing how legal change occurs, such change can only happen organically. People don't 'accept' but rather 'live by'[67] the norms they need to foster a better way of living together. That aspiration in turn generates a practice whose perceived social value (vector 5) may call for its institutionalisation (vector 6).[68] These institutions may in turn foster novel practices (vector 7).

Whereas vectors 5 to 7 are well-rehearsed in legal theory, the contrast between the kinds of habits that are capable of generating normative practices versus

[64] '[P]ractice should be regarded as an elevation of habit rather than a departure from it': Maike Albertzart, 'Principle-based moral judgement' (2013) 16 *Ethical Theory and Moral Practice* 339.

[65] Marmor, 'Legal conventionalism' 194.

[66] '[N]othing [...] keeps our practices in line except the reactions and responses we learn in learning them': John McDowell, 'Non-cognitivism and rule following' in *Mind, Value and Reality* (Harvard UP 1998).

[67] Waldron reminds us of the non-propositional character of this 'constitutive know-how', 'for it reflects the fact that at this stage of social development rules have no presence in society apart from their being practiced and their having a shared normativity – their "internal aspect" – in the minds and actions of those who practice them': Jeremy Waldron, 'All we like sheep' (1999) 12 *Canadian Journal of Law & Jurisprudence* 169 177.

[68] It is beyond the scope of this work to delve into the debate relating to the best way of characterising the nature of such practices, conventional or otherwise: While Shapiro's 'planning theory' (Shapiro, 'Law, plans, and practical reason'; Shapiro, *Legality*) expands upon Bratman's 'shared cooperative activity' concept, Andrei Marmor (Marmor, 'Legal conventionalism'), for his part rejects the idea that conventionalism necessarily relies on the concept of coordination problems and constructs an alternative model of 'constitutive conventions', which arise out of some general practical concerns leading to the adoption of a partly autonomous conventional practice. Gerald Postema (Postema, 'Morality in the first person plural') decisively distances himself from the game-theoretic model (to which he referred initially) when he introduces his 'constructive conventionalism', which emphasises the importance of moral and political concerns on the part of the people involved in establishing conventional rules (and in particular conventional rules of recognition).

those habits that can be fostered by legal institutions is rarely studied. Vectors 8 and 9 come with normative implications that are unpacked in section III.C.

8. Other legal norms or institutions prompt widespread disengagement from social / community issues that would have otherwise triggered reflective practices within that community.

   Example: Social security norms and institutions may demobilise those members of a community who would have otherwise engaged reflectively in practices aimed at addressing the plight of the least well-off (in which case those legal institutions might be said to facilitate 'normative holidays').

9. In some cases, those in charge of continuously adapting and generating legal norms in a particular domain have no 'practical commitment to the overall activity of the institution but instead will have a practical commitment only to the activity they must perform in order to avoid sanctions or receive a wage from the institution they serve'.[69] In such cases, they may be able to contribute to the modification of the applicable legal regime in that domain without any deliberative engagement on their part, automatically (and habitually) adapting to various cues.

   Example: Some among the team of senior civil servants in charge of adapting and generating social security norms are so bored or disengaged from the institution they have served for years that they are able to automatically react to whatever cue indicates their input is needed for the adaptation of the legal regime in place.

B. Division of Normative Labour and its Moral Risks

> Without law, social order requires considerable buy-in from the general population: The people are regulated by norms that are more or less accepted. [...] With the emergence of law, however, people are also regulated by norms that meet officials' criteria of validity and are enforced by specialized agencies. This division of labor can alienate people from the most important rules that govern their lives – rules that threaten to become remote, technical, and arcane. That is one more reason why the rule of law is not an unqualified human good: It is in the nature of law to pose such risks, and the rule of law cannot eliminate them. Leslie Green, 'Positivism and the inseparability of law and morals'[70]

To understand the way in which people might get 'alienated' from the most important rules that govern their lives, it is helpful to start from the way Hart

[69] 'In such instances, they will not have a practical commitment to the overall activity of the institution but instead will have a practical commitment only to the activity they must perform in order to avoid sanctions or receive a wage, regardless of whether that activity contributes to the overall activity of the institution. Insofar as there is any practical commitment at all to the joint activity of the institution, it is an entirely derivative commitment. Let us call this condition in which an agent performs the tasks as if she were practically committed to the J (or, as it were, the sub-Js) of the institution without actually being so committed alienation from the institution': Smith, 'The law as a social practice'.

[70] Green, 'Positivism and the inseparability of law and morals'.

formulated similar concerns. In *The Concept of Law*, Hart emphasises the contrast between a 'pre-legal' society, where 'acceptance' of the rules has to be widespread, to one where:

> [because] there is a union of primary and secondary rules [...] the acceptance of the rules as common standards for the group may be split off from the relatively passive matter of the ordinary individual acquiescing in the rules by obeying them for his part alone.[71]

The above 'split' is made possible by the fact that established legal orders *can* be sustained on the basis of official acceptance alone, thanks to their institutional structure. Because of this structure, it may well be the case that an established legal system (as opposed to a simpler regime of primary rules) is particularly conducive to a society that is 'deplorably sheeplike' – and where the sheep might all end up 'in the slaughterhouse'.[72]

> The step from the simple form of society [...] into the legal world [...] brings its solid gains at a certain cost. The gains are those of adaptability to change, certainty and efficiency, and these are immense; the cost is the risk that the centrally organised power may well be used for the oppression of numbers with whose support it can dispense, in a way that the simpler regime of primary rules could not.[73]

Because it is concomitant with the 'division of normative labour' that is made possible by established legal systems' institutional structure, this risk of oppression is likened by Green to 'standard patterns of decay that are explained by the nature of the thing that is decaying'.[74] Green's focus is on showing that the moral import of this risk disproves Hart's separability thesis, since it 'marks a connection between law and morality of a reverse kind'.[75] Perhaps because of this focus, Green does not dwell on how exactly people get 'alienated [...] from the most important rules that govern their lives'.

On this front, Wilkinson rightly questions the extent to which 'widespread acceptance can be said to *preclude* the vice of alienation, if acceptance is given no further specification'.[76] Given the minimalist way in which Hart defines it (acceptance may be based on 'an unreflecting inherited or traditional attitude, or the mere wish to do as others do'[77]), acceptance is certainly no safeguard against the 'sheeplike' predicament Hart worries about. To make sense of the type of engagement that may make a slaughterhouse ending less likely, one must look at the opposite of such engagement,

[71] Hart, *The Concept of Law*.
[72] Ibid.
[73] Ibid.
[74] Green, 'Positivism and the inseparability of law and morals'.
[75] Ibid.
[76] Michael A Wilkinson, 'Is law morally risky? Alienation, acceptance and Hart's concept of law' (2010) 30 *Oxford Journal of Legal Studies* 441, 451.
[77] Hart, *The Concept of Law*.

and unpack the kind of alienation deemed concomitant with the emergence of law's institutional structure.

C. Legal Institutional Structures, Alienation Risks and Habit Rigidification

Among the 'five variants of alienation' described by Melvin Seeman, 'powerlessness' encapsulates one aspect of the alienation we are concerned with (an alternative analysis of alienation and its relationship to rigidified habits is developed in chapter seven). In its Marxist origins, alienation referred to the extent to which 'the prerogative and means of decision are expropriated [from the worker] by the ruling entrepreneurs'.[78] Extended beyond the industrial sphere by Weber, this type of alienation aptly captures the way in which the transition from a customary order to a fully fledged legal structure may be said to take away from most 'the prerogative and means' of shaping a legal landscape that is not deemed to be 'theirs' anymore. This aspect of alienation ties in with what Hart bemoaned as:

> the failure on the part of ordinary men to realise that the forms of law and human society were at bottom merely human artefacts, not natural necessities but things actually made by men, and hence things which could be unmade and remade.[79]

Yet today that failure to come to terms with our role (and responsibility) as authors of those practices that can ultimately give rise to law stems at least in part from another variant of alienation. It is one that is connected – but not reducible to – what Seeman describes as 'meaninglessness':

> This second type of alienation, then, refers to the individual's sense of understanding the events in which he is engaged. We may speak of high alienation, in the meaninglessness usage, when the individual is unclear as to what he ought to believe – when the individual's minimal standards for clarity in decision-making are not met.[80]

As a society evolves from a tight-knit, small community, the number and complexity of the issues to be addressed to continually seek (better) ways of living together is daunting. The 'minimal standards for clarity in decision-making' mentioned above are arguably rarely met. Legal institutions are designed to tackle such complexity. Freeing the individual from the task of balancing a complex set of reasons,[81] law is to mediate between its subjects and the reasons that apply to them.[82] The 'secondary rules' that come with legal

[78] Melvin Seeman, 'On the meaning of alienation' (1959) *American Sociological Review* 783, 784.

[79] HLA Hart, 'Bentham and the Demystification of the Law' (1973) 36 *Modern Law Review* 2, 6.

[80] Seeman, 'On the meaning of alienation'.

[81] A task for which the individual may lack information or expertise.

[82] 'The advantage of normally proceeding through the mediation of rules is enormous. It enables a person to consider and form an opinion on the general aspects of recurrent situations in advance

institutions establish how legal change may occur. To relinquish responsibility for this key aspect of 'normative labour' comes at a price, for it is all too tempting to relax and enjoy the benefits of institutional authority (rather than actively partake in it).

Raz vividly captures those benefits in his 'service conception of authority': when law succeeds in its claim to authority, it is supposed to give us reasons for action that replace the set of dependent reasons, and thus simplify our practical reasoning. To a large extent the efficiency of a legal system depends on this 'de-mobilisation' of practical reasoning – and its concomitant fostering of habituated behaviour. Yet there is another side to Raz's theory. Law's claim to authority is to succeed only if it is deemed legitimate. We are not meant to relax for too long. We are supposed to keep checking[83] that law still has a 'sufficiently high normal justification score',[84] ie that it does better enable us to comply with the demands of 'right reason'.[85] In so doing, the hope is that we may – to use Wilkinson's phrase – 'reclaim law's authority'.[86]

The worry is that in practice fewer and fewer of us will bother; that more and more of us will surrender to the comfort of demobilised practical reasoning. The particular degree of surrender – and the danger that stems from it – depends in large part on the extent to which legal institutions are designed in a way that fosters bottom-up, critical engagement. The more authoritarian, rigidly top-down those structures are, the more they will discourage the learning processes necessary to the dynamic re-articulation of the implicit norms that structure legal practices. This is bad news for the evolution of the legal systems themselves, which will get out of touch with the needs and aspirations they are supposed to answer to. It is also bad news, importantly, for the extent to which we remain capable of continuously honing the perceptual and evaluative habits

of their occurrence. It enables a person to achieve results which can be achieved only through an advance commitment to a whole series of actions, rather than by case to case examination': Joseph Raz, *The Morality of Freedom* (Clarendon Press 1986) 58.

[83] '[T]he thesis allows maximum flexibility in determining the scope of authority. It all depends on the person over whom authority is supposed to be exercised: his knowledge, strength of will, his reliability in various aspects of life, and on the government in question [...] The test is as explained before: does following the authority's instructions improve conformity with reason? For every person the question has to be asked afresh, and for every one it has to be asked in a manner which admits of various qualifications': ibid.

[84] Emran Mian, 'The curious case of exclusionary reasons' (2002) 15 *Canadian Journal of Law and Jurisprudence* 99, 107.

[85] 'In such cases conformity with the underlying reasons is secured by complying with the rule, or rather a better degree of conformity than can otherwise be achieved is so obtained. This can justify complying with the rule even when it requires action which the underlying reasons do not. Such compliance may still be the best strategy to maximise conformity with the underlying reasons': Joseph Raz, *Practical Reason and Norms* (rev. ed, with postscript edn, Princeton UP 1990) 194.

[86] 'Contrary to Raz's image of law as an official authority, in the modern democratic order we are all implicit "mouthpieces" of the law, an insistence on which might begin to inculcate a sense of legal and social responsibility and perhaps in more radical guise, a social purpose, to reclaim law's authority': Wilkinson, 'Is law morally risky?'.

that condition our 'responsiveness to the other'. When the incentives to leave the comforts of one's 'demobilised bubble' are low, opportunities for the kind of encounter[87] that might jolt us out of our moral torpor are correspondingly low. What is compromised, in such a scenario, is not just the vitality of our law-making practices. Just like a muscle that has gone limp through lack of exercise, normative agency can get atrophied too.

To refer back to the figure in section II.C: the resulting retrenchment to increasingly rigid, habitual frames of thought which condone the adoption of whatever legal framework is applicable is described in vector 8. The risks inherent in this retrenchment are captured in a prescient way by de Tocqueville:[88]

> Thus, the ruling power, having taken each citizen one by one into its powerful grasp and having molded him to its own liking, spreads its arms over the whole of society, covering the surface of social life with a network of petty, complicated, detailed, and uniform rules through which even the most original minds and the most energetic of spirits cannot reach the light in order to rise above the crowd. It does not break men's wills but it does soften, bend, and control them; rarely does it force men to act but it constantly opposes what actions they perform; it does not destroy the start of anything but it stands in its way; it does not tyrannize but it inhibits, represses, drains, snuffs out, dulls so much effort that finally it reduces each nation to nothing more than a flock of timid and hardworking animals with the government as shepherd.[89]

[87] These encounters are described in chapter five.

[88] There is a striking similarity with von Humboldt's analysis of the same risks, which will be referred to in the next chapter: '[T]he evil results of a too extensive solicitude on the part of the State, are still more strikingly shown in the suppression of all active energy, and the necessary deterioration of the moral character.[…] The man who is often led, easily becomes disposed willingly to sacrifice what remains of his capacity for spontaneous action. He fancies himself released from an anxiety which he sees transferred to other hands, and seems to himself to do': Wilhelm von Humboldt, *The Limits of State Action* (CUP 1969) 1402 (loc).

[89] Alexis de Tocqueville, *Democracy in America* (Penguin 2003).

7

Algorithmic Habits and Social Transformations

> Acts are free not insofar as the subject is always the same, an essence, an identity, but insofar as the subject is transformed by and engaged through its acts, becomes through its acts.
>
> Elizabeth Grosz, 'Habit today'[1]

THE ALGORITHMIC SYSTEMS considered in this chapter have in common with legal systems their claim to simplify our practical reasoning. In both cases, the quality of the habits needed to bring such systems into existence stands in sharp contrast with the 'ways of having habits' often fostered by such systems. Law's institutionalised adaptation to change can encourage growing degrees of 'agency surrender'. The resulting estrangement from the political and social practices that empower us to continually shape our legal landscape may not, at first sight, have much in common with the extent to which some of the algorithmic systems considered here can have the opposite effect.

In *Revolutionary Routines*, Carolyn Pedwell evocatively highlights the extent to which transformative movements such as Black Lives Matter have successfully leveraged 'the affordances of digital technology to produce a new way of seeing [...] Through citizen-produced documentation of police brutality shared widely via networked media, Black Lives Matter has countered law enforcement's iterative injunction to "move on, there's nothing to see here"'.[2] As a mobilisation tool, social media platforms have tremendous transformative potential. Yet these platforms' profile-based optimisation of user content also have a less visible, transformation-hindering effect. Section I unpacks the concept of 'profile-based optimisation', while section II analyses this transformation-hindering effect as a form of alienation. At stake is a compromised inner mobility: instead of being 'transformed by and engaged through its acts',[3] 'the subject's acts' converge to

[1] Elizabeth Grosz, 'Habit today: Ravaisson, Bergson, Deleuze and us' (2013) 19 *Body & Society* 217.

[2] Carolyn Pedwell, *Revolutionary Routines* (McGill-Queen's UP 2021) 142, quoting Nicholas Mirzoeff, *The Appearance of Black Lives Matter* ([NAME] Publications 2018).

[3] Grosz, 'Habit today'.

shore up an identity that has taken a life of its own through mutually reinforcing, optimised content and contacts. In contrast to the emphasis on autonomous, deliberative agency that is encouraged by a manipulation-focused framework, an analysis in terms of alienation is concerned with the factors that halt experimentation (and thus transformative capabilities).

Sections III and IV conclude by considering two types of 'interventions': they are both meant to revive and widen the scope for normative experimentation within data-reliant infrastructures. 'Ensemble contestability' features, outlined in section III, are to enable collective, critical engagement with optimisation tools. This critical engagement is made possible by outlining the outputs of differently trained, 'ghost' optimisation systems and introducing ways for users to interactively assess those counterfactual outcomes. 'Bottom-up data trusts', outlined in section IV, are designed to enable groups to regain agency over the data that makes these optimisation tools possible in the first place. Empowering people to have a say over their personal data can not only become a lever for social and political change. Data trusts' 'bottom-up' design also opens the door to the development of a variety of participation habits that are far removed from the widespread passivity encouraged by current top-down approaches to data governance.

I. INFERRED TRAITS AND OPTIMISATION ENDEAVOURS

A. Profile-based, Personalised Optimisation Tools

Few of us would be able to get through our lives without, at some point or another, 'profiling'[4] the things, animals, or people we encounter. We might associate dogs of a certain size or demeanour with characteristically aggressive behaviour, and as a result keep our distance on the pavement. This assumed correlation between dog size and aggressive behaviour is highly fallible: it is likely to stem from a very small data sample. Yet the fear associated with the event that led to that assumed correlation means that it is unlikely to be challenged for some time. We all make countless inferences of this kind: we might associate particular voice pitches or dress styles with distinct personalities, particular shop windows with distinct kinds of goods, and so on.

In most cases, the accuracy of our predictions will be rather poor, since we simply do not have the time or energy to collect (let alone process) large enough data samples. The multitude of data collection devices we interact with on a

[4] For a thorough analysis of the concept of 'profiling', its roots and implications, see Mireille Hildebrandt, 'Defining profiling: A new type of knowledge?' in Mireille Hildebrandt and Serge Gutwirth (eds), *Profiling the European Citizen: Cross-Disciplinary Perspectives* (Springer Netherlands 2008).

daily basis, however, means that today many of those inferences can be made with a high degree of accuracy. The vast amounts of data we (un)willingly provide on a daily basis are drawn upon to establish all sorts of correlations. Some are deemed more useful than others. If it can be shown that there is a strong correlation between attending a particular kind of gym and buying a barbecue at the first sign of sunshine, that information will be valuable to companies advertising barbecues. Some online platforms – such as social media platforms – are in a privileged position when it comes to being able to draw the kind of 'gym–barbecue' correlation that is so valuable to advertisers, provided they succeed in what has become their primary imperative: to maximise user engagement.

This 'maximise user engagement' imperative in turn gives rise to the need for yet more predictions: what type of online content is most likely to lead 'user X' to engage for longer with the platform? It might be a subtle combination of particular news headlines with photos of friends and news of their recent travels. For others it might be reports of recent neighbourhood burglaries combined with a call for protests. In all cases, the traits[5] inferred from the machine-readable behaviour of user X – user X's 'profile' – will guide the content selection so as to maximise user engagement.

This chapter analyses the impact of profile-based, personalised optimisation tools on our capacity for critical agency and ongoing transformation. Social media platforms are far from the only relevant example. Sophisticated recommender systems will recommend we read a book, listen to a tune, or approach a potential date based on their 'fit' with the traits inferred from our machine-readable behaviour. Online education platforms are looking to deploy 'personalised homework' based on each child's profile, which may include a variety of inferred psychological traits. In contrast to social media platforms, these optimisation endeavours may be driven by aims that have little to do with user engagement. Given that these aims may be as noble as can be (personalised education is but one example), how are we to assess – if at all – these personalised optimisation tools?

Because the optimisation of user X's online environment takes place seamlessly in a way that is designed to invisibly 'push her emotional buttons', assessments of the legitimacy of these personalised optimisation interventions often proceed from the assumption that what is at stake is some form of manipulation. To show why this manipulation framework is not as helpful as is often assumed, the next section outlines its key elements through the prism of social media, as an example that has captured much attention so far.

[5] Michael Kosinski, David Stillwell and Thore Graepel, 'Private traits and attributes are predictable from digital records of human behavior' (2013) 110 *Proceedings of the National Academy of Sciences*.

B. Manipulation as Hidden and Non-deliberative Interventions

Most social media users have little understanding of what data social media platforms have about them, and why their online environment – from ads to newsfeeds – is shaped the way it is. Even after the introduction of a variety of so-called 'transparency features',[6] the way in which social media platforms leverage their users' data remains opaque.[7] Given this enduring opacity, Susser and others[8] argue that those platforms are powerful manipulation tools. Unlike persuasion and coercion, which are both relatively forthright in their endeavour to influence or restrict another person's decision-making processes, manipulation *covertly* exploits the manipulee's traits or vulnerabilities in order to invisibly steer her decision-making in a given direction. This emphasis on covertness is controversial – its centrality is notably questioned by Sunstein[9] and Barnhill[10] – but pivotal. Those who question the importance of covertness as a constitutive criterion of manipulation tend to confuse covert influence with merely non-deliberative influence.

This confusion is common. It is largely attributable to the impact of rationalist accounts[11] of autonomy. According to such accounts, autonomy presupposes that one's choices be the result of rational, deliberative processes – free of interference from their habitual, intuitive counterparts. As such, any attempt to influence through non-deliberative means is likely to count as 'manipulative'. While Sunstein is aware of the issues underlying such an overly wide understanding of manipulation, he hesitates to consider 'nondeliberative efforts to

[6] To take Facebook as an example, these 'transparency features' include a 'why am I seeing this?' button that is meant to explain why a particular ad is shown to a particular user. There is an 'Ad preferences page' that seeks to reveal what inferences Facebook has made about a particular user, and how. Most recently, the 'Download your information' feature has been made to include more of the latter inferences. While this introduction of 'transparency features' is laudable in terms of overall direction, it should not be mistaken for a cure, nor taken at face value. For a critique, see notably Athanasios Andreou and others, *Investigating ad transparency mechanisms in social media: A case study of Facebook's explanations* (2018), who conducted controlled ad campaigns four years ago to show how misleading so-called 'transparency features' (they were different then) can be. See also Laura Edelson and others, *Universal Digital Ad Transparency* (2021); Rasia Haji and Wolfgang G Stock, 'User settings for advertising optimization on Facebook: Active customer participation or settings blindness?' (2021) 59 *Telematics and Informatics* 101548.

[7] For a recent, and particularly pertinent critique, see Paddy Leerssen, 'The soap box as a black box: Regulating transparency in social media recommender systems' (2020) 11 *European Journal of Law and Technology*.

[8] Daniel Susser, Beate Roessler and Helen Nissenbaum, 'Technology, autonomy and manipulation' (2019) 8 *Internet Policy Review*.

[9] Cass R Sunstein, 'Fifty shades of manipulation' (2016) *Journal of Marketing Behavior*.

[10] Anne Barnhill, 'What is manipulation?' in Christian Coons and Michael Weber (eds), *Manipulation: Theory and Practice* (OUP 2014).

[11] This impact can be seen at play in Wood's influential definition: 'What is characteristic of manipulative behaviour is that it influences people's choices in ways that circumvent or subvert their rational decision-making processes': Allen W Wood, 'Coercion, manipulation, exploitation' in Christian Coons and M Weber (eds), *Manipulation: Theory and Practice* (OUP 2014).

alter properly nondeliberative judgments'[12] as instances of persuasion rather than manipulation. Yet cases of non-deliberative influence are widespread and mostly unproblematic. Chapter two emphasised the extent to which our receptivity to all sorts of non-deliberative influences typically supports – rather than compromises – intentional action. The vast majority of human interactions are shaped through non-deliberative means: the art of understanding and steering these non-deliberative interactions is called 'emotional intelligence', not manipulation.

This emphasis on the centrality of deliberative agency can also be seen at play in the procedural, post-hoc endorsement tests that are sometimes deemed able to retrospectively legitimise instances of manipulation. These procedural tests make sense if the preservation of deliberative agency is all that is at stake. Yet as soon as we worry not only about the competency but also the authenticity of that endorsement process, we are back to considering the extent to which that process itself may be impacted by outside forces that lack authentic endorsement. As Christman acknowledges:

> most of our commitments, tendencies, emotional predilections, and forms of thought, have developed in us without any ongoing reflective consideration or judgment by our own reasons-responsive faculties. We merely find ourselves with such traits and come to endorse them as constitutive of who we in fact are.[13]

To avoid an infinite reflective endorsement regress, Christman puts forward a counterfactual 'alienation test' that can be informed by non-deliberative elements too. If, were I to reflect about the way one of my acquired traits has come about, I would not feel alienated from this characteristic, then autonomy may be said to 'obtain' in relation to that trait. In scenarios where the outside influence operates in a punctual way, that test is appealing: when we acquire a certain trait due to a well-defined, targeted type of influence, there may be enough left of us that is free of such influence[14] to anchor a counterfactual alienation test, even months later. Yet when the scope of the influence at stake is such that it is near-impossible to delineate which of my 'traits' were affected and which were not, the above test starts to show its limits.

Consider the following social media scenario:

> Having picked up the news that one of my social media contacts has been burgled, my newsfeed prioritises burglary and crime reports, times the appearance of burglary protection adverts in order to coincide with moments when my online activity

[12] Sunstein, 'Fifty shades of manipulation'.

[13] John Christman, *The Politics of Persons: Individual Autonomy and Socio-historical Selves* (Cambridge University Press 2009) 139.

[14] Christman puts it slightly differently: 'the hypothetical reflection we imagine here must be such that it is not the product of social and psychological conditions that prevent adequate appraisal of oneself': ibid.

suggests increased anxiety,[15] and prioritises right-wing leaning political content and videos. New contacts with similar burglary experiences and/or safety concerns are suggested. These measures succeed in giving me a vastly exaggerated sense of burglary risk, which eventually leads me to buy a burglar alarm. But things don't end there. What may have started as a commercial promotion endeavour becomes a self-reinforcing intervention with comprehensive effects. The platform's user engagement maximisation imperative means I am 'served' more and more 'insecurity' content which, over time, not only shapes my political views, but also my wider circle of friends and acquaintances.

Three months have passed. I receive an email offering me the option of returning my burglar alarm for a full refund, as the online alarm adverts that led to my purchase were found to be overly manipulative by the relevant watchdog. Thanks to social media prompts, I have since become friends with other safety-conscious mums and learned about and joined my neighbourhood watch. I am actively campaigning for increased security controls at the borders and random ID checks in the streets. What if I not only have no regret over this alarm purchase, but I also embrace the security-focused trait that prompted this purchase? What if, now that I know I was induced to have an exaggerated sense of burglary risk for purely commercial purposes, I still endorse both my decision to purchase a burglar alarm and my organising my life around pervasive security concerns? What if I now actively dismiss any left-leaning news content, or old acquaintances' invites?

When one looks at the above scenario through manipulation lenses, an exonerating conclusion is likely to follow: the targeted, aggressive advertising that led to the burglary alarm purchase is as clear a case of manipulation as any, and there are no immediate reasons to dismiss its post-hoc endorsement as either incompetent or inauthentic. Is any remaining sense of unease – any intuition that something is amiss – tracking any pertinent feature of the above scenario? The next section argues that it does, and that the manipulatory mis-selling of burglar alarms acts as a distraction in the above scenario.

Most users of social media – or users of recommender systems and dating apps – will never be at the receiving end of anything resembling as clear-cut a case of manipulation as the mis-selling practices described above. Some nevertheless argue that the hidden and non-deliberative way in which these platforms personalise content warrants an analysis in terms of manipulation.[16] I argue that what goes amiss is better characterised in terms of alienation, since what can be compromised is our capacity for both inner and 'outer' (collective) transformations.

[15] For an account of the way in which Facebook researchers endeavoured to test a so-called 'emotional contagion' hypothesis by modifying – without consent – the content users were exposed to, see Adam DI Kramer, Jamie E Guillory and Jeffrey T Hancock, 'Experimental evidence of massive-scale emotional contagion through social networks' (2014) 111 *Proceedings of the National Academy of Sciences* 8788.

[16] Susser, Roessler and Nissenbaum, 'Technology, autonomy and manipulation'.

II. PRECLUDED TRANSFORMATIONS: ALIENATION THROUGH REIFICATION

Given our 'homophilic'[17] tendency to engage with things or people that are most like us,[18] the algorithms designed to automate content recommendation or selection can lead to our being exposed to an increasingly narrow range of views (and people).[19] Concerns about the potential for 'internet technology'[20] to foster increased socio-political homogeneity[21] (accelerated by 'filtering' technologies'[22]) are far from new. They have notably given rise to an ongoing debate about the existence – and detrimental effects[23] – of so-called 'echo chambers'.[24]

In contrast to the consequentialist framework underlying the above studies, this section analyses the impact of personalised optimisation tools on the extent to which we retain a capacity to transform ourselves, both individually and collectively. This capacity is central to this book's thesis. 'Habitual ethics' remains a live possibility, rather than a contradiction in terms, because and to the extent that we develop habits that are malleable enough to remain at the service of the evolving demands of our ethical life.

Just as our remaining minimally responsive to 'the other' (chapter five) can be compromised by a variety of environmental factors, our underlying capacity for critical, transformative agency cannot be taken for granted either. To foster

[17] Miller McPherson, Lynn Smith-Lovin and James M Cook, 'Birds of a feather: Homophily in social networks' (2001) 27 *Annual Review of Sociology* 415.

[18] '[S]ocial media platforms and their respective affordances (such as Twitter hashtags, or Facebook pages and groups) can be understood as engines of homophily': Axel Bruns, 'Filter bubble' (2019) 8 *Internet Policy Review* 4.

[19] 'In recent years, a growing trend in personalized filtering research is to consider factors, other than accuracy, that contribute to the quality of filtering, because an overt focus on accuracy has limitations': Sayooran Nagulendra and Julita Vassileva, 'Providing awareness, explanation and control of personalized filtering in a social networking site' (2016) 18 *Information Systems Frontiers* 145, 145.

[20] Robert D Putnam, *Bowling Alone: The Collapse and Revival of American Community* (Simon & Schuster 2000) 178.

[21] For an analysis focusing on conformity to the majority opinion, see Jaclyn Cameron and Nick Geidner, 'Something old, something new, something borrowed from something blue: Experiments on dual viewing TV and Twitter' (2014) 58 *Journal of Broadcasting & Electronic Media* 400.

[22] Putnam, *Bowling Alone.*

[23] For an analysis in terms of polarised politics: Cass R Sunstein, *#republic: Divided Democracy in the Age of Social Media* (Princeton UP 2018). Empirical accounts analysing the purported link between social media usage and polarisation paint a more nuanced picture, in part because of variation in the way 'polarisation' is defined. For a recent, critical overview of the debate, see Pablo Barberá, 'Social media, echo chambers, and political polarization' in Nathaniel Persily and Joshua A Tucker (eds), *Social Media and Democracy: The State of the Field and Prospects for Reform* (CUP 2020).

[24] Daniel Geschke, Jan Lorenz and Peter Holtz, 'The triple-filter bubble: Using agent-based modelling to test a meta-theoretical framework for the emergence of filter bubbles and echo chambers' (2019) 58 *British Journal of Social Psychology* 129C; Thi Nguyen, 'Echo chambers and epistemic bubbles' (2020) 17 *Episteme* 141.

such 'critical agency',[25] Sen argues, the 'power to question accepted norms is essential if groups are to settle axiological choices and be 'active participant[s] in change'.[26] What follows highlights the importance of both imagination (section II.A) and the possibility of ongoing experimentation (section II.C) in preserving one's 'power to be active participants in change'. We are much more familiar with the dangers that result from the narrowing of imaginative horizons than we are with those that result from an environment that is engineered to 'halt experimentation'. Section II.B highlights why.

A. Narrowing of Imaginative Horizons

To be capable of bringing about change, one needs to be able to imagine[27] how one could develop differently (both as an individual and as a group) and on that basis possibly change who we are becoming: while we are in large part the product of the environment within which we grow up, we are also endowed with a capacity for transformation, both individually and collectively. Yet by 'narrow[ing] the range of the repertoires on which we can draw in our imaginative projects and so [curtailing] our imaginative explorations of alternative possibilities',[28] content personalisation ends up endangering that crucial, transformative aspect of human agency.

When content and contact recommendations faithfully reflect my inferred traits and beliefs, what could otherwise be an eclectic range of random encounters becomes an ever narrower set of potential life experiences. Will Thumbelina's 'better made than filled' head ('very different from her mother's') 'find the new genius, the inventive intelligence, an authentic cognitive subjectivity',[29]

[25] Aware of the variety of meanings associated with the term 'agency', Sen uses it 'in its older – and 'grander' – sense as someone who acts and brings about change, and whose achievements can be judged in terms of her own values and objectives': Amartya Sen, *Development as Freedom* (Oxford Paperbacks 2001).

[26] Ibid.

[27] Defined as the capacity to transcend the simple perceptual field and hence endow the natural world with properties drawn from self-understanding, imagination plays a key role in Vico's moral sociology: Giambattista Vico, *The New Science of Giambattista Vico* (3rd edn, Cornell UP 1984). As it allows the human being to 'divorce him or herself from the immediate world of causes and reactions', imagination can be defined as 'the capacity to apply the structure of 'what if?' to the world in order to conceptualize it as lacking something' hence introducing the need to work on it: David E Rose, 'Society and the origin of moral law: Giambattista Vico and non-reductive naturalism' in Bert Musschenga and Anton van Harskamp (eds), *What Makes Us Moral? on the Capacities and Conditions for Being Moral* (Springer 2014) 901.

[28] Catriona Mackenzie, 'Imagining oneself otherwise' in Catriona Mackenzie and Natalie Stoljar (eds), *Relational Autonomy: Feminist Perspectives on Autonomy, Agency, and the Social Self* (OUP 1999) 144. In a related vein, Julie Cohen emphasises the extent to which digital manipulation compromises what she calls 'play' – 'the modality through which situated subjects advance their own contingent goals, constitute their communities, and imagine their possible futures': Julie Cohen, *Configuring the Networked Self* (Yale UP 2012).

[29] Michel Serres, *Thumbelina: The Culture and Technology of Millennials* (Rowman & Littlefield 2014) 19.

as foreseen by Michel Serres? '[S]ince she no longer has to work hard to gain knowledge',[30] the 'millennial' portrayed by Serres is seen as having the opportunity to 'cultivate a more intuitive mode of engagement attuned to the visceral experience and flow of everyday life'.[31] Yet will that flow remain varied and visceral[32] enough for those intuitions to be adequately challenged?

If it wasn't for the 'maximise user engagement' imperative that has come to preside over so many of our online experiences, this question may not have become so salient. In its original inception, the internet put an exhilarating array of viewpoints and forms of life at one's fingertips. The possibility of personalised optimisation – from the foods we eat to the people we meet – is however feeding an insatiable appetite for more of the 'optimal'. Why leave a process as consequential as dating practices to random encounters when an algorithm may be able to finetune the selection of potential dates on the basis of traits and dispositions I may not even be aware of?

Any such optimised existence won't leave much room for encounters that throw doubt on deeply held beliefs or aspirations. The undermining effect of such a smooth experience is insidious: the anxiety that can be generated by encountering what Srinivasan describes as a 'shadow me' – a 'me who believes the opposite of much of what I believe, who values what I disvalue'[33] – can prove salutary. It may impart us with a 'broader sense of possibility'; one that allows us to 'stand back from the intellectual [and emotional] commitments that we have inherited and ask ourselves in a new spirit of enquiry what we should think of them'.[34]

The need for such an open 'spirit of enquiry' is intimately connected to von Humboldt's critique of any institutional structure that endangers what he calls 'Selbsttätigkeit'. Sometimes translated as 'self-realisation',[35] the development of the powers and capacities necessary for the latter is only possible, von Humboldt assumes,[36] in an environment that maximises the extent to which one

[30] Ibid.

[31] Carolyn Pedwell, 'Re-mediating the human: Habits in the age of computational media' in Tony Bennett and others (eds), *Assembling and Governing Habits* (Routledge 2021).

[32] For a critique of Dewey's suggestion that 'the problem of racial prejudice' could be addressed via a 'transformation of the foreign into the familiar' achieved through more interaction between different cultures, see Shannon Sullivan and her arguing that Dewey fails to understand the real nature and impact of 'racial friction': Shannon Sullivan, *Revealing Whiteness: The Unconscious Habits of Racial Privilege* (Indiana UP 2006) 36–37 (with thanks to Carolyn Pedwell).

[33] Srinivasan describes a 'shadow me' as a 'me who believes the opposite of much of what I believe, who values what I disvalue, and who articulates the world in terms of concepts that are alien to my own': Amia Srinivasan, 'Genealogy, epistemology and worldmaking' (2019) *CXIX Proceedings of the Aristotelian Society* 128.

[34] Quentin Skinner, *Visions of Politics*, vol 1 (CUP 2002) 116, quoted by Srinivasan, 'Genealogy, Epistemology and Worldmaking'.

[35] Raymond Geuss discusses Humboldt's particular understanding of 'self-realisation' in Raymond Geuss, *Outside Ethics* (Princeton UP 2009) 75.

[36] The idea that full development requires encounters with a wide variety of circumstances is a revolutionary one at the time. Because of the difficulties inherent in defining 'development', empirical verification is challenging. Contemporary empirical psychology studies that delve into the effects of monotony on psychological development come closest.

is exposed to a wide variety of situations and worldviews. Thus von Humboldt devotes *The Limits of State Action* to the delineation of the conditions that enable such 'self-realisation', away from the State's homogenising influence.[37] In a – Romantic – Aristotelian[38] vein, von Humboldt asserts that 'the true end of Man [...] is the highest and most harmonious development of his powers to a complete and consistent whole'.[39] To do this, 'freedom is the first and indispensable condition [...] but there is besides another essential – intimately connected with freedom, it is true – a variety of situations'.[40]

Unlike 'content-neutral' autonomy-based arguments, which emphasise the need for awareness of 'options'[41] to structure a truly autonomous life, the 'variety of situations' von Humboldt calls for is driven by the full development of one's capacities rather than autonomy[42] as an end:

> '[A]s State interference increases, the agents to which it is applied come to resemble each other, as do all the results of their activity. And this is the very design which States have in view. They desire comfort, ease, tranquillity; and these are most readily secured to the extent that there is no clash of individualities. But what man does and must have in view is something quite different – it is variety and activity. Only these develop the many-sided and vigorous character; and, there can be no one, surely, so far degraded, as to prefer, for himself personally, comfort and enjoyment to greatness; and he who draws conclusions for such a preference in the case of others, may justly be suspected of misunderstanding human nature, and of wishing to make men into machines.'[43]

Today we may not have 'made men into machines', but 'through habits users [have arguably] become their machines: they stream, update, capture, upload, grind, link, save, trash, and troll'.[44] The resulting exposure to a homogenised range of experiences will affect our capacity to pre-reflectively envisage different

[37] For a brilliant outline of the role which Humboldt's valuing of diversity plays in his critique of State interference, see Raymond Geuss, *History and Illusion in Politics* (CUP 2001) 80.

[38] von Humboldt's concept of 'Selbsttätigkeit' arguably finds some of its roots in Aristotle's concept of 'energeia', even if this emphasis on individual powers and creativity can also be seen as a sign of Goethe's influence – hence the 'romantic' Aristotelian vein (for an in depth discussion of the extent to which von Humboldt's theory draws upon Aristotle's 'energeia', see Josef Voss, 'Aristote et la théorie énergétique du langage de Wilhelm von Humboldt' (1974) 72 *Revue philosophique de Louvain* 482.

[39] Wilhelm von Humboldt, *The Limits of State Action* (Kindle edn, CUP 1969) 16.

[40] Ibid.

[41] Joseph Raz, *The Morality of Freedom* (Clarendon Press 1986).

[42] This emphasis on the development of one's capabilities – rather than autonomy – as an end distinguishes von Humboldt's capability account from most contemporary versions, including that of Susan Brison, whose specification of a 'capability set' (intentionally left incomplete) is seen as essential to 'autonomy': Susan J Brison, 'Relational autonomy and freedom of expression' in Catriona Mackenzie and Natalie Stoljar (eds), *Relational Autonomy: Feminist Perspectives on Autonomy, Agency, and the Social Self* (OUP 1999).

[43] von Humboldt, *The Limits of State Action.*

[44] Wendy Hui Kyong Chun, *Updating to Remain the Same: Habitual New Media* (MIT Press 2016).

futures – different ways of structuring our living together. Is it reasonable to wish otherwise? Have we not, in some sense, always been 'our machines' (where we once 'ploughed, seeded, moulded and carried', we now 'stream, update etc'?) If that is so, is the above, 'self-realisation', critique of optimisation tools to be dismissed as both overly romantic and unworkable, given the rapidly changing, complex environments we navigate on a daily basis?

B. Habitats and their Inherent Narrowing of Encountered Worldviews

This question brings us back to the reason why habits are mostly empowering us, rather than holding us back: we cannot be open to change all at once.

> If we were simply receptive to change, without limit, then we would be incapable of habit. Each new action or experience would transform us, so that we would have no character or integrity to call our own. We would be empty, entirely subject to circumstance, blown hither and thither by the winds of change.[45]

The above quote was called upon in chapter five to explain our reliance on a variety of defence mechanisms that mould the degree and quality of our responsiveness to the other. The need to preserve an 'integrity to call our own' does entail a limit to our receptivity, which must be rooted in a stable frame of reference. What if the optimisation tools under scrutiny have become, for many at least, what provides precisely such stability? As novel 'habitats', they become 'the taken-for-granted base of our habits'.[46]

From that perspective, to criticise personalised optimisation tools for their narrowing of encountered worldviews is to criticise them for precisely what they are they bound to do as habitats. Every habitat shapes 'not only habits of life, but patterns of thought and valuation'.[47] As habitats, these tools would thus provide the stable frame from within which we may contemplate changes in our environment, and the extent to which these changes call for any adaptation.

Yet social media platforms and recommender tools of various kinds are also unlike most habitats in at least one important respect: they do not lend themselves to open co-construction. To inhabit a structure – whether built from scratch or discovered – is to initiate a two-way relationship of influence whose exact nature and scope is uncertain. Just as the way I shall shape and contribute to some habitat is uncertain, there is normally some element of surprise in the way some habitat will shape me (since it partly depends on my mode of

[45] Clare Carlisle, *On Habit* (Routledge 2014).
[46] John Durham Peters, *The Marvelous Clouds: Towards a Philosophy of Elemental Media* (University of Chicago Press 2015) 1.
[47] Marshall McLuhan, *Understanding Media: The Extensions of Man* (MIT Press 1994) 12.

habitation). The same cannot be said of the way social media platforms mould us. Not only do some go as far as to claim that these platforms '"pre-compute" the nature of "our" future habits before they actually come into being'.[48] None of these platforms and tools are designed to allow any form of constructive input.

This one-way relationship of influence based on our past machine-readable behaviour prompts the unhealthy rigidification of habits: habits that I once co-negotiated with and within my environment become unquestionable 'givens'. The next section delves into the way in which the alienation that results from such engineered rigidification rubs against our capacity for transformative agency by halting the possibility of experimentation.

C. Habitat Co-construction and the Possibility of Experimentation

The concept of 'alienation as powerlessness'[49] unpacked in the context of the risks inherent in law's institutional structure (chapter six) is closely related to the kind of alienation that results from our being 'hooked'[50] to tools designed to maximise user engagement. Here what is compromised are 'the prerogative and means' of continually (re)shaping our way of inhabiting a landscape: this landscape has been unilaterally optimised in accordance with the traits and propensities inferred from our machine-readable past. Not only are we not in a position to anticipate how we are being 'read', we are also unable to anticipate how that reading translates into architecture modifications.[51] Yet this double opacity is but the first of the layers facilitating 'alienation as powerlessness'. Were increasing transparency demands[52] to go a lot further than they presently do,[53] they would still not necessarily alleviate the type of alienation at play. To understand why, Jaeggi's analysis of alienation as 'halting of experimentation'[54] is particularly helpful.

[48] Pedwell, 'Re-mediating the Human', referring to Mark BN Hansen, *Feed Forward: On the Future of Twenty-First Century Media* (Chicago UP 2015) and Louise Amoore, *Cloud Ethics: Algorithms and the Attributes of Ourselves and Others* (Duke UP 2020).

[49] Melvin Seeman, 'On the meaning of alienation' (1959) *American Sociological Review* 783.

[50] Nir Eyal, *Hooked: How to Build Habit-Forming Products* (Penguin 2014).

[51] For a brilliant analysis of this double opacity and its normative implications, see Mireille Hildebrandt, *Smart Technologies and the End(s) of Law: Novel Entanglements of Law and Technology* (Elgar 2015).

[52] Motahhare Eslami and others, 'User Attitudes towards Algorithmic Opacity and Transparency in Online Reviewing Platforms', *Proceedings of the 2019 CHI Conference on Human Factors in Computing Systems* (Association for Computing Machinery 2019); Leyla Dogruel, 'Too much information!? Examining the impact of different levels of transparency on consumers' evaluations of targeted advertising' (2019) 36 *Communication Research Reports* 383.

[53] Andreou and others, *Investigating ad transparency mechanisms*; Leerssen, 'The soap box as a black box'.

[54] 'Relationships are refined and alienating when they cannot be understood as providing a field for possible action and experimentation. And, with respect to rigidification, it can be said that

To grasp the significance of this alienation analysis for our purposes, we need to recall chapter two's account of the factors that might disrupt what should be a cycle of dynamic responses to environmental 'affordances'. Rietveld and others' analysis of 'affordance' as 'a relation between (a) an aspect of the (sociomaterial) environment and (b) an ability available in a "form of life"'[55] is marked by a degree of optimism[56] about the extent to which all living beings remain dynamically responsive to states of disequilibrium in their relationship with their environment.

In contrast with such optimism, Jaeggi emphasises that 'it cannot be taken for granted that we generally perceive situations as the object of practical questions or that they "come into view for us" as such'.[57] Along this line, chapter two notably highlighted the extent to which a 'lack of aspiration'[58] can disrupt this cycle of dynamic responses; chapter three introduced us to the professional who sees 'the usual person in the usual place'; and chapter six highlighted the 'moral risk' inherent in the extent to which law, as a normative framework, can also 'mask practical questions':

> at the same time, the concept of masking is supposed to indicate that what is at issue is not merely a subjective misapprehension but something that can be true of a situation as well as of the agent who finds herself in it.[59]

The 'situations' made possible by personalised optimisation tools go one crucial step further than the many normative frameworks that define the self's relationship to others (from law and professional codes to social and moral norms). Such optimised environments solidify that relationship in a way that can be said to preclude onwards experimentation. How so? In both optimised and non-optimised environments, the process of socialisation contributes to a degree of habit rigidification:[60] we align ourselves with dominant patterns of behaviour, in the same way as well-trodden paths get greater footfall. What differs is the extent to which chance encounters and real-world events can turn into opportunities for experimentation.

alienation does not consist in the solidifying of relationships per se – what is alienating is the halting of experimentation': Rahel Jaeggi, *Alienation* (Columbia UP 2014).

[55] Erik Rietveld, Damiaan Denys and Maarten Van Westen, 'Ecological-Enactive Cognition as engaging with a field of relevant affordances' in *The Oxford Handbook of 4E Cognition* (OUP 2018) 5. The term 'form of life' is, of course, borrowed from Wittgenstein.

[56] '[A]ll living beings are affective beings and there will always be a field of significant affordances soliciting the human being': ibid 12.

[57] Jaeggi, *Alienation.*

[58] Julia Annas, *Intelligent Virtue* (Kindle Edition edn, OUP 2011) loc 221–22.

[59] Jaeggi, *Alienation.*

[60] 'This solidifying [...] can also occur in relations that, at the beginning, we consciously decided to enter into. Rigidification leads to what I have called the masking of practical questions. Even if someone has at some point posed such practical questions, she can at a later point stop posing them' (ibid).

Just as the 'moral risk' inherent in law's institutionalised adaptation to change[61] can be moderated – in some democracies at least – by demonstrations, political campaigns and acts of civil disobedience, some personal or metaphorical encounters do succeed in reaching otherwise 'enclaved' individuals.[62] These events and encounters can engender what Reed describes as an experience of 'self-doubt'.[63] For the latter experiences to generate a process of gradual intuitions refinement, and thereby hone our perceptual and evaluative habits, we need to be able to 'toy' with a variety of stances. To construct discussion fora that support such an iterative, inherently fallible learning process is never easy.[64] Within an algorithmically optimised environment that transforms a 'person's doing' – our past machine-readable behaviour – into a 'being', the construction of such fora becomes downright impractical. There is no such thing as 'toying' with a stance when the latter becomes irretrievably associated with the profile used to optimise both our online and offline experiences.

Here it helps to consider both the parallels and differences with the alienation that results from being trapped in roles we feel unable to challenge:

> Men fix women to feminine roles and vice versa – less harmless. In such cases specific social roles and specific patterns of behaviour are hypostasised and made into a person's 'being'. Here a part (a single role) is taken to be the whole (the person), and the specific patterns of behaviour tied to it are reified into qualities that become inseparably tied to the person. A person's doing is made into a being [...] – a field of possibility is taken away from her, the possibility of (also) determining herself differently – the possibility to be (also) something different.[65]

In both optimised and non-optimised environments, the alienated person lacks the resources necessary to being able to challenge the expectations (or stigma) associated with that role. That role comes to define her in ways she feels powerless to resist, in a striking parallel with the 'sense of self' vulnerability scenarios highlighted in chapter three. Yet in those scenarios – as in most 'non-optimised' environments – events or encounters with others can nevertheless unmask a field of possibilities in a way that allows for gradual, experiment-based learning. It is the possibility of such iterative experimentation that is taken away in profile-based, optimised environments. It is because and to the extent that we cannot

[61] See chapter six.

[62] Whether they be personal or metaphorical, such encounters can lead to what Lear refers to as 'ironic disruptions', which unsettle the beliefs and aspirations that structured our participation in various social practices, whether as a citizen, teacher or member of a faith group, to refer to two of Lear's examples. These unsettling events or encounters can lead to a feeling that 'none of this' is truly being a teacher, that among 'all the teachers, there never was a teacher', or 'among all the Christians, no Christian': Jonathan Lear, *A Case for Irony* (Harvard UP 2011) 4–24.

[63] Robert C Reed, 'Euthyphro's elenchus experience: Ethical expertise and self-knowledge' (2013) 16 *Ethical Theory and Moral Practice* 245.

[64] Chapter five notably referred to the inter-disciplinary discussion fora that have become commonplace within medical practice.

[65] Jaeggi, *Alienation*.

make things 'always again become different from how [they are]'[66] that tools like social media platforms often rob the encounters they do facilitate of their transformative power.

This need not be so. The next section explores the potential inherent in 'ensemble contestability', as a tool designed to help individuals (and groups) 'negotiate [...] what they reciprocally make each other into'.[67]

III. ENSEMBLE CONTESTABILITY

A. Case Study

This section[68] compares four different ways of designing a system that is trained to predict educational needs[69] and personalise remote assignments of high school students. Each design instantiates a particular way of interpreting the demand for an 'interpretable'[70] system. This education provision example is chosen for two reasons. First, the fact that desired outcomes are not necessarily known is important. In contrast to mortgage risk assessment or job recruitment tools, where users are faced with a binary 'approval / non-approval' outcome (it is clear which of the two outcomes users would rather have), users' incentives to critically engage with the outputs of a tool like this education optimisation example are less evident. Many of the efforts to emphasise the importance of features such as 'counterfactual explanations'[71] have focused on tools such as mortgage assessments. This narrow focus has contributed to a lack of attention to the challenges inherent in fostering contestability of long-term, non-binary optimisation tools.

The other reason behind this choice of example is negative: in many of the other long-term, non-binary optimisation tools, users' and service providers' incentives have too few points of intersection (if any). As an example, it is difficult to conceive of social media platform users whose reasons to rely on those platforms are aligned with the 'maximise user engagement' imperative that presides over the design of these platforms. This discrepancy makes

[66] Ibid.

[67] Ibid.

[68] This section borrows from Sylvie Delacroix, 'Diachronic interpretability and machine learning systems' (2022) forthcoming *Journal of Cross-disciplinary Research in Computational Law*.

[69] For a survey of the potential (and pitfalls) inherent in data-intensive technologies deployed within an education context, see Mireille Hildebrandt, 'Learning as a Machine: Crossovers between humans and machines' (2017) 4 *Journal of Learning Analytics* 18.

[70] The contrast between different ways of understanding 'interpretability' is discussed in Delacroix, 'Diachronic interpretability'.

[71] Sandra Wachter, Brent Mittelstadt and Chris Russell, 'Counterfactual explanations without opening the black box: Automated decisions and the GDPR' (2017) 31 *Harvard Journal of Law & Technology* 841.

it implausible to consider the development of tools that go beyond 'mere' individual, punctual explanation features, whose limits will be illustrated in examples 1 and 2 below. While 1 and 2 (wrongly) assume that normative agency is adequately preserved through the individual provision of 'explanations', 3 and 4 may be seen as driven by a concern to facilitate contestability at an individual (3) and collective (4) level respectively. The latter, collective contestability mechanisms are argued to be key to preserving the 'prerogative and means' of (re)shaping a socio-cultural landscape that is increasingly structured by algorithmic optimisation tools.

1. Because of a medical condition that makes school attendance difficult, Sophie's twin children, Aisha and Paul, are following a remote high school learning program that claims to deliver superior results compared to traditional remote schooling. It does so by optimising the timing and selection of educational content based on Aisha and Paul's respective profiles. When Aisha asks why she gets far less challenging science lessons than Paul, the course coordinator sends her a link to a website that can generate a simple approximation of the decision-making algorithm that informed the content selection decision (just how much that algorithm was relied on is left unsaid). To produce such a 'local' approximation of the overall model, one needs to narrow down the domain (and extent) of the variables deemed relevant. This narrowing-down process is judgement-based, and will significantly affect the substance, accuracy[72] and clarity of the explanation.[73]
   Assessment: Aisha does not know what to make of the 'explanation' she has been given. Neither of these explanations empower her to effect change.
2. In response to her query regarding the science lessons, the course coordinator explains to Aisha that had her recent psychological test results been different, she would probably have been given harder materials. As it stands, her psychological profile suggests that she does not respond well to very challenging content or tasks. As such, the content and tasks she is assigned are designed to be only marginally harder than what she has successfully achieved previously. The course coordinator also includes an (anonymised) reference to other past pupils who were given very similar science content, so that she may compare herself and possibly reach out to them.

[72] This accuracy issue is sometimes referred to as the 'fidelity' of an explanatory approximation of a machine learning system. The degree of fidelity depends on how well it mimics the system it is meant to explain. See notably Alan B Tickle and others, 'The truth will come to light: Directions and challenges in extracting the knowledge embedded within trained artificial neural networks' (1998) 9 *IEEE Transactions on Neural Networks* 1057, 1058.

[73] The difficulties and limitations inherent in the production of such 'local' models are outlined in detail in Wachter, Mittelstadt and Russell, 'Counterfactual explanations'.

Assessment: The counterfactual explanation given in 2 is problematic not only because it does not do anything to improve Aisha's degree of agency within her education program. It may also become a harmful, self-fulfilling prophecy.

3. The course coordinator refers Aisha to a set of three different education personalisation algorithms. In contrast to the system Z favoured by the course coordinator, system X does not allow psychological tests results to influence the selection of content and tasks. System Y comes in two versions: one trained on data generated by girls-only schools, and one trained on data generated by boys-only schools. Aisha is struck by the very different content recommendations issued by each system. As a result, she starts questioning the extent to which she is well served by the 'not too challenging' approach.
   Assessment: Aisha may ask her course coordinator to switch to the system trained on data generated by girls-only schools for a while, to see how she fares, as she suspects she is not that averse to challenging content.
4. Not only is Aisha's questioning the adequacy of the 'not too challenging' science content fed back into system Z, the students are also regularly switched from one personalisation system to another. Every time this switch takes place, students are notified and asked to reflect upon the extent to which they felt adequately challenged, motivated etc. They then provide such feedback in both a formalised (scale of 1 to 10) and non-formalised way, describing in their own words their experience. Similar but separate feedback is open to both parents and course coordinators. Students, teachers, parents and the wider community are encouraged to discuss their views on the criteria and objectives that should drive education in discussion boards, online fora etc, which soon feed into wider societal debates.
   Assessment: The rationale behind 4 – rather than 3 – takes its roots in the extent to which our drive to experiment and 'perceive a situation as the object of practical questions' (to refer back to Jaeggi's analysis) will soon dry out if it is not nurtured by wider, emergent societal debates. Aisha's questioning stance in 3 cannot be taken for granted. Unless debates about the shape and values underlying the provision of education are fostered, the comparison between differently trained systems may become akin to the comparison between different types of candies: we may not be bothered to care, or we may tire of the 'normative labour' involved in having an opinion. Because it places end-users and their feedback 'in the learning loop', this method is sometimes referred to as 'interactive machine learning' or 'IML'.[74] Aside from potentially improving the system's

[74] 'Although humans are an integral part of the learning process (the provide labels, rankings etc.), traditional machine learning systems used in these applications are agnostic to the fact that inputs/outputs are from/for humans. In contrast, interactive machine learning places end-users in the learning loop (end users is an integral part of the learning process), observing the result of learning and

learning performance (assuming adequate monitoring), such a method has the advantage of addressing the 'normative holiday' risk mentioned in earlier chapters.

B. From 'Passive' and Individualist Explanations to Ensemble Contestability

Example 4 in the previous section seeks to create built-in opportunities for collective feedback and debate about the nature and design of non-binary, long-term optimisation tools. This debate would remain very abstract without an ability to compare the outcomes of models trained differently. This is where so-called 'ensemble contestability' features come in. They are thus called to flag their borrowing from parts of 'ensemble models' techniques.

These techniques rely on the parallel running of one learning algorithm (or 'base learner') on different data subsets. These techniques' degree of rigour depends in large part on the way these data subsets are selected (and subsequent outcome differences resolved). When combined with 'bootstrap sampling' methodologies,[75] these ensemble techniques can notably help reduce the risk of overfitting.[76]

As a concrete way of taking on board the need to develop systems that not only make possible but foster contestability, 'ensemble contestability' features only loosely borrow from the above techniques. Because the aim has little to do with the risk of overfitting, the learning algorithms that are run in parallel could just as well be trained in a slightly different fashion[77] rather than on different data subsets (they may for instance have different constraints imposed on the optimisation process). What matters is that the resolution process is taken out. Rather than combining the results of each 'base learner' (whether through 'voting', 'averaging' or otherwise), emphasis would be placed on documenting the factors that lead to each of the base learners' outcomes, in an 'agonistic Machine Learning' spirit, to borrow Hildebrandt's phrase.[78]

providing input meant to improve the learning outcome. Canonical applications of IML include scenarios involving humans interacting with robots to teach them to perform certain tasks, humans helping virtual agents play computer games by giving them feedback on their performance': Wendell Wallach and Colin Allen, *Moral Machines: Teaching Robots Right from Wrong* (OUP 2008).

[75] There are various ways of extracting those data subsets from the larger data set. 'Bootstrap sampling' or 'bagging' (which randomly draws data subsets, thus allowing one data point to potentially re-appear in several subsets) is frequently relied on.

[76] In statistics, overfitting is 'the production of an analysis that corresponds too closely or exactly to a particular set of data, and may therefore fail to fit additional data or predict future observations reliably' (OxfordDictionaries.com).

[77] Such techniques are sometimes referred to as multiple classifier systems.

[78] Mireille Hildebrandt, 'Privacy as protection of the incomputable self: From agnostic to agonistic machine learning' (2019) 20 *Theoretical Inquiries in Law* 83 suggests that 'one way of protecting our privacy is to require what I call "agonistic machine learning', i.e., demanding that companies or

By facilitating the comparison of 'shadow'[79] systems, such 'ensemble contestability' features would put end-users in a position where they may appreciate concretely the impact of different training datasets and/or different optimising constraints. This 'ensemble contestability' aspect would ideally be accompanied by interactive features. These features would allow end-users to 'interrogate, investigate, scrutinize the system'.[80] Again, the importance of this interactive dimension stems from the nature of the practices within which the ML agent is deployed. The (re)articulation of the conflicting values at the heart of education or criminal justice practices does not proceed *ex nihilo*. It is nurtured by the 'imperfect rationalisations'[81] characteristic of our intuitive, ethical grasp of a situation (chapter two). The habits that structure these 'imperfect rationalisations' need to be continuously honed. To convey what is at stake in fostering interactive contestability, the following passage from Williams' 'Conflict of values' is worth quoting in full:

> [T]he public order, if it is to carry conviction, and also not to flatten human experience, has to find ways in which it can be adequately related to private sentiment, which remains more 'intuitive' and open to conflict than public rules can be. For the intuitive condition is not only a state which private understanding can live with, but a state which it must have as part of its life, if that life is going to have any density or conviction and succeed in being that worthwhile kind of life which human beings lack unless they feel more than they can say, and grasp more than they can explain.[82]

To design ML systems meant for ethically or legally significant contexts that are equipped with such interactive, 'ensemble contestability' features may sound like a tall order. Particularly so if 'AI researchers [are used to] building explanatory agents for [them]selves, rather than for the intended users'.[83] Hopefully the above has hinted at the extent to which such design choices are not just a matter of instrumental success. They are also a matter of preserving what is distinctive, and inherently valuable, about those ethically and legally significant practices: at their heart are our ongoing, collective efforts to continually (re)shape our axiological habitats.

governments that base decisions on machine learning must explore and enable alternative ways of datafying and modelling the same event, person or action'.

[79] I am grateful to Eric Meissner for suggesting this term.

[80] '[U]nlike simple contestation in which disagreement or attempts to shape the decision-making process may be asynchronous, pursued through outside channels, or otherwise externalized, contestability is built into the system to support iteration on the decision-making process. This makes contestability a deep system property: the ability to interrogate, investigate, scrutinize the system throughout the process of coming to a joint decision between human and algorithm. It must surface information to the user but also support interaction with and co-construction of the decision making process': Kristen Vaccaro and others, *Contestability in algorithmic systems* (2019).

[81] Bernard Williams, 'Conflicts of value' in *Moral Luck: Philosophical Papers* (CUP 1981).

[82] Ibid 82.

[83] Tim Miller, Piers Howe and Liz Sonenberg, 'Explainable AI: Beware of inmates running the asylum or: How I learnt to stop worrying and love the social and behavioural sciences' (2017) arXiv preprint arXiv:171200547.

IV. BOTTOM-UP DATA TRUSTS

When one switches from personalised education provision systems to current social media platforms, the 'habitat co-construction' ideal that informs ensemble contestability sounds like a quixotic idea at best. Power asymmetries are too great – and too entrenched – for the introduction of such ensemble contestability features to have any degree of plausibility. If such habitat co-construction endeavours are to get off the ground, we need to target what makes these platforms' power[84] possible in the first place: personal data collection.

In Europe, the duties imposed by the GDPR on data controllers stem in part from an acknowledgement of the power imbalances – and concomitant vulnerabilities[85] – at stake. While some early voices in data privacy law advocated extensive reliance on property law,[86] today the 'law and doctrine on human rights' are 'generally regarded as providing the principal normative basis'[87] for the GDPR. This turn to human rights reflects the fundamental nature of the harms that can ensue from – and vulnerabilities concomitant with – the exploitation of personal data. Not only are such harms and vulnerabilities ill-addressed through post-hoc, material compensation; they are also difficult, if not impossible, to attend to through individual vigilance alone.

Today the exercise of the data rights granted by the GDPR arguably demands a degree of pro-active engagement that is out of reach for many individuals. Aside from the fact that obtaining an adequate response to an access request (on the basis of one's 'right to access'[88]) is often an arduous process, many people remain unaware of their data rights. A study analysing the replies to a number of access requests highlights that 'in most cases a request for information about specific data in an initial data request is ignored, while follow up requests get an individualised reply more often. Sometimes a follow up request does receive an answer with data that was previously withheld'.[89] Most importantly, despite the fact that a right to access has been in place for nearly 20 years, some large organisations processing personal data reported that they had never received an access request. As a way forward, this study argues that 'collective use of the

[84] Soshana Zuboff is one of the many scholars who have delved into the social, cultural and structural factors that have contributed to endowing social media platforms with considerable regulatory power: Shoshana Zuboff, *The Age of Surveillance Capitalism* (Profile Books 2019).

[85] The nature of these vulnerabilities is strikingly similar to the 'sense of self' vulnerability outlined in chapter three.

[86] Alan F Westin, *Privacy and Freedom* (Atheneum 1967).

[87] Lee A Bygrave, *Data Privacy Law* (OUP 2014).

[88] The right of access (Article 15 of the GDPR) is wider in scope than the right to portability (Article 20 of the GDPR), which is limited to information that has been 'provided' to a controller, actively or passively, and processed on the basis of consent (or performance of a contract).

[89] Rene Mahieu, and Hadi Asghari, and Michel van Eeten, 'Collectively exercising the right of access: Individual effort, societal effect' (2018) 7 *Internet Policy Review*.

right of access can help shift the power imbalance between individual citizens and organisations in favour of the citizen'.[90]

As a concrete way of addressing the above concerns, a data trust[91] is a legal structure that enables groups of individuals to pool their data rights (or data) into an organisation – the data trust. Acting as an independent, professional[92] layer between the data collectors and us – the data subjects – the data trustee is then tasked with leveraging those rights to obtain better terms and conditions from service providers and/or negotiate (and monitor) a variety of data sharing agreements. Bound by a fiduciary obligation of undivided loyalty towards the beneficiaries of the trust, data trustees act as stewards of the data rights vested in the trust.[93] This stewardship role is compatible with a wide variety of bottom-up participatory models: some data trusts may reflect a preference for wide delegation, while others will be run in a manner similar to a cooperative. The possibility of choice[94] opens the door to a level of debate and grassroots engagement that stands in sharp contrast to that enabled by today's 'one size fits all' approach to data governance.

What matters, for the purpose of this book, is the construction of an infrastructure that encourages bottom-up participatory practices and normative experimentation. Without such an infrastructure, opportunities to learn from and challenge the data-reliant tools that form such a big part of our shared habitat are all too likely to give way to widespread retrenchment to ossified modes of thought and behaviour. When the rigidification of the habits underlying these modes of thoughts or behaviour is such as to compromise the possibility of onwards individual and collective transformation, the resulting alienation is arguably graver than the 'law-enabled' kind surveyed in chapter six.

[90] Ibid. Along a similar line, Veale and others discuss both the desirability and challenges inherent in the development of some automated platform 'to enable data subjects to utilise their rights': Michael Veale and others, 'Automating data rights' in David Eyers and others (eds), *Towards Accountable Systems* (Dagstuhl Reports, Schloss Dagstuhl 2018).

[91] Sylvie Delacroix and Neil D Lawrence, 'Bottom-up data trusts: Disturbing the "one size fits all" approach to data governance' (2019) 9 *International Data Privacy Law* 236

[92] On the need for such 'professional' status, see Sylvie Delacroix, 'To protect our social selves, we need data trustees' (*Centre for International Governance Innovation*, 2020), www.cigionline.org/articles/protect-our-social-selves-we-need-data-trustees, accessed 12 September 2021.

[93] For more details see https://datatrusts.uk and Delacroix and Lawrence, 'Bottom-up data trusts'.

[94] Individuals and groups may switch from one trust to another as and when their aspirations change.

Conclusion

OF THE THREE main answers to the provocative question mark in the title of this book, one is typically voiced with more indignation than the others. Those who dismiss the possibility of 'habitual ethics' as a contradiction in terms will be keen to emphasise the extent to which our capacity for ethical agency is precisely what enables us to rise above the causal determinants of our lives, including the random habits we pick up along the way. To assert the possibility (or worse, desirability) of habitual ethics would be to downplay the importance of this human capacity to call into question commonly accepted practices.

The two other types of answers are more blasé than indignant. If ethics is nothing but a set of evaluative attitudes that we develop as we try to find our way around the world, there is nothing remarkable about the possibility of 'habitual ethics'. Just like other attitudes, one would expect some of those attitudes to become habitual under the weight of repetition. From this perspective, the above, indignant stance proceeds from a naïve endeavour to imbue ethics with a degree of objectivity it simply cannot have.

At the other end of the meta-ethical spectrum, the possibility of 'habitual ethics' can be deemed almost as unremarkable. That our capacity for ethical discernment relies on the gradual, habit-dependent education of our senses is all but a given for a large, Aristotelian strand of moral philosophy. From that perspective, there is no need for this book's provocative question mark; nor is there any need for quite so much emphasis on the preservation of habit plasticity. Just like we had better get rid of bad habits, we will want to cling on to the good ones: habit adaptability is beside the point.

Because it celebrates the habit-dependent, pre-reflective intelligence without which we would be incapable of all sorts of things – including ethical agency – this book does have key elements in common with the Aristotelian strand just mentioned. Yet this book's delineation of the conditions that can compromise this pre-reflective intelligence proceeds from a less optimistic stance when it comes to the adequacy of our 'habituated' grasp of normative significance. It is not just that we need to keep honing the habits of thought and perception that make certain features of our environment stand out. This is true of all the skills that have a significant non-cognitive dimension (chapter two). It is also that what this honing process needs to 'track' does not always present itself as an easily articulated goal or given feature of our environment.

The 'responsiveness to the other' articulated in chapter five emphasises the necessarily uncertain nature of what it is we need to be attentive to in order to live up to our ethical responsibility. There is no telling in advance who the 'overlooked other' is. Looking back, it is easy to be mortified by the myriad 'others' whom our past practices have turned a blind eye to. It is less easy to carry forward the implications of this fallibility for our present practices. Because any abstract, reasons-based analysis of a situation is liable to perpetuate habitual salience, it needs to be complemented by an ethics of attention. This ethics of attention demands a way of having habits that is flexible enough to be receptive to the presence of the otherwise unacknowledged 'other'.

Chapter three outlined the challenges inherent in sustaining such an ethics of attention in the context of professional practice. Rising to the demands entailed by the situational vulnerability that often characterises lay-professional encounters demands a willingness to engage with each client / pupil / patient in a way that leaves the exact nature of one's duties as a professional open to redefinition. Such openness is not without costs: it needs to be balanced with the need for some emotional defence mechanisms. The need for such defence stems from the same roots as those which make us reliant on habit in the first place. In the never-ending process of self-(re)construction, we need 'a structure weak enough to yield to an influence, but strong enough not to yield all at once'.[1]

Barricading our ethical selves behind a wall of carefully curated, unyielding reasons won't help. The dangers inherent in such barricading strategies can be felt on a quotidian basis, though they are poignantly illustrated in some of the diaries of Holocaust perpetrators. Chapter four opened some of these diaries. The 'it is a weakness not to be able to stand the sight of dead people; the best way of overcoming it is to do it more often. Then it becomes a habit'[2] (this concludes a German pharmacist's endeavour to justify the horrors he participates in) triggered much of the research at the heart of this book.

When one considers what might stop us from waking up to the ethical demands of a particular situation – and possibly the need for change – habit features prominently. This has contributed to moral and legal philosophy's frequent disdain for habit, which is often 'left' to the province of sociology. Yet as soon as one considers more carefully the wide spectrum of the habitual – and the different ways of having a habit – the above disdain appears ill-judged.

This dismissive stance not only results in a poor grasp of the moral risks inherent in institutional structures whose lack of opportunities for co-construction limit the extent to which our perceptual and evaluative habits can be continuously honed (chapters six and seven). Haughty indifference towards the

[1] William James, *Psychology: Briefer Course* (Harvard UP 1984).

[2] Herlinde Pauer-Studer and J David Velleman, 'Distortions of Normativity' (2011) 14 *Ethical Theory and Moral Practice* 329.

habitual also results in implausible accounts of social, moral and legal normativity (they are implausible because and to the extent that they presuppose deliberative agency all the way through). Chapter one emphasised the central role played by pre-reflective agency in any 'liberal' naturalist narrative that takes us from human beings with needs, desires and aspirations all the way to internalised standards of right and wrong.

The second part of this book considered two types of 'macro', systemic factors that can compromise the extent to which our pre-reflective selves are in a position to support – or trigger – the deliberative work involved in many social transformations. Chapter six focused on the design of legal institutions. When these institutions work effectively, they free us of significant normative labour. The ways in which they do so is crucial. While some institutions are designed in such a way as to foster high degrees of critical engagement, others are less so. In such contexts, just as the opportunities for the continued honing of our 'imperfectly rationalised intuitions' become scarce, the temptation to surrender to the comfort of demobilised practical reasoning gets higher. Since the resulting retrenchment to habitual modes of thought is unlikely to be accompanied by opportunities to learn from and challenge one's environment, habit rigidification often follows. Unlike the goal-oriented habits that nurture legal practice, such rigid habits are easily exploited by 'unscrupulous shepherds bent on a slaughterhouse ending', to use Hart's metaphor.

The type of retrenchment facilitated by the algorithmic systems considered in chapter seven is harder to pin down. In an environment that has been invisibly optimised according to our machine-readable past, the uncertainty that normally characterises the way an agent is moulded by (and moulds) her 'habitat' is replaced by carefully orchestrated endeavours to maximise user engagement with online platforms. This orchestration leaves little room for the kind of learning and experimentation that hinges on encounters with 'the other'.

This need not be so. It is never too late to insist on designing structures that foster rather than hinder bottom-up, critical engagement. The 'bottom-up data trusts' outlined in chapter seven are but one example of the kind of infrastructure that needs to be in place if we are to learn novel forms of participation. Yet it is a particularly salient one, given the extent to which the current top-down regime of data governance has all but reinforced a powerful habit of passivity: who hasn't ever clicked away yet another 'data consent' pop-up? To counteract such deeply ingrained, habitual retrenchment from civic life, the downcast cataloguing of the various factors that contribute to such retrenchment won't do.

The last chapter's resolutely practical stance – in an otherwise largely philosophical inquiry – should be read as an invitation. Just as the 'ensemble contestability' features that are put forward as a way to not only enable but incentivise the contestability of algorithmic tools deployed in morally loaded contexts won't go very far without active input from system designers, there are myriad ways in which we can each change some feature of our environment so as to challenge the habitual retrenchment mentioned above. No matter how fancy, philosophical inquiry won't make the question mark in this book's title redundant: only we can, provided we insist on practices that foster rather than impede the 'work of attention'.

Bibliography

Aboulafia M, 'Introduction' in Aboulafia M (ed), *Habermas and pragmatism* (Routledge 2002).

Adams CD and Dickinson A, 'Instrumental responding following reinforcer devaluation' (1981) 33 *The Quarterly Journal of Experimental Psychology* Section B 109.

Albertzart M, 'Principle-based moral judgement' (2013) 16 *Ethical Theory and Moral Practice* 339.

Amoore L, *Cloud Ethics: Algorithms and the Attributes of Ourselves and Others* (Duke UP 2020).

Anderson JH and Honneth A, 'Autonomy, vulnerability, recognition, and justice' in Christman J and Anderson J (eds), *Autonomy and the Challenges to Liberalism: New Essays* (CUP 2005).

Andreou A and others, *Investigating ad transparency mechanisms in social media: A case study of Facebook's explanations* (NDSS 2018 – Network and Distributed System Security Symposium, San Diego, United States, February 2018).

Anleu SR and Mack K, 'Magistrates' everyday work and emotional labour' (2005) 32 *Journal of Law and Society* 590.

Annas J, *Intelligent Virtue* (Kindle edn, OUP 2011).

Anscombe GEM, 'Rules, rights, and promises' (1978) 3 *Midwest Studies in Philosophy* 318.

Anscombe GEM, *Intention* (2nd edn, Harvard University Press 2000).

Apel K-O, 'Regarding the relationship of morality, law and democracy: On Habermas's Philosophy of Law (1992) from a transcendental-pragmatic point of view' in Aboulafia M, Bookman M and Kemp C (eds), *Habermas and Pragmatism* (Taylor & Francis Group 2002).

Arendt H, *Eichmann in Jerusalem: A Report on the Banality of Evil* (Penguin 1994).

Arendt H, *Responsibility and Judgment* (Schocken Books 2003).

Ayer AJ, 'On the analysis of moral judgements', *Philosophical Essays* (Springer 1972).

Ayer AJ, *Language, Truth and Logic* (Penguin 2001).

Baker LR, *Naturalism and the First-person Perspective* (OUP 2013).

Bankowski Z and Del Mar M, *The Moral Imagination and the Legal Life: Beyond Text in Legal Education* (Routledge 2016).

Barberá P, 'Social media, echo chambers, and political polarization' in Persily N and Tucker JA (eds), *Social Media and Democracy: The State of the Field and Prospects for Reform* (CUP 2020).

Bargh JA, 'Auto-motives: Preconscious determinants of social interaction' in *Handbook of Motivation and Cognition: Foundations of Social Behavior, Vol 2* (The Guilford Press 1990).

Bargh JA, 'The four horsemen of automacity: Awareness, intention, efficiency, and control in social cognition' in Wyer RS and Srull TK (eds), *Handbook of Social Cognition, Vol 1* (Erlbaum 1994).

Bargh JA, 'The automaticity of everyday life' in Wyer RS (ed), *The Automaticity of Everyday Life*, Advances in social cognition, Vol 10 (Lawrence Erlbaum Associates Publishers 1997).

Bargh JA and Gollwitzer PM, 'Environmental control of goal-directed action: Automatic and strategic contingencies between situations and behavior' in *Integrative Views of Motivation, Cognition, and Emotion*, Nebraska symposium on motivation, Vol 41 (University of Nebraska Press 1994).

Barnhill A, 'What is manipulation?' in Coons C and Weber M (eds), *Manipulation: Theory and Practice* (OUP 2014).

Barrington K and Pilley P, *Playing it Straight* (S Paul 1968).

Barzun CL, 'Jerome Frank, Lon Fuller, and a romantic pragmatism' (2017) 29 *Yale Journal of Law & the Humanities* 129.

Bauman Z, *Modernity and the Holocaust* (Cornell UP 1989).

Bennett J, *Empathic Vision: Affect, Trauma, and Contemporary Art* (Stanford UP 2005).

Bennett J, *The Enchantment of Modern Life: Attachments, Crossings, and Ethics* (Princeton UP 2016).

Bennett T and others, 'Habit and habituation: Governance and the social' (2013) 19 *Body & Society* 3.

Benson HH, *Socratic Wisdom: The Model of Knowledge in Plato's Early Dialogues* (OUP 2000).

Bernacer J and Murillo JI, 'The Aristotelian conception of habit and its contribution to human neuroscience' (2014) 8 *Frontiers in Human Neurosciences* 883.

Blackburn S, *Ruling Passions* (Clarendon Press 1998).

Blackburn S, 'Normativity a la mode' (2001) 5 *Journal of Ethics: An International Philosophical Review* 139.

Bloom P, *Against Empathy: The Case for Rational Compassion* (Random House 2017).

Boncompagni A, *Wittgenstein and Pragmatism: On Certainty in the Light of Peirce and James* (Palgrave Macmillan 2016).

Bourdieu P, *Outline of a Theory of Practice* (CUP 1977).

Boyd D and Kohlberg L, 'The is-ought problem: A developmental perspective' (1973) 8 *Zygon®* 358.

Bratman ME, 'Shared cooperative activity' (1992) 101 *The Philosophical Review* 327.

Braude HD, *Intuition in Medicine: A Philosophical Defense of Clinical Reasoning* (University of Chicago Press 2012).

Brett N, 'Human habits' (1981) 11 *Canadian Journal of Philosophy* 357.

Bridges J, 'Rule-following skepticism, properly so called' in Conant J and Kern A (eds), *Varieties of Skepticism: Essays after Kant, Wittgenstein, and Cavell* (De Gruyter 2014).

Brink DO, *Moral Realism and the Foundations of Ethics* (CUP 1989).

Brison SJ, 'Relational autonomy and freedom of expression' in Mackenzie C and Stoljar N (eds), *Relational Autonomy: Feminist Perspectives on Autonomy, Agency, and the Social Self* (OUP 1999).

Bruns A, 'Filter bubble' (2019) 8 *Internet Policy Review*.

Bygrave LA, *Data Privacy Law* (OUP 2014).

Cameron J and Geidner N, 'Something old, something new, something borrowed from something blue: Experiments on dual viewing TV and Twitter' (2014) 58 *Journal of Broadcasting & Electronic Media* 400.

Carlisle C, 'Creatures of habit: The problem and the practice of liberation' (2006) 38 *Continental Philosophy Review* 19.

Carlisle C, 'Between freedom and necessity: Felix Ravaisson on habit and the moral life' (2010) 53 *Inquiry* 123.

Carlisle C, *On Habit* (Routledge 2014).

Chanan M, 'The Idea of Freedom' (*Solus Enterprises, Chanan Films*, 1972) www.youtube.com/watch?v=zJHIwnr3UlI.

Chase WG and Simon HA, 'The mind's eye in chess' (1973) Proceedings of the Eighth Annual Carnegie Symposium on Cognition, Held at the Carnegie-Mellon University, Pittsburgh, Pennsylvania, 19 May 1972.

Chemero A, 'An outline of a theory of affordances' (2003) 15 *Ecological Psychology* 181.

Chemero A, *Radical Embodied Cognitive Science* (MIT Press 2009).

Chesterton GK, 'The twelve men' in Chesterton GK (ed), *Tremendous Trifles* (Sheed & Ward 1955).

Chilovi S and Pavlakos G, 'The explanatory demands of grounding in law' (2021) *Pacific Philosophical Quarterly*.

Christian B and Griffiths T, *Algorithms to Live by: The Computer Science of Human Decisions* (Macmillan 2016).

Christman J, *The Politics of Persons: Individual Autonomy and Socio-historical Selves* (CUP 2009).

Chun WHK, *Updating to Remain the Same: Habitual New Media* (MIT Press 2016).

Clark A, *Being There: Putting Brain, Body, and World Together Again* (MIT Press 1997).

Clarke SG and Simpson E, *Anti-theory in Ethics and Moral Conservatism* (SUNY Press 1989).

Cohen AA, *The Tremendum: A Theological Interpretation of the Holocaust* (Continuum Publishing Co 1993).

Cohen J, *Configuring the Networked Self* (Yale UP 2012).

Colapietro V, 'Doing – and undoing – the done thing: Dewey and Bourdieu on habituation, agency, and transformation' (2004) 1 *Contemporary Pragmatism* 65.
Coleman J, 'Incorporationism, conventionality, and the practical difference thesis' in Coleman J (ed), *Hart's Postscript, Essays on the Postscript to the Concept of Law* (OUP 2001).
Coleman J, *The Practice of Principle: In Defence of a Pragmatist Approach to Legal Theory* (OUP 2001).
Costall A, 'Socializing affordances' (1995) 5 *Theory & Psychology* 467.
Cowley C, 'A new rejection of moral expertise' (2005) 8 *Medicine, Health Care, and Philosophy* 273.
Cowley C, 'Expertise, wisdom and moral philosophers: A response to Gesang. Jul 2012' (2012) 26 *Bioethics* 337.
Coxon AH (ed), *The Fragments of Parmenides* (Van Gorcum 1986).
Crandall B and Getchell-Reiter K, 'Critical decision method: A technique for eliciting concrete assessment indicators from the intuition of NICU nurses' (1993) 16 *Advances in Nursing Science* 42.
Crosthwaite JAN, 'Moral expertise: A problem in the professional ethics of professional ethicists' (1995) 9 *Bioethics* 361.
Csikszentmihalyi M, *Flow: The Psychology of Optimal Experience* (Harper and Row 1990).
Damasio A, *Descartes' Error: Emotion, Reason and the Human Brain* (Random House 2008).
Dancy J, 'Nonnaturalism' in Copp D (ed), *The Oxford Handbook of Ethical Theory* (OUP 2006).
Darwall SL, 'Internalism and agency' (1992) 6 *Philosophical Perspectives* 155.
Davidson D, *Essays on Actions and Events* (Clarendon Press 1980).
De Caro M and Macarthur D, 'Science, naturalism, and the problem of normativity' in De Caro M and Macarthur D (eds), *Naturalism and Normativity* (Columbia UP 2010).
De Caro M and Macarthur D (eds), *Naturalism and Normativity* (Columbia UP 2010).
de Montaigne M, *The Complete Essays* (Penguin Classics 1991).
de Tocqueville A, *Democracy in America* (Penguin 2003).
Del Mar M, 'The education of attention and encounter in the legal academy' in Bankowski Z and Del Mar M (eds), *The Moral Imagination and the Legal Life: Beyond Text in Legal Education* (Routledge 2016).
Delacroix S, 'Montaigne's inquiry into the sources of normativity' (2003) 16 *Canadian Journal of Law and Jurisprudence* 271.
Delacroix S, 'Schmitt's critique of Kelsenian normativism' (2005) 18 *Ratio Juris* 30.
Delacroix S, *Legal Norms and Normativity: An Essay in Genealogy* (Hart Publishing 2006).
Delacroix S, 'Meta-ethical agnosticism in legal theory: Mapping a way out' (2010) 1 *Jurisprudence* 225.
Delacroix S, 'Automated systems and the need for change' in Markou C and Deakin S (eds), *Is Law Computable?* (Hart Publishing 2020).
Delacroix S, 'To protect our social selves, we need data trustees' (Centre for International Governance Innovation, 2020), www.cigionline.org/articles/protect-our-social-selves-we-need-data-trustees accessed 12 September 2021.
Delacroix S, 'Professional Responsibility: Conceptual Rescue and Plea for Reform' [2022] 42 *Oxford Journal of Legal Studies* 1.
Delacroix S, 'Diachronic interpretability and machine learning systems' (2022) forthcoming *Journal of Cross-disciplinary Research in Computational Law*.
Delacroix S and Denvir C, 'Virtually teaching ethics' in Denvir C (ed), *Modernizing Legal Education* (CUP 2020).
Delacroix S and Lawrence ND, 'Bottom-up data trusts: Disturbing the "one size fits all" approach to data governance' (2019) 9 *International Data Privacy Law* 236.
DeSouza N, 'Pre-reflective ethical know-how' (2013) 16 *Ethical Theory and Moral Practice* 279.
Dewey J, *Human Nature and Conduct: An Introduction to Social Psychology* (G Allen & Unwin 1922).

Dogruel L, 'Too much information!? Examining the impact of different levels of transparency on consumers' evaluations of targeted advertising' (2019) 36 *Communication Research Reports* 383.

Douskos C, 'Deliberation and automaticity in habitual acts' (2018) 9 *Ethics in Progress*.

Dreyfus HL, *Alchemy and Artificial Intelligence* (Rand Corporation Santa Monica, California 1965).

Dreyfus HL, 'Heidegger's critique of the Husserl/Searle account of intentionality' (1993) *Social Research* 17.

Dreyfus HL, *Overcoming the Myth of the Mental: How Philosophers Can Profit from the Phenomenology of Everyday Expertise* (American Philosophical Association 2005).

Dreze J and Sen A, *India: Development and Participation* (OUP on Demand 2002).

Dror IE, 'The paradox of human expertise: Why experts get it wrong' in Kapur N (ed), *The Paradoxical Brain* (CUP 2011).

Durkheim E, *The Division of Labor in Society* (Simon and Schuster 2014).

Edelson L and others, *Universal Digital Ad Transparency* (2021).

Eisenach JA, Hanser AS and Gingrich N, *Readings in Renewing American Civilization* (McGraw-Hill 1993).

Eriksen C, *Moral Change: Dynamics, Structure, and Normativity* (Springer 2020).

Eslami M and others, 'User Attitudes towards Algorithmic Opacity and Transparency in Online Reviewing Platforms', *Proceedings of the 2019 CHI Conference on Human Factors in Computing Systems* (Association for Computing Machinery 2019).

Everitt BJ and Robbins TW, 'Neural systems of reinforcement for drug addiction: from actions to habits to compulsion' (2005) 8 *Nature Neuroscience* 1481.

Everitt BJ and Robbins TW, 'Drug addiction: Updating actions to habits to compulsions ten years on' (2016) 67 *Annual Review of Psychology* 23.

Eyal N, *Hooked: How to Build Habit-Forming Products* (Penguin 2014).

Faraji M, 'Learning with surprise: Theory and applications' (PhD thesis, École Polytechnique Fédérale de Lausanne 2016).

Faraji MJ, Preuschoff K and Gerstner W, 'Balancing new against old information: The role of puzzlement surprise in learning' (2018) 30(1) *Neural Computation* 34.

Feltovich PJ, Prietula MJ and Ericsson KA, 'Studies of expertise from psychological perspectives' (2006) *The Cambridge Handbook of Expertise and Expert Performance* 41.

Fineman MA, 'The vulnerable subject: Anchoring equality in the human condition' (2008) 20 *Yale Journal of Law and Feminism* 1.

Fink H, 'Three Sorts of Naturalism' (2006) 14 *European Journal of Philosophy* 202.

Fink H, 'Against ethical exceptionalism – through critical reflection on the history of use of the terms "ethics" and "morals" in philosophy' (2020) 21 *SATS*.

Finnegan W, 'Defending the Unabomber' *New Yorker* (March 16), www.newyorker.com/magazine/1998/03/16/defending-the-unabomber.

Foot P, *Natural Goodness* (Clarendon Press 2003).

Frensch PA and Sternberg RJ, 'Expertise and intelligent thinking: When is it worse to know better?' (1989) 5 *Advances in the Psychology of Human Intelligence* 157.

Fricker M, *Epistemic Injustice: Power and the Ethics of Knowing* (OUP 2007).

Fritz Z, Slowther A-M and Perkins GD, 'Resuscitation policy should focus on the patient, not the decision' (2017) 356 *BMJ* j813.

Fuller L, 'Positivism and fidelity to law: A reply to Professor Hart' (1958) 71 *Harvard Law Review* 630.

Garchar K, 'Imperfection, practice and humility in clinical ethics' (2012) 18 *Journal of Evaluation in Clinical Practice* 1051.

Gardner B, 'A review and analysis of the use of "habit" in understanding, predicting and influencing health-related behaviour' (2014) 9 *Health Psychology Review* 277.

Gesang B, 'Are moral philosophers moral experts?' (2010) 24 *Bioethics* 153.

Geschke D, Lorenz J and Holtz P, 'The triple-filter bubble: Using agent-based modelling to test a meta-theoretical framework for the emergence of filter bubbles and echo chambers' (2019) 58 *British Journal of Social Psychology* 129.

Geuss R, *History and Illusion in Politics* (CUP 2001).

Geuss R, *Outside Ethics* (Princeton UP 2009).

Gibson JJ, *The Ecological Approach to Visual Perception* (Houghton Mifflin 1979).

Giddens A, *Capitalism and Modern Social Theory: An Analysis of the Writings of Marx, Durkheim and Max Weber* (CUP 1971).

Gigerenzer G and Brighton H, 'Can hunches be rational' (2007) 4 *Journal of Law, Economics and Policy* 155.

Ginsborg H, 'Primitive normativity and skepticism about rules' (2011) 108 *Journal of Philosophy* 227.

Ginsborg H, 'Normativity and concepts' in D Star (ed), *The Oxford Handbook of Reasons and Normativity* (OUP 2018).

Glazer T, 'Epistemic violence and emotional misperception' (2019) 34 *Hypatia* 59.

Green L, 'Positivism and the inseparability of law and morals' (2008) 83 *NYUL Rev* 1035.

Grice P, *Studies in the Ways of Words* (Harvard UP 1989).

Grosz E, 'Habit today: Ravaisson, Bergson, Deleuze and us' (2013) 19 *Body & Society* 217.

Gulley N, *The Philosophy of Socrates* (MacMillan 1968).

Gurwitsch A, *Human Encounters in the Social World* (Duquesne UP 1979).

Habermas J, 'Reconciliation through the public use of reason' in C Cronin (ed), *The Inclusion of the Other: Studies in Political Theory* (Polity 1999) 58.

Habermas J, *The Future of Human Nature* (Polity 2003).

Haji R and Stock WG, 'User settings for advertising optimization on Facebook: Active customer participation or settings blindness?' (2021) 59 *Telematics and Informatics* 101548.

Hann G and Fertleman C, *The Child Protection Practice Manual* (OUP 2016).

Hansen MBN, *Feed Forward: On the Future of Twenty-First Century Media* (Chicago University Press 2015).

Hart HLA, 'Signs and words' (1952) 2 *The Philosophical Quarterly* 59.

Hart HLA, 'Analytical jurisprudence in mid-twentieth century: A reply to Professor Bodenheimer' (1956) 105 *University of Pennsylvania Law Review* 953.

Hart HLA, 'Positivism and the separation of law and morals' (1958) 71 *Harvard Law Review* 593.

Hart HLA, 'Social solidarity and the enforcement of morality' (1967) 35 *The University of Chicago Law Review* 1.

Hart HLA, 'Bentham and the demystification of the law' (1973) 36 *Modern Law Review* 2.

Hart HLA, *Essays in Jurisprudence and Philosophy* (Clarendon Press 1983).

Hart HLA, *The Concept of Law* (2nd edn, Clarendon Press 1994).

Hatley J, McLane J and Diehm C (eds), *Interrogating Ethics: Embodying the Good in Merleau-Ponty* (Duquesne UP 2006).

Heft H, *Ecological Psychology in Context: James Gibson, Roger Barker, and the Legacy of William James's Radical Empiricism* (Lawrence Erlbaum 2001).

Heidegger M, *The Basic Problems of Phenomenology* (Indiana UP 1988).

Hershovitz S, 'Wittgenstein on rules: The phantom menace' (2002) 22 *Oxford Journal of Legal Studies* 619.

Hetherington MJ, 'Putting polarization in perspective' (2009) 39 *British Journal of Political Science* 413.

Hildebrandt M, 'Defining profiling: A new type of knowledge?' in Hildebrandt M and Gutwirth S (eds), *Profiling the European Citizen: Cross-Disciplinary Perspectives* (Springer Netherlands 2008).

Hildebrandt M, *Smart Technologies and the End(s) of Law: Novel Entanglements of Law and Technology* (Elgar 2015).

Hildebrandt M, 'Learning as a machine: Crossovers between humans and machines' (2017) 4 *Journal of Learning Analytics* 18.
Hildebrandt M, 'Privacy as protection of the incomputable self: From agnostic to agonistic machine learning' (2019) 20 *Theoretical Inquiries in Law* 83.
Hochschild AR, *The Managed Heart* (University of California Press 2012).
Hogarth RM, *Educating Intuition* (University of Chicago Press 2001).
Hogarth RM, Lejarraga T and Soyer E, 'The two settings of kind and wicked learning environments' (2015) 24 *Current Directions in Psychological Science* 379.
Inbar Y, Pizarro D and Bloom P, 'Disgusting smells cause decreased liking of gay men' (2012) 12 *Emotion* 23.
Jaeggi R, *Alienation* (Columbia UP 2014).
Jaeggi R, *Critique of Forms of Life* (Harvard UP 2018).
James W, *Psychology: Briefer Course* (Harvard UP 1984).
James W, 'Pragmatism: A new name for some old ways of thinking' in *Pragmatism and Other Writings* (Penguin Classics 2000).
Joyce R, 'Expressivism and motivation internalism' (2002) 62 *Analysis* 336.
Kaczynski T, 'The Unabomber's manifesto: Industrial society and its future' (1995), http://besser.tsoa.nyu.edu/howard/Anarchism/Unabom/manifesto2.html.
Kahneman D, *Thinking, Fast and Slow* (Macmillan 2011).
Kahneman D and Klein G, 'Conditions for intuitive expertise: A failure to disagree' (2009) 64 *American Psychologist* 515.
Kass SJ, Cole KS and Stanny CJ, 'Effects of distraction and experience on situation awareness and simulated driving' (2007) 10 *Transportation Research* Part F: Traffic Psychology and Behaviour 321.
Kearney R, *Poetics of Imagining: Modern to Post-Modern* (Fordham UP 1998).
Kelsen H, *General Theory of Law and State* (Harvard UP 1949).
Kelsen H, *Pure Theory of Law* (University of California Press 1967).
Kennett J, 'Autism, empathy and moral agency' (2002) 52 *The Philosophical Quarterly* 340.
Kierkegaard S, *Works of Love* (Princeton UP 1995).
Kitcher P, *The Ethical Project* (Harvard UP 2011).
Kitcher P, *Preludes to Pragmatism: Toward a Reconstruction of Philosophy* (OUP 2012).
Klee E, Dressen W and Riess V, *"The Good Old Days": The Holocaust as Seen by Its Perpetrators and Bystanders* (Konecky & Konecky 1991).
Klein G, 'Naturalistic decision making' (2008) 50 *Human Factors: The Journal of the Human Factors and Ergonomics Society* 456.
Kohlberg L, 'Continuities in childhood and adult moral development revisited' in Baltes P and Schaie KW (eds), *Life-Span Developmental Psychology: Personality and Socialization* (Academic Press 1973).
Kohlberg L, 'Moral stages and moralization' in Lickona T (ed), *Moral Development and Behavior: Theory, Research, and Social Issues* (Holt, Rinehart and Winston 1976).
Kohlberg L, 'Kohlberg on moral development and moral education' in Munsey B (ed), *Moral Development, Moral Education, and Kohlberg: Basic Issues in Philosophy, Psychology, Religion, and Education* (Religious Education Press 1980).
Kohlberg L, *The Meaning and Measurement of Moral Development*, The Heinz Werner lectures (Clark UP 1981).
Kohlberg L and Mayer R, 'Development as the aim of education' (1972) 42 *Harvard Educational Review* 449.
Kosinski M, Stillwell D and Graepel T, 'Private traits and attributes are predictable from digital records of human behavior' (2013) 110 *Proceedings of the National Academy of Sciences*.
Kramer AD, Guillory JE and Hancock JT, 'Experimental evidence of massive-scale emotional contagion through social networks' (2014) 111 *Proceedings of the National Academy of Sciences* 8788.

Kripke SA, *Wittgenstein on Rules and Private Language: An Elementary Exposition* (Blackwell 1982).
Krishna N, 'Is goodness natural?' (2017) *Aeon* (28 November 2017).
Lacey N, *The Nightmare and the Noble Dream: A Life of HLA Hart* (OUP 2004).
Lally P and others, 'How are habits formed: Modelling habit formation in the real world' (2010) 40 *European Journal of Social Psychology* 998.
Lear J, *A Case for Irony* (Harvard UP 2011).
Leerssen P, 'The soap box as a black box: Regulating transparency in social media recommender systems' (2020) 11 *European Journal of Law and Technology*.
Leiboff M, *Towards a Theatrical Jurisprudence* (Routledge 2019).
Leiter B, *Naturalizing Jurisprudence: Essays on American Legal Realism and Naturalism in Legal Philosophy* (OUP 2007).
Leiter B, 'Normativity for naturalists' (2015) 25 *Philosophical Issues* 64.
Leiter B, *Moral Psychology with Nietzsche* (OUP, USA 2019).
Lenman J, 'Moral naturalism' (plato.stanford.edu, 2006).
Levinas E, *Totality and Infinity: An Essay on Exteriority* (Duquesne UP 1969).
Levy N and Bayne T, 'Doing without deliberation: automatism, Automaticity, and moral accountability' (2004) 16 *International Review of Psychiatry* 209.
Lewis DK, *Convention: A Philosophical Study* (Harvard UP 1963).
Lipshitz RM and others, 'Naturalistic decision making and organizations: Reviewing pragmatic science' (2006) 27 *Organization Studies* 925.
Lovibond S, *Ethical Formation* (Harvard UP 2002).
Luban D, 'Lawyers as upholders of human dignity (when they aren't busy assaulting it)' (2005) *University of Illinois Law Review* 815.
Lutz M and Lenman J, 'Moral naturalism' (*The Stanford Encyclopedia of Philosophy*, 2021), plato.stanford.edu/archives/spr2021/entries/naturalism-moral.
Mackenzie C, 'Imagining oneself otherwise' in Mackenzie C and Stoljar N (eds), *Relational Autonomy: Feminist Perspectives on Autonomy, Agency, and the Social Self* (OUP 1999).
Mackenzie C, 'The importance of relational autonomy and capabilities for an ethics of vulnerability' in Mackenzie C, Rogers W and Dodds S (eds), *Vulnerability: New Essays in Ethics and Feminist Philosophy* (OUP 2014).
Mackie JL, *Ethics: Inventing Right and Wrong* (Penguin Books 1990).
Mahieu RLP, Asghari H and van Eeten M, 'Collectively exercising the right of access: individual effort, societal effect' (2018) 7 *Internet Policy Review*.
Maier C, 'The unmasterable past: History, Holocaust, and German national identity' (1992) 21 *Theory and Society* 290.
Manning E, *The Minor Gesture* (Duke UP 2016).
Marmor A, 'Legal conventionalism' in Coleman J (ed), *Hart's Postscript, Essays on the Postscript to the Concept of Law* (OUP 2001).
McDowell J, *Mind and World: With a New Introduction by the Author* (Harvard UP 1996).
McDowell J, 'Précis of "Mind and World"' (1996) 7 *Philosophical Issues* 231.
McDowell J, 'Non-cognitivism and rule following' in *Mind, Value and Reality* (Harvard UP 1998).
McDowell J, 'Projection and truth in ethics' in *Mind, Value and Reality* (Harvard UP 1998).
McDowell J, 'Two sorts of naturalism' in *Mind, Value and Reality* (Harvard UP 1998).
McDowell J, 'Responses' in Smith NH (ed), *Reading McDowell: On Mind and World* (Routledge 2002).
McLuhan M, *Understanding Media: The Extensions of Man* (MIT Press 1994).
McPherson M, Smith-Lovin L and Cook JM, 'Birds of a feather: Homophily in social networks' (2001) 27 *Annual Review of Sociology* 415.
Mele AR, 'Motivation: Essentially motivation-constituting attitudes' (1995) 104 *The Philosophical Review* 387.

Mello M, 'The non-trial of the century: Representations of the Unabomber' (1999) 24 *Vermont Law Review* 417.
Merleau-Ponty M, *Nature: Course notes from the Collège de France* (Northwestern UP 2003).
Merleau-Ponty M, *Phenomenology of Perception* (Routledge 2012).
Mian E, 'The curious case of exclusionary reasons' (2002) 15 *Canadian Journal of Law and Jurisprudence* 99.
Michaels CF, 'Affordances: Four points of debate' (2003) 15 *Ecological Psychology* 135.
Mill JS, *Utilitarianism* (Cambridge Library Collection – Philosophy, CUP 2014 [1863]).
Miller T, Howe P and Sonenberg L, 'Explainable AI: Beware of inmates running the asylum or: How I learnt to stop worrying and love the social and behavioural sciences' (2017) arXiv preprint arXiv:171200547.
Mirzoeff N, *The Appearance of Black Lives Matter* ([NAME] Publications 2018).
Montgomery J, 'The virtues and vices of professionalism' in Bhugra D and Malik A (eds), *Professionalism in Mental Healthcare: Experts, Expertise and Expectations* (CUP 2011).
Moors A and De Houwer J, 'Automaticity: A theoretical and conceptual analysis' (2006) 132 *Psychological Bulletin* 297.
Moors A and De Houwer J, 'What is automaticity? An analysis of its component features and their interrelations' (2007) *Social Psychology and the Unconscious: The Automaticity of Higher Mental Processes* 11.
Murdoch I, *The Sovereignty of Good* (Routledge 2013).
Nagulendra S and Vassileva J, 'Providing awareness, explanation and control of personalized filtering in a social networking site' (2016) 18 *Information Systems Frontiers* 145.
Nanay B, '"Know thyself" is not just silly advice: it's actively dangerous' *Aeon* (16 October 2017), aeon.co/ideas/know-thyself-is-not-just-silly-advice-its-actively-dangerous.
Nguyen CT, 'Echo chambers and epistemic bubbles' (2020) 17 *Episteme* 141.
Nussbaum M, *Frontiers of Justice: Disability, Nationality, Species Membership* (Harvard UP 2006).
O'Tousa D and Grahame N, 'Habit formation: Implications for alcoholism research' (2014) 48 *Alcohol* 327.
Owens D, 'Habitual agency' (2017) 20 *Philosophical Explorations* 93.
Pan X and others, 'A study of professional awareness using immersive virtual reality: The responses of general practitioners to child safeguarding concerns' (2018) 5 *Frontiers in Robotics and AI* 1.
Pan X and Slater M, 'Confronting a moral dilemma in virtual reality: A pilot study' (Proceedings of the 25th BCS Conference on Human-Computer Interaction).
Pattie C and Johnston R, 'Talking with one voice? Conversation networks and political polarisation' (2016) 18 *The British Journal of Politics and International Relations* 482.
Pauer-Studer H and Velleman JD, 'Distortions of normativity' (2011) 14 *Ethical Theory and Moral Practice* 329.
Pedwell C, 'Re-mediating the human: Habits in the age of computational media' in Bennett T and others (eds), *Assembling and Governing Habits* (Routledge 2021).
Pedwell C, *Revolutionary Routines* (McGill-Queen's UP 2021).
Peters JD, *The Marvelous Clouds: Towards a Philosophy of Elemental Media* (University of Chicago Press 2015).
Plato, *Laws* (CUP 2016).
Poggi G, *Durkheim* (OUP 2000).
Pollard B, 'Naturalizing the space of reasons' (2005) 13 *International Journal of Philosophical Studies* 69.
Posner MI and Snyder CRR, 'Attention and cognitive control' in Solso RL (ed), *Information Processing and Cognition: The Loyola Symposium* (Erlbaum 1975).
Postema GJ, 'Coordination and convention at the foundations of law' (1982) 11 *Journal of Legal Studies* 165.
Postema GJ, 'Morality in the first person plural' (1995) 14 *Law and Philosophy* 35.
Postema GJ, 'Norms, reasons and law' (1998) 51 *Current Legal Problems* 149.

Postema GJ, 'Custom, normative practice, and the law' (2012) 62 *Duke Law Journal* 707.
Priaulx N, Weinel M and Wrigley A, 'Rethinking moral expertise' (2014) 24 *Health Care Analysis* 1.
Price H, 'Carnap, Quine, and the fate of metaphysics' (1997) 5 *Electronic Journal of Analytic Philosophy*.
Price H, 'Naturalism and the fate of the M-Worlds' (1997) 7 *Proceedings of the Aristotelian Society* 247.
Prinz JJ, *The Emotional Construction of Morals* (Oxford UP 2007).
Proust M, *In Search of Lost Time*, vol 5 (Vintage 1996).
Putnam H, *Reason, Truth, and History* (CUP 1981).
Putnam H, *The Collapse of the Fact/ Value Dichotomy and Other Essays* (Harvard UP 2002).
Putnam H, *Ethics Without Ontology* (Harvard UP 2004).
Putnam RD, *Bowling Alone: The Collapse and Revival of American Community* (Simon & Schuster 2000).
Queloz M, *The Practical Origins of Ideas: Genealogy as Conceptual Reverse-Engineering* (OUP 2021).
Quirk M, *Intuition and Metacognition in Medical Education: Keys to Developing Expertise* (Springer 2006).
Radcliff PB, *Interpreting the 20th Century: The Struggle over Democracy* (Teaching Company 2004).
Railton P, *Facts, Values, and Norms: Essays Toward a Morality of Consequence* (CUP 2003).
Railton P, 'Moral factualism' (2006) *Contemporary Debates in Moral Theory* 201.
Railton P, 'Practical competence and fluent agency' in *Reasons for Action* (CUP 2009).
Railton P, 'The affective dog and its rational tale: Intuition and attunement' (2014) 124 *Ethics* 813.
Rawls AW, 'Durkheim's theory of modernity: Self-regulating practices as constitutive orders of social and moral facts' (2012) 12 *Journal of Classical Sociology* 479.
Raz J, *The Morality of Freedom* (Clarendon Press 1986).
Raz J, *Practical Reason and Norms* (rev edn, with postscript edn, Princeton UP 1990).
Raz J, 'Intention and value' (2017) 20 *Philosophical Explorations* 109.
Redding P, 'Two directions for analytic Kantianism' in De Caro M and Macarthur D (eds), *Naturalism and Normativity* (Columbia UP 2010).
Reed E, *Encountering the World: Toward an Ecological Psychology* (OUP 1996).
Reed RC, 'Euthyphro's elenchus experience: Ethical expertise and self-knowledge' (2013) 16 *Ethical Theory and Moral Practice* 245.
Reiljan A, ' "Fear and loathing across party lines" (also) in Europe: Affective polarisation in European party systems' (2020) 59 *European Journal of Political Research* 376.
Rietveld E, 'Situated normativity: The normative aspect of embodied cognition in unreflective action' (2008) 117 *Mind* 973.
Rietveld E, 'McDowell and Dreyfus on unreflective action' (2010) 53 *Inquiry* 183.
Rietveld E, De Haan S and Denys D, 'Social affordances in context: What is it that we are bodily responsive to' (2013).
Rietveld E, Denys D and Van Westen M, 'Ecological-Enactive Cognition as engaging with a field of relevant affordances' in *The Oxford Handbook of 4E Cognition* (OUP 2018).
Ritchie J, *Understanding Naturalism* (Routledge 2014).
Romdenh-Romluc K, 'Habit and attention' in Jensen RT and Moran D (eds), *The Phenomenology of Embodied Subjectivity* (Springer 2014).
Romdenh-Romluc K, 'Merleau-Ponty: Actions, habits, and skilled expertise' in Dahlstrom D, Elpidorou A and Hopp W (eds), *Philosophy of Mind and Phenomenology: Conceptual and Empirical Approaches* (Routledge 2015).
Rose DE, 'Society and the origin of moral law: Giambattista Vico and non-reductive naturalism' in Musschenga B and van Harskamp A (eds), *What Makes Us Moral? on the Capacities and Conditions for Being Moral* (Springer 2014).
Rovira A and others, 'The use of virtual reality in the study of people's responses to violent incidents' (2009) 3 *Frontiers in Behavioral Neuroscience* 59.

Ryle G, *The Concept of Mind: 60th Anniversary Edition* (Taylor & Francis 1949/2009).

Sangiovanni A, *Humanity without Dignity: Moral Equality, Respect and Human Rights* (Havard UP 2017).

Sartorio C, 'Situations and responsiveness to reasons' (2018) 52 *Noûs* 796.

Sbicigo JB, Janczura GA and de Salles JF, 'The role of attention in perceptual and conceptual priming' (2017) 10 *Psychology & Neuroscience* 117.

Scanlon TM, *Being Realistic About Reasons* (OUP 2014).

Schiff J, 'The varieties of thoughtlessness and the limits of thinking' (2012) 12 *European Journal of Political Theory* 99.

Schnall S and others, 'Disgust as embodied moral judgment' (2008) 34 *Personality and Social Psychology Bulletin* 1096.

Seeman M, 'On the meaning of alienation' (1959) *American Sociological Review* 783.

Selinger E, Dreyfus H and Collins H, 'Interactional expertise and embodiment' (2007) 38 *Studies in History and Philosophy of Science* Part A 722.

Sellars W, 'Empiricism and the philosophy of mind' (1956) 1 *Minnesota Studies in the Philosophy of Science* 253.

Sen A, *Development as Freedom* (Oxford Paperbacks 2001).

Serres M, *Thumbelina: The Culture and Technology of Millennials* (Rowman & Littlefield 2014).

Shapiro SJ, 'Law, plans, and practical reason' (2002) 8 *Legal Theory* 387.

Shapiro SJ, *Legality* (Harvard UP 2011).

Shiffman M, 'Review of *Simone Weil: Attention to the Real*', ndpr.nd.edu/reviews/simone-weil-attention-to-the-real.

Skinner Q, *Visions of Politics*, vol 1 (CUP 2002).

Slater M and others, 'A virtual reprise of the Stanley Milgram obedience experiments' (2006) 1 *PLOS ONE* e39.

Smith MN, 'The law as a social practice: Are shared activities at the foundations of law?' (2006) 12 *Legal Theory* 265.

Spiro M, 'Culture and personality: The natural history of a false dichotomy' (1951) 14 *Psychiatry* 19.

Srinivasan A, 'Genealogy, epistemology and worldmaking' (2019) *CXIX Proceedings of the Aristotelian Society*.

Sullivan S, *Revealing Whiteness: The Unconscious Habits of Racial Privilege* (Indiana UP 2006).

Sunstein CR, 'Fifty shades of manipulation' (2016) *Journal of Marketing Behavior*.

Sunstein CR, *#republic: Divided Democracy in the Age of Social Media* (Princeton UP 2018).

Susser D, Roessler B and Nissenbaum H, 'Technology, autonomy and manipulation' (2019) 8 *Internet Policy Review*.

Sutton J, 'Batting, habit and memory: The embodied mind and the nature of skill' (2007) 10 *Sport in Society* 763.

Taylor C, 'Foundationalism and the inner-outer distinction' in Smith NH (ed), *Reading McDowell: On Mind and World* (Routledge 2002).

Teloh H, *The Development of Plato's Metaphysics* (Pennsylvania State UP 1981).

Thomson JJ, 'The right and the good' (1997) 94 *The Journal of Philosophy* 273.

Thomson JJ, *Normativity* (Open Court 2008).

Tickle AB and others, 'The truth will come to light: Directions and challenges in extracting the knowledge embedded within trained artificial neural networks' (1998) 9 *IEEE Transactions on Neural Networks* 1057.

Tribus M, *Thermodynamics and Thermostatics: An Introduction to Energy, Information and States of Matter, with Engineering Applications* (D Van Nostrand 1961).

Vaccaro K and others, *Contestability in Algorithmic Systems* (2019) CSCW'19, Austin, TX, USA, November 2019.

van den Herik JC and Rietveld E, 'Reflective situated normativity' (2021) *Philosophical Studies*.

Van Grunsven J, 'Enactivism and the paradox of moral perception' (2021) *Topoi*.

Varela FJ, *Ethical Know-How: Action, Wisdom, and Cognition* (Stanford UP 1992).

Veale M and others, 'Automating data rights' in Eyers D and others (eds), *Towards Accountable Systems* (Dagstuhl Reports, Schloss Dagstuhl 2018).
Velleman JD, 'The voice of conscience' (1999) 99 *Proceedings of the Aristotelian Society* 57.
Verplanken B and Wood W, 'Interventions to break and create consumer habits' (2006) 25 *Journal of Public Policy & Marketing* 90.
Vico G, *The New Science of Giambattista Vico* (3rd edn, Cornell UP 1984).
von Humboldt W, *The Limits of State Action* (CUP 1969).
Voss J, 'Aristote et la théorie énergétique du langage de Wilhelm von Humboldt' (1974) 72 *Revue philosophique de Louvain* 482.
Wachter S, Mittelstadt B and Russell C, 'Counterfactual explanations without opening the black box: Automated decisions and the GDPR' (2017) 31 *Harv JL & Tech* 841.
Wakefield J and Dreyfus H, 'Intentionality and phenomenology of action' in Lepore E and Van Gulick R (eds), *John Searle and His Critics* (Blackwell 1991).
Waldron J, 'All we like sheep' (1999) 12 *Canadian Journal of Law and Jurisprudence* 169.
Wallach, W and Allen C, *Moral Machines: Teaching Robots Right from Wrong* (OUP 2008).
Weber M, *Economy and Society: An Outline of Interpretive Sociology* (University of California Press 1978).
Weil S, *Gravity and Grace* (University of Nebraska Press 1997).
Westaby C, '"Feeling like a sponge": The emotional labour produced by solicitors in their interactions with clients seeking asylum' (2010) 17 *International Journal of the Legal Profession* 153.
Westaby C and Jones E, 'Empathy: An essential element of legal practice or "never the twain shall meet"?' (2018) 25 *International Journal of the Legal Profession* 107.
Westin AF, *Privacy and Freedom* (Atheneum 1967).
Wilkinson MA, 'Is law morally risky? Alienation, acceptance and Hart's Concept of Law' (2010) 30 *Oxford Journal of Legal Studies* 441.
Williams B, 'Conflicts of value' in *Moral Luck: Philosophical Papers* (CUP 1981).
Williams B, 'Internal and external reasons' in Williams B (ed), *Moral Luck: Philosophical Papers 1973–1980* (CUP 1981).
Williams B, *Ethics and the Limits of Philosophy* (Fontana Masterguides 1985).
Williams B, 'Naturalism and genealogy' in Harcourt E (ed), *Morality, Reflection and Ideology* (OUP 2000).
Wittgenstein L, *Philosophical Investigations* (Blackwell 1958).
Wittgenstein L, *The Blue Book* (Harper & Row 1960).
Wolf S, *Freedom Within Reason* (OUP 1990).
Wood AW, 'Coercion, manipulation, exploitation' in Coons C and Weber M (eds), *Manipulation: Theory and Practice* (OUP 2014).
Wood W and Neal DT, 'A new look at habits and the habit-goal interface' (2007) 114 *Psychological Review* 843.
Wood W and Rünger D, 'Psychology of habit' (2016) 67 *Annual Review of Psychology* 289.
Woolley A and Kostopoulou O, 'Clinical intuition in family medicine: More than first impressions' (2013) 11 *The Annals of Family Medicine* 60.
Yin HH and Knowlton BJ, 'The role of the basal ganglia in habit formation' (2006) 7 *Nature Reviews Neuroscience* 464.
Zsambok CE and Klein G, *Naturalistic Decision Making* (Psychology Press 2014).
Zuboff S, *The Age of Surveillance Capitalism* (Profile Books 2019).

Index

www.ingramcontent.com/pod-product-compliance
Ingram Content Group UK Ltd.
Pitfield, Milton Keynes, MK11 3LW, UK
UKHW020821290926
15470UKWH00003B/1289

9 781509 920419